CONFESSIONS AT ANY COST
Police Torture in Russia

Human Rights Watch
New York · Washington · London · Brussels

Copyright © November 1999 Human Rights Watch.
All Rights Reserved.
Printed in the United States of America.

ISBN: 1-56432-244-0
Library of Congress Card Number: 99-068011

Addresses for Human Rights Watch
350 Fifth Avenue, 34th Floor, New York, NY 10118-3299
Tel: (212) 290-4700, Fax: (212) 736-1300, E-mail: hrwnyc@hrw.org

1630 Connecticut Avenue, N.W., Suite 500, Washington, DC 20009
Tel: (202) 612-4321, Fax: (202) 612-4333, E-mail: hrwdc@hrw.org

33 Islington High Street, N1 9LH London, UK
Tel: (171) 713-1995, Fax: (171) 713-1800, E-mail: hrwatchuk@gn.apc.org

15 Rue Van Campenhout, 1000 Brussels, Belgium
Tel: (2) 732-2009, Fax: (2) 732-0471, E-mail:hrwatcheu@skynet.be

Web Site Address: http://www.hrw.org

Listserv address: To subscribe to the list, send an e-mail message to majordomo@igc.apc.org with "subscribe hrw-news" in the body of the message (leave the subject line blank).

Human Rights Watch is dedicated to
protecting the human rights of people around the world.

We stand with victims and activists to prevent
discrimination, to uphold political freedom, to protect people from inhumane
conduct in wartime, and to bring offenders to justice.

We investigate and expose
human rights violations and hold abusers accountable.

We challenge governments and those who hold power to end abusive practices
and respect international human rights law.

We enlist the public and the international
community to support the cause of human rights for all.

HUMAN RIGHTS WATCH

Human Rights Watch conducts regular, systematic investigations of human rights abuses in some seventy countries around the world. Our reputation for timely, reliable disclosures has made us an essential source of information for those concerned with human rights. We address the human rights practices of governments of all political stripes, of all geopolitical alignments, and of all ethnic and religious persuasions. Human Rights Watch defends freedom of thought and expression, due process and equal protection of the law, and a vigorous civil society; we document and denounce murders, disappearances, torture, arbitrary imprisonment, discrimination, and other abuses of internationally recognized human rights. Our goal is to hold governments accountable if they transgress the rights of their people.

Human Rights Watch began in 1978 with the founding of its Europe and Central Asia division (then known as Helsinki Watch). Today, it also includes divisions covering Africa, the Americas, Asia, and the Middle East. In addition, it includes three thematic divisions on arms, children's rights, and women's rights. It maintains offices in New York, Washington, Los Angeles, London, Brussels, Moscow, Dushanbe, Rio de Janeiro, and Hong Kong. Human Rights Watch is an independent, nongovernmental organization, supported by contributions from private individuals and foundations worldwide. It accepts no government funds, directly or indirectly.

The staff includes Kenneth Roth, executive director; Michele Alexander, development director; Reed Brody, advocacy director; Carroll Bogert, communications director; Barbara Guglielmo, finance director; Jeri Laber special advisor; Lotte Leicht, Brussels office director; Patrick Minges, publications director; Susan Osnos, associate director; Maria Pignataro Nielsen, human resources director; Jemera Rone, counsel; Wilder Tayler, general counsel; and Joanna Weschler, United Nations representative. Jonathan Fanton is the chair of the board. Robert L. Bernstein is the founding chair.

The regional directors of Human Rights Watch are Peter Takirambudde, Africa; José Miguel Vivanco, Americas; Sidney Jones, Asia; Holly Cartner, Europe and Central Asia; and Hanny Megally, Middle East and North Africa. The thematic division directors are Joost R. Hiltermann, arms; Lois Whitman, children's; and Regan Ralph, women's.

The members of the board of directors are Jonathan Fanton, chair; Lisa Anderson, Robert L. Bernstein, David M. Brown, William Carmichael, Dorothy Cullman, Gina Despres, Irene Diamond, Adrian W. DeWind, Fiona Druckenmiller, Edith Everett, Michael E. Gellert, Vartan Gregorian, Alice H. Henkin, James F. Hoge, Stephen L. Kass, Marina Pinto Kaufman, Bruce Klatsky, Joanne Leedom-Ackerman, Josh Mailman, Yolanda T. Moses, Samuel K. Murumba, Andrew Nathan, Jane Olson, Peter Osnos, Kathleen Peratis, Bruce Rabb, Sigrid Rausing, Orville Schell, Sid Sheinberg, Gary G. Sick, Malcolm Smith, Domna Stanton, and Maya Wiley. Robert L. Bernstein is the founding chair of Human Rights Watch.

ACKNOWLEDGMENTS

This report is based on almost two years of research that began in July 1997. During that time, Diederik Lohman, director of Human Rights Watch's Moscow office, Alexander Petrov, deputy director of the Moscow office, and Rachel Denber, deputy director of Human Rights Watch's Europe and Central Asia division, conducted fact-finding missions in Irkutsk and Nizhnii Novgorod provinces as well in the cities of Arkhangel'sk, Novgorod, St. Petersburg, and Ekaterinburg. In addition, considerable research was carried out in Moscow. The report was written by Diederik Lohman and edited by Rachel Denber; Mike McClintock, deputy program director; and Dinah PoKempner, deputy general counsel. Additional editorial comments were provided by Elizabeth Andersen, advocacy director, Europe and Central Asia division. Invaluable assistance was provided by Liudmila Belova, associate for the Moscow office; Alex Frangos, coordinator for the Europe and Central Asia division; Alexandra Perina and Natasha Zaretsky, associates for the Europe and Central Asia division; Meredith Moss-Quinn and Amy Bramley, interns for the Moscow office; and Patrick Minges, publications director, Human Rights Watch.

We are deeply grateful to torture victims who agreed to retell their traumatic and painful stories. We extend a special thanks to the numerous human rights defenders and organizations in Russia's regions, without whom this report would not have been possible. In particular, we thank Igor Kaliapin and Sergei Shimovolos of the Nizhnii Novgorod Society for Human Rights; Anna Pastukhova and Petr Diakonov of the Memorial Society, in Ekaterinburg; Sergei Kuznetsov of the Public Committee for the Protection of the Rights of Detainees, in Ekaterinburg; Alexander Liuboslavskii of the Alexander Liuboslavskii Public Charitable Fund for the Defense of Human Rights, in Irkutsk; Nina Davydovskaia of the Novgorod Regional Center for Human Rights; Galina Dundina of the Human Rights Center of Arkhangel'sk Province and all those other regional activists who put us in contact with torture victims, their relatives and lawyers, and local authorities, and who gave us invaluable insights relating to their own experiences working with torture victims.

We also thank the numerous experts on torture, prisons, Russian criminal law, law enforcement practices, and other topics. In particular, we thank Valerii Abramkin and Liudmila Al'pern of the Moscow Center for Prison Reform; Andrei Babushkin of the Committee for Civil Rights; Sergei Ezhov of the Society for Assistance to the Convicted; Svetlana Gannushkina of the Memorial Human Rights Center; Judge Vasilii Martyshkin of the Supreme Court of the Republic of Mordovia; Karina Moskalenko of the International Protection Center; Rein Odink of the Amsterdam City Court; Andrei Savchenko and Alexander Sokolov of the Memorial Human Rights Center in Moscow; Elena Topil'skaia of the Leningrad province procuracy; and Olga Tretiakova of the *Pravda severa* newspaper in Arkhangel'sk.

Human Rights Watch is profoundly grateful to the Henry M. Jackson Foundation, the Carnegie Corporation of New York, the John Merck Fund, and the Moriah Fund for their generous support of our work on Russia and of our Moscow office; and to the J.M. Kaplan Fund, which made possible the translation of this report.

GLOSSARY OF TERMS

Chastnoe opredelenie: A separate ruling issued by a court (in conjunction with a verdict) to state agencies, public organizations, or officials when the presiding judge has established that these agencies bear special responsibility to address human rights violations or other violations of the law, circumstances that promoted the crime that was the subject of the judge's verdict, or other reasons that explain why the crime was committed the crime.
CIS: Commonwealth of Independent States.
Convention against Torture: The United Nations Convention against Torture and other Cruel, Inhuman or Degrading Treatment or Punishment.
CPT: The Council of Europe Committee for the Prevention of Torture and Inhuman or Degrading Treatment or Punishment.
Detention report (protokol zaderzhaniia): A report confirming that a suspect has been detained before the procuracy has issued a warrant.
ECHR: The European Convention on Human Rights.
GAI (Gosudarstvennaia avtoinspektsiia): State automobile inspection
GOM (Gorodskoe otdelenie militsii): City police department
ICCPR: The International Covenant on Civil and Political Rights.
IVS (Izoliator vremennogo soderzhaniia): Temporary holding cell at a police station.
Fel'dsher: Senior nurse.
Konvertik (The envelope): Torture through a form of trussing, in which the detainee is forced to sit with his head between his bent knees and hands tied to his feet.
KPZ (Kamera predvaritel'nogo zakliucheniia): Soviet era term for a temporary holding cell at a police station (old name).
Lastochka (The swallow): A form of body suspension, the victim's hands are cuffed behind his back and attached to an iron bar or pipe, from which he hangs without his legs touching the ground.
MVD (Ministerstvo vnutrennikh del): Ministry of Internal Affairs.
OMON (Otriad militsii osobogo naznacheniia): Riot police.
Procuracy (prokuratura): State agency responsibility for both criminal investigation and prosecution, and human rights protection.
ROVD (Raionnoe otdelenie vnutrennikh del): District police department.
RUOP (Rainnoe upravlenie po bor'be s organizovannoi prestupnost'iu): District level organized crime police.
SIZO (Sledstvennyi izoliator): Pretrial detention center.
Skoraia pomoshch: Ambulance.
Slonik (The elephant): Torture by near asphyxiation. Police officers force an old-fashioned gas mask over the head of their victim and cut the oxygen supply. This

type of torture is called *"slonik"* because of the resemblance of the gas mask's hose to an elephant's trunk.
Travmapunkt: Medical emergency room.
Uchastkovyi vrach: General practitioner.
UNHCR: United Nations High Commissioner on Refugees
Visiak: (plural: *visiaki*) Crimes that police are unable to solve for long periods.

TABLE OF CONTENTS

SUMMARY 1
   Torture 1
   Accountability 4
   Lack of Redress 6
   Cycle of Abuse 7

RECOMMENDATIONS 9
   To the Russian authorities 9
      On the Matter of Acknowledging and Preventing Torture and Establishing
         the Rule of Law 9
      On the Matter of Reforming the Criminal Justice System 12
      On the Matter of Accountability 13
   To the International Community 15
      The United Nations 15
      The Council of Europe 15
      The Organization for Security and Cooperation in Europe 16
      The European Union 17
      The U.S. Government 18

A PERSISTENT PATTERN OF TORTURE AND ILL-TREATMENT 20
   The Methodology of Torture 21
   Sustained Beatings 24
   "Slonik" and Plastic Bags 28
   Electroshock 32
   Suspension and Trussing 33
   Torture by Proxy 35
   Threats of Violence 39

MEDICAL EVIDENCE OF TORTURE 43
   Access to a Forensic Expert 44
      Access to a Medical Doctor for Former Detainees 46
      Detainees' Access to Medical Doctors 48
   Death in Custody or Permanent Physical Damage 50

THE DETENTION PROCESS 54
   Informal Detentions 57
   Detention on Administrative Charges 59
   Torture and Ill-treatment at the Time of Detention 62
   Access to Lawyers 63

TORTURE AND CONFESSION EVIDENCE 68
    The Process of Securing Confessions 68
    Reliance on Confession Evidence 71
    Judicial Refusal to Exclude Coerced Confessions 75

THE VICTIMS 78
    Minors 78
        Oleg Fetisov, Ekaterinburg 79
        Igor Afon'kin, Baikal'sk, Irkutsk province 80
        Aleksei Alekseev, Ekaterinburg 81
    Women 82

THE LEGAL FRAMEWORK 85
    Prohibition and Criminalization of Torture and Ill-Treatment 85
    Forced Confessions in Court/The Right not to Testify against Oneself .. 88
    Investigation of Torture Allegations 89
    Redress and Compensation 91

HOLDING RUSSIA TO ITS INTERNATIONAL OBLIGATIONS 94
    United Nations 94
        Committee against Torture 94
        Special Rapporteur on Torture 95
            Ill-treatment and Coercion to Confess 95
            Detention Policies, Court Review, and Length of Detention 96
            Conditions in Detention 97
            Recommendations 98
    Council of Europe 98
        Parliamentary Assembly Monitoring Procedure 98
        Committee for the Prevention of Torture 100
        Directorates for Human Rights and Legal Affairs 101
    Organization for Security and Cooperation in Europe 101
    European Union and Member States 101
    United States of America 102

CRISIS IN THE CRIMINAL JUSTICE SYSTEM 103
    The Police Force 103
        Personnel, Recruitment, and Turnover 104
        Material Difficulties and Workload 106
        Police Extortion and Violence 107
    The Procuracy 108
    The Judiciary 110
    The Legal Profession 111

STALLED REFORM 112
   Institutional Reform 112
   Problems Reforming the Procuracy 113
   Reforms of the Judiciary 114
      Pressure to Convict 118
   Crime Policy Reform 122
   Absence of Public Monitoring over Places of Detention 126
   A Predisposition to Brutal Methods 127

ACCOUNTABILITY 131
   The Procuracy Inquiry 131
      Superficiality 132
      Delays 137
   Criminal Investigation and Court Action 139
      The Case of Vitalii Sokolov (Nizhnii Novgorod province) 140
      The Case of the Timofei Petrov 141
      The Case of Oleg Fetisov 142
      The Case of Sergei Kolosovskii 143
      The Case of Mikhail Sobolev 144
      The Case of Andrei Getsko 145
   Convictions 146
      The Case of Oleg Igonin 147
   Complaints to the Russian Ombudsman 148
   Compensation for Damage 150
   Fear as a Deterrent to Complaints 150

RUSSIA'S OFFICIAL REACTION TO TORTURE 153
   President and Presidential Structures 153
   Ministry of Internal Affairs 154
   Procuracy General 157
   State Duma 159

APPENDIX A: UNITED NATIONS COMMITTEE AGAINST TORTURE
.... 160
   Excerpts from the U.N. Convention against Torture and Other Cruel, Inhuman
      or Degrading Treatment or Punishment 160
   Concluding Observations on Russia's Second Periodic Report to the U.N.
      Committee against Torture 161

APPENDIX B: EUROPEAN COMMITTEE FOR THE PREVENTION OF TORTURE AND INHUMAN OR DEGRADING TREATMENT OR PUNISHMENT 167
Excerpts from the European Convention for the Prevention of Torture
.... 167
The Committee's November 1998 Visit 169
The Committee's September 1999 Visit 171

APPENDIX C: LETTER FROM RUSSIA'S OMBUDSMAN
TO THE MINISTER OF INTERNAL AFFAIRS 174

APPENDIX D: RESPONSE FROM THE MINISTRY OF INTERIOR TO RUSSIA'S OMBUDSMAN 177

APPENDIX E: DECISION OF THE PRESIDENTIAL HUMAN RIGHTS CHAMBER OF APRIL 7, 1998 180

APPENDIX F: SEPARATE RULING OF SUPREME COURT
JUDGE VASILII MARTYSHKIN ON TORTURE IN MORDOVIA
.... 183

SUMMARY

Torture and ill-treatment of detainees at the time of and immediately after arrest is rampant in Russia today. In the first hours after detention, police regularly beat their captives, nearly asphyxiate them, or subject them to electroshock in the pursuit of confessions or testimony incriminating others. With the exception of a few particularly grave cases in which public exposure led to prosecutions, police carry out torture with complete impunity as the provincial and federal procuracies close their eyes to evidence of abuse. The courts commonly accept forced confessions at face value, and use them as a basis for convictions. Despite overwhelming evidence that torture has become an integral part of police practice, the Russian government and law enforcement agencies generally—with some notable exceptions—deny that torture or ill-treatment is a problem, and are not taking any measures to end these abusive practices.

Torture

More than fifty interviews with torture victims and dozens of interviews with lawyers, relatives, former police officers, judges, and procurators in five regions of Russia reveal the systematic use of torture and ill-treatment as a means to coerce confessions and other testimony from criminal suspects. In April 1998, the Presidential Chamber on Human Rights, a gathering of administration officials, parliamentarians, and nongovernmental organizations, adopted a statement saying that:

> torture and cruel, degrading forms of treatment or punishment with respect to citizens in the organs [of the Ministry] of Internal Affairs during the pretrial stages of criminal justice administration have a massive and systematic character which makes it one of the most serious problems of abuse of power and violations of human rights.

Some knowledgeable sources, including Russia's federal human rights ombudsman and a leading Russian judge, estimate that up to 50 percent of criminal suspects in Russia may be subjected to torture or ill-treatment. Another judge told Human Rights Watch she believed that as many as 80 percent of criminal suspects who refuse to confess may be tortured in the course of a criminal investigation. Some former police officers said they believe it is impossible to solve crimes without torture.

The most widespread method of police torture in Russia is prolonged beating. Asphyxiation, suspension by the arms or legs, and electroshock are also common. In addition, police use trusted prisoners in pretrial cells as proxies to beat and threaten suspects into cooperating with an investigation. Police almost always combine physical torture with threats of further physical harm and other psychological abuse. In some cases, torture has led to the victim's death or permanent disability.

Our research found several forms of prolonged beatings. Police punch, kick, and use nightsticks or other instruments, aiming for the victim's head, back, legs, kidney area, and heels. In some cases, police put books or criminal case binders on detainees' heads before beating there to avoid leaving traces. Torture by near asphyxiation is used less frequently than sustained beatings but almost always in combination with them. Police officers handcuff their victim to a chair and force an old-fashioned gas mask or a plastic bag over the head. Subsequently, the oxygen supply is cut; at this point, in many cases, police beat the suspect, causing him to hyperventilate. Some victims reported losing consciousness, with police reviving them, demanding they write a confession, and repeating the procedure if they resist. This is called "elephant," or *"slonik"* in Russian, a reference to the resemblance of a person in a gas mask to the head of an elephant. In July 1995, a public scandal ensued when it was confirmed that a detainee in Saransk died as a result of this torture. Torture by electroshock leaves few marks and, according to Russian human rights organizations, is used frequently. Police use what ex-prisoners call an electric "cranking" machine, which, according to descriptions, resembles an old-fashioned field telephone. The machine produces a current that is transmitted through electrodes attached to the ears of the detainee.

Police also torture detainees by suspending them or painfully binding them. For the *"lastochka"* (swallow) position, the victim's hands may be cuffed behind his back and attached to an iron bar or pipe so that the detainee hangs without his or her legs touching the ground, while police beat the victim with nightsticks. In a variation on "lastochka," the detainee is forced face down on the ground and his or her legs are tied tightly with a rope to the handcuffed hands. These positions cause grave pain in the joints, cut off the blood supply to the wrists and can dislocate arms or shoulders. In the *"konvertik"* (envelope) position, the detainee is forced to sit with his or her head between bent knees and his or her hands tied to his or her feet. In Nizhnii Novgorod, a detainee died in the mid-1990s after being held in this position for a long period and subjected to sustained beatings. A forensic examination found forty bruises from nightsticks on his body.

An inseparable part of police torture in Russia is psychological abuse aimed at utterly disorienting the victim. This abuse might consist of strings of insults, which one victim said included "you're a horse," "a pig," "we'll break you," "confess!," "you drunk!," together with threats of continued physical violence, or threats to the suspect's family. These might include threats to "do with you whatever we like"; to kill, rape, or otherwise physically injure the person; to have the person sentenced to death (even if they are not charged with a crime that carries the death penalty); to throw the person into a "pressing room" where "criminals will take care of you"; and to harm the person's family. Threats against family members may be particularly effective because the detainee is isolated from the outside world and has no way of knowing what is happening to them.

More than fifty interviews with torture victims did not produce a single case in which lawyers were present at interrogations in which torture or ill-treatment occurred. Police routinely refuse to grant detainees access to a lawyer in the hours after detention, often allowing the presence of a lawyer only after a confession has been secured. In several cases, police called in friendly lawyers who ignored evidence of torture. Asking for a lawyer can be risky because such requests sometimes provoke increased violence by police officers. Police were found frequently to force their victims to write in their confession that they had voluntarily refused the assistance of a lawyer.

Police detectives use criminal suspects and defendants who are trusted and given special privileges in police cells and pretrial detention centers—known as IVSs and SIZOs—to beat, rape, or otherwise force suspects and defendants into confessing or providing needed testimony. This widespread phenomenon is called the "pressing room" or "press hut" (*press-khata* in Russian) because police trustees "press" the detainee within the confines of the pretrial cell. In exchange for their services, these prisoners, who serve both as police enforcers and informers, receive privileges, such as access to narcotics and women.

Most torture victims Human Rights Watch interviewed were adult males. We also interviewed five minors who described being tortured, and relatives and lawyers of other minors told us of more such cases. In some cases, the detainees were tortured for petty crimes. Oleg Fetisov, a minor in Ekaterinburg, was tortured by near asphyxiation and beatings in 1996 for stealing a jacket from another schoolboy. Unable to withstand the torture, he jumped out of a third-floor window. He was taken to a hospital with a fractured skull, pelvic bone, and arm; a small cerebral hemorrhage; a damaged knee; and a concussion.

In several of the cases Human Rights Watch investigated, torture led to the death of or permanent injury to the detainee. Oleg Igonin was tortured to death by gas-mask asphyxiation in 1995. Boris Botvinnik lost more than 90 percent of his eyesight after police tortured him in 1996, beating and asphyxiating him at his Moscow apartment. A medical examination confirmed that the damage to his vision may have been caused by beatings to the back of the head.

In the course of our research, we found four cases of detainees who leapt or fell from police precinct windows—a peculiar hallmark of torture in Russia. One man from Arkhangel'sk province, fell to his death. The other young men told Human Rights Watch they jumped to escape the torture that they were no longer able to withstand. Two of them were tortured by electroshock, one was asphyxiated in a gas mask. Twenty-four-year-old "Dmitrii Ivanov" (not his real name) from a town in Central Russia fell fifteen meters to the ground after police beat him and subjected him to electroshock. He fell on his back on a parked car, breaking his back. Despite undergoing surgery, Ivanov will never be able to walk again and was not even able to sit up when Human Rights Watch interviewed him. Twenty-three year old Aleksei Mikheev from Nizhnii Novgorod jumped out of a police station's upper window after he was tortured with electroshock, landing on a parked motorcycle. As of this writing, he was paralyzed from the waist down and recovery prospects were uncertain.

Accountability

Due to conflicts of interest inherent in the procuracy—the state agency that bears responsibility for criminal investigation and prosecution, and human rights protection—strong corporate solidarity in the police force, pressures on prosecutors, and intimidation of the victims themselves, the overwhelming majority of the abusive police officers who torture criminal suspects are not held accountable. Some prosecutions of torture cases take place, but this appears to be limited to exceptional cases in which the torture victim dies, is maimed or, as in the cases of suspects who fall from high windows, attains public notoriety. Informal procuracy inquiries into torture complaints, which a torture victim usually files prior to his trial, frequently do not lead to a criminal investigation against abusive police officers, and complaints filed during the defendant's trial are usually dismissed without serious consideration. Criminal investigations of police abuse have yielded a mixed record, and few victims of torture are known to have received compensation for the injuries they suffered. In some cases, torture victims reported that police or procuracy officials threatened them with repercussions if they were to complain about their treatment. Victims can also seek accountability through the Russian ombudsman's office, which started to work on torture when it was established in 1998. However, it is too early to assess the effectiveness of this complaint procedure. While international remedies, like appeals to the European Court of Human Rights, are theoretically open to torture victims, international bodies appear not yet to have heard any torture cases from Russia.

Our research and that of numerous human rights groups in Russia's regions show that the informal inquiries conducted by the procuracy into complaints of abuse are exceedingly superficial. These are conducted primarily by young and inexperienced procurator's assistants, who often reportedly do no more than forward complaints to the chiefs of police precincts for a response, take these responses at face value, and neither interview the complainant nor seek other evidence of abuse. The procedure frequently ends with a letter informing the complainant in a few stark sentences that because his complaint "was not confirmed by the facts," no criminal proceedings will take place, without further explanation.

Most torture complaint procedures end after this procedure, since many complainants are not aware of their right to study the records of the procurator's inquiry and to challenge it. If victims of police abuse do challenge the outcome of the initial inquiry, they face lengthy delays as the complaint wends its way up the hierarchy of procuracies—district, city, province, and federal. As the process drags on, evidence of torture (wounds, burns, and the like) disappears and the likelihood of a criminal investigation of the torture claim diminishes.

Torture victims who seek justice can become intimidated by police and procuracy threats. For example, procuracy officials reportedly threatened Dmitrii Ivanov's mother with repercussions if she were to lodge a complaint about the torture of her son. She was told that if she were to pursue the torture complaint, her son's "status could easily be changed from witness to defendant." After this threat, she gave up all attempts to bring to justice the police officers whose abuse resulted in her son being crippled.

In the minority of cases in which criminal proceedings are begun, abusive police may threaten and intimidate the complainants or case investigators, or the procuracy itself can undermine the investigation. In the case of Oleg Fetisov, who was fifteen-years-old when police tortured him, the procuracy began a criminal investigation into the boy's torture allegations and even charged the police officer with exceeding authority. The case, however, never went to court. It was transferred to another procuracy, ostensibly to ensure greater objectivity, and eventually closed. In 1997, procurators in Ekaterinburg began a criminal investigation against police officer Sergei Kolosovskii for asphyxiating a suspect. Local police officers launched a campaign on behalf of their colleague, with the support of several newspapers. The procurator in charge of the case told Human Rights Watch that large numbers of armed police sat demonstratively in the corridor outside his office as well as in the courtroom to intimidate procuracy and court employees. In court, Kolosovskii was acquitted of one charge; the second charge was sent back for further investigation. In Nizhnii Novgorod, a district procuracy started a criminal investigation into the arbitrary arrest and torture of Timofei Petrov in 1996. For three months, the alleged torturers intensely harassed Petrov and finally reportedly offered him money to drop his complaint. Petrov, apparently tired of the harassment, accepted the money as an informal settlement and withdrew his complaint, after which the procuracy closed the criminal case.

The record on those torture and ill-treatment cases that reach the courts is mixed, ranging from acquittals to lenient to appropriate sentences. Human Rights Watch is aware of the conviction of twenty-five police officers for torture or ill-treatment in seven criminal cases over a period of six years. The most significant conviction to date took place in February 1998, when the Supreme Court of Mordovia found seven police officers guilty of acts constituting torture and related crimes. This case began with the 1995 torture death of nineteen-year-old Oleg Igonin in Mordovia, which drew unprecedented attention from the Russian media. The media followed the case through to the historic conviction of several police officers for a range of related crimes three years later. On July 25, 1995, A. Daev, Ye. Sazonov and A. Guliaikin, detectives from the Lenin police precinct in Saransk, asphyxiated and beat A. Lavrent'ev, a minor, and demanded that he confess to armed robbery and name his accomplices. After Lavrent'ev named Oleg Igonin as his alleged co-offender, the Saransk precinct chiefs instructed their subordinates to detain Igonin. The three detectives and their colleague Kuflin detained Igonin at his home at 2:00 a.m., brought him to the police station, did not register him with the duty officer or write a detention report, and forced him to write a confession. Police asphyxiated Igonin with a gas mask on various occasions, until Igonin died at around 4:00 a.m. at the station.

Lack of Redress

Most torture victims are unable to get immediate access to medical professionals, let alone official forensic medical experts. As a result, medical evidence of torture is almost always lost. The procuracy and courts, which are obliged under Russian and international law to exclude any confessions or testimony received under duress, routinely ignore evidence of torture, and courts often base convictions on coerced testimony.

Russian criminal procedure, physicians' reluctance to have anything to do with the police, and simple financial constraints combine to make it unlikely that a torture victim will obtain medical documentation of torture. Forensic medical experts may examine people only at the request of certain law enforcement officials and judges. Torture victims and their lawyers cannot approach these forensic experts directly. They can, of course, request the investigator or judge in the case to order a forensic examination, but the latter can simply dismiss the request, claiming it is not germane to the criminal case. For example, Boris Botvinnik and his lawyer asked investigators, and later the judge, numerous times to order a forensic examination. Despite the fact that a hospital in Volgograd diagnosed Botvinnik with head trauma, both investigators and the judge refused these repeated requests.

Torture victims may also seek a medical examination by a regular doctor, but such a doctor's conclusions are often not accepted in court. In addition, victims who remain in temporary holding facilities at police stations face problems gaining access to such doctors, as most of these facilities do not employ medical personnel. Detainees at pretrial detention centers, which do employ permanent medical staff, may distrust these staff members. Even victims who have been released face problems getting a medical examination as many medical doctors are reluctant to examine people who claim they were tortured by the police.

When confronted with a torture complaint, judges at trial generally appeared to question the defendant on the issue, often summoned the alleged perpetrators for questioning, and sometimes requested medical documents. Some judges subsequently dismissed the torture complaint without further inquires, while others sent it back to the procuracy for further investigation or instructed the procuracy to investigate it. However, Human Rights Watch's research did not identify any case in which evidence allegedly obtained under torture was excluded in court.

Cycle of Abuse

The torture experience is part of a cycle of abuse, which starts at the time of arrest and continues through conviction or beyond. These abuses range from arbitrary detention to life-threatening conditions in detention to refusal to acknowledge judicial errors.

Our research shows that police frequently make improper use of detention procedures when detaining suspects. For example, police may ask an individual to come to the police station for an ostensibly voluntary visit, rather than issuing a summons. The nature of these visits leaves the procedural status of the individual unclear and relieves police officers of the obligation to process any detention or arrest report that documents the individuals presence in custody and to inform the individual of his or her rights. However, force may be used to bring the individual to the police station in case he or she refuses to come, testifying to the not-so-voluntary nature of what effectively becomes a detention without a warrant. Police also frequently detain suspects on administrative charges for misdemeanors like swearing in public or petty hooliganism. However, once the detainee is in custody, police may question him or her on much more serious criminal charges, taking advantage of the more limited safeguards provided in law for those held on administrative charges. While criminal suspects—in law, if not in practice—are guaranteed immediate access to a lawyer, the law is much less clear on the right to counsel for those held on administrative charges.

Most torture victims are kept in pretrial detention centers from the time they are charged until a court verdict has attained legal force, which often takes years. The conditions in these pretrial detention centers are so horrific that the U.N. Special Rapporteur on Torture called them "torturous." The cells are severely overcrowded—in many centers, detainees sleep in shifts and cannot sit down all at once. There is an acute lack of fresh air, no privacy, poor lighting, and the hygienic situation is such that the special rapporteur called these cells "incubators for diseases."

In our research, we came across several apparent miscarriages of justice—cases in which defendants were convicted on the basis of confessions obtained under duress. In these cases, the procuracy was often slow to admit its mistakes, causing apparently innocent individuals—including some facing the death penalty—to continue to be held in prison. In an egregious example, as of this writing, the Procuracy General refused to submit the case of Sergei Mikhailov, a man who was apparently wrongly convicted for raping and murdering a minor, to the Supreme Court, even though three independent procuracy investigators had established that Mikhailov did not commit the crimes, and another suspect had been identified.

RECOMMENDATIONS

To the Russian authorities
On the Matter of Acknowledging and Preventing Torture and Establishing the Rule of Law

- **Acknowledge that torture in pretrial detention is a problem of serious dimensions and create a committee to investigate such torture.** Acknowledge the scale of police torture, initiate broad public and internal debate involving the Ministry of Internal Affairs, the Procuracy General, the State Duma, the presidency, the ombudsman and relevant nongovernmental organizations about causes of and solutions for the problem. A committee should be created, involving the above-mentioned actors, to draw up plan of action to end torture practices. This plan should form the basis for a public and comprehensive government program aimed at combating torture and ill-treatment;

- **Work in good faith.** Police detectives, police and procuracy investigators, procurators, and judges should work in good faith, placing their responsibilities before the law over their institutional interests. Thus, investigators should conduct criminal investigations fully and objectively; procurators should vet investigations for objectivity, comprehensiveness and lawfulness; procurators should investigate torture complaints fully and objectively; and courts should consider evidence in criminal cases fully and objectively;

- **Produce a bill of rights.** The government or Ministry of Internal Affairs should produce a bill of rights for defendants, including the right not to testify against oneself, the right to a lawyer, the right not to be tortured or ill-treated, the right to be informed of the reasons for one's arrest, the right to know the location to which one is being taken, the right to know the identity of any law enforcement officials with whom one deals, and the like, and should instruct police officers to give copies of the bill of rights to any person they detain or call in for informal questioning. This bill should further be hung in a visible place in any cell or investigation room;

- **End misleading detentions.** The Ministry of Internal Affairs should issue instructions calling on all police officers to strictly observe due process when detaining persons. "Voluntary" visits to the police office for informal questioning should be truly voluntary and should take place only during working hours. Police should not mislead individuals or their relatives about the nature and purpose of such questioning. In case of detention or arrest under articles 89, 90 or 122 of the criminal procedure code, police should present an arrest or detention warrant at the earliest possible time. Police should always identify themselves and inform those in custody of their rights. Police should always allow detainees to call a lawyer immediately. At the request of the detained person, police should promptly provide his family with information regarding the whereabouts of their relative and any request made for a lawyer. Police should never use administrative detention as a means of detaining individuals when there are not sufficient grounds for holding them as criminal suspects. The Ministry of Internal Affairs should meticulously investigate any credible complaints about violation of these rules and apply strict disciplinary measures against offending officers;

- **Transparency for interrogation staff.** To enable detainees to identify an alleged abuser, all interrogators, as well as medical and other staff coming into contact with detainees under interrogation, should wear badges bearing their name and/or identification number;

- **Instruct medical personnel.** The Ministry of Justice should adopt legislation requiring medical personnel in detention facilities to pay close attention to injuries on detainees or other signals of mistreatment that may be due to abuse by a public servant, to examine and document such injuries or signs in the greatest possible detail, and to promptly report such cases to the proper authorities;

- **Criminalize torture properly.** The legislature should introduce, as recommended by the U.N. Committee against Torture, a separate crime of torture in the Russian criminal code, using the definition of torture as contained in article 1 of the Convention against Torture. Russia should further adopt amendments to its criminal code to ensure that article 117 criminalizes the causing of physical or psychological suffering by non-violent means. It should also amend article 302 of the criminal code to explicitly include torture by persons other than officials when performed at the instigation, or with the acquiescence, of officials;

- **Prompt judicial review of detention.** To protect against arbitrary detention, detainees should be brought before a judge or judicial authority within forty-eight hours (the procuracy cannot be considered judicial authority). The judge should assess the lawfulness and necessity of the detention, as well as the treatment received by the detainee, and authorize any continuation of detention;

- **Lawyers at police stations.** Lawyers' collegia and the Ministry of Internal Affairs should take steps to ensure that an independent duty lawyer is present at all police stations during working hours. Police officials should be instructed to introduce any person who is brought to the police station (voluntarily or following a detention or arrest) to the duty lawyer. At the request of the individual, the lawyer should be allowed to be present during (informal) questioning;

- **Establish a training program.** Establish a training program for law enforcement agents on international and domestic human rights standards; law enforcement agents should be held accountable for deviations from these standards. This program should pay special attention to, inter alia, the problems of torture and ill-treatment, unlawful detentions, and proper professional conduct. It should convey a clear explanation to all police and procuracy officers of what acts constitute torture;

- **The ombudsman.** The ombudsman should continue to actively monitor the problem of torture and carefully investigate all complaints received. He should exercise his right, granted in the law on the ombudsman, to make suggestions and recommendations to the Ministry of Internal Affairs, the Procuracy General, the State Duma, and the Russian government to end widespread torture practices in Russia. He should call on the State Duma to appoint a special parliamentary commission to investigate the problem of torture and to schedule parliamentary hearings on the issue aimed at developing a set of concrete measures for ending torture practices and preventing them in the future. And he should intervene in the case of Sergei Mikhailov and demand immediate transfer of his case to the Supreme Court for review of his death sentence;

- **Invite international experts to investigate torture and the fairness of criminal proceedings.** The government should invite U.N. Special Rapporteur Nigel Rodley to return to Russia and request the OSCE's Advisory Panel of Experts on the Prevention of Torture to scrutinize the findings in Human Rights Watch's report and to advise the government and its institutions on how to implement them;

- **Submit third periodic report to the United Nations Committee against Torture.** The government should submit its third periodic report on the implementation of the United Nations Convention against Torture, which was due in 1996, as a matter of priority;

- **Publicize findings of international bodies.** Make public the findings of the November 1998 visit to Russia by the Committee for the Prevention of Torture of the Council of Europe as well as the findings of forthcoming visits by this body; and

- **Withdraw reservations to the European Convention on Human Rights.** Reservations to article 5(3 and 4), the right to be brought promptly before a judge upon detention, and the right to speedy proceedings to determine the lawfulness of his detention should be withdraws as a matter of priority.

On the Matter of Reforming the Criminal Justice System

- **New criminal procedure code.** The legislature should adopt a new criminal procedure code that is fully consistent with principles enshrined in the Russian constitution and United Nations standards (including the International Covenant on Civil and Political Rights, the Basic Principles on the Role of Lawyers, the Guidelines on the Role of Prosecutors, and the Basic Principles on the Independence of the Judiciary); in particular, a new code should create mechanisms to realize the equality of arms (between the prosecution and the defense) and the presumption of innocence. The law should further regulate the use and length of detention in a manner that is consistent with Russia's obligations under the ICCPR and other United Nations standards;

- **Reform the procuracy.** In accordance with requirements for Russia's admission to the Council of Europe, the legislature should reform the procuracy to ensure that policing and judicial tasks are performed by separate bodies that are fully independent of each other;

- **Introduce public control.** The government should introduce legislation and develop mechanisms to permit independent bodies and nongovernmental organizations to monitor police and detention facilities, including interrogation rooms. They should be authorized to conduct unannounced visits. Legislation should strengthen the independence of medical examiners and other authorities in a position to evaluate human rights practices in police and prison facilities, so that they may work independently from prosecutors and police;

- **Improve access to forensic experts.** The legislature should amend the current criminal procedure code and the draft criminal procedure code to allow suspects, defendants, and their lawyers direct access to forensic medical examinations without an investigator's or judge's authorization; and

- **Appoint specialized forensic experts.** State forensic medical centers should appoint specialists for cases of torture and ill-treatment from among forensic doctors at regional forensic medical centers. These specialists should confer regularly with international medical experts on torture and medical documentation of torture.

On the Matter of Accountability
- **Procuracy inquiries into torture complaints should be a priority.** Until the procuracy is reformed as recommended above, the procurator general should instruct procuracies throughout the country to process investigations of complaints about torture and ill-treatment as a matter of priority. As a rule, experienced procuracy officials should lead such investigations and should promptly begin criminal proceedings. Torture complaints should never be investigated by the team that is also in charge of investigating the underlying criminal case against the complainant. The complaint should also never be sent to the head of the agency against which the complaint is directed. Preferably, complaints should be investigated by the procuracy of a neighboring province, city, or district, or by a higher-level procuracy;

- **Investigate complaints thoroughly.** The procurator general should issue instructions containing a set of minimum requirements for informal inquiries regarding torture complaints. These instructions should oblige investigating officials to ask detailed, oral questions of the complainant, the alleged torturers, the complainant's lawyer, and any witness the complainant indicates. The contents of these interviews should be recorded in detail. Officials should demand all medical documents from the IVS, SIZOs, hospital emergency rooms, or other physicians. If the complainant has not been examined by a medical doctor, the official should order a forensic expert assessment. In conducting the investigation, officials should pay particularly close attention to the circumstances under which the individual was taken into custody, the manner in which the detention was recorded in precinct logs, and whether there was an inappropriate use of administrative detention procedures. The Ministry of Internal Affairs should always either transfer from active duty officers who are under investigation for torture or suspend them, and fire them if convicted;

- **Appoint special procurators for torture complaints.** The Procuracy General should appoint specific officials at Russia's regional procuracies who would be responsible for overseeing the handling of torture complaints in the regions. These officials should keep statistics on torture and ill-treatment complaints. These officials should investigate practices at precincts that are the subject of multiple complaints to establish whether such complaints are well-founded, to determine the cause of persistent complaints, and to take corrective steps;

- **The Ministry of Internal Affairs should gather statistics.** The Ministry of Internal Affairs should submit an annual report to the head of state reflecting the number of reported cases of police brutality or torture in each of Russia's regions and the resulting disciplinary measures, criminal charges, and convictions. Regional internal affairs directorates should maintain such statistics;

- **Track prosecution of abusive officials.** The government should establish a system to track closely the progress and outcome of prosecutions against law enforcement officials in torture cases and the performance of procurators in such cases. In addition, the work of procurators in human rights cases should be part of their official job evaluations;

- **Study judicial practice on torture complaints.** The government should authorize an independent government body to review the work of judges as it relates to torture. This body should document credible cases in which judges accept evidence obtained through human rights violations or otherwise fail to ensure that due process rights have been observed in all aspects of the cases that come before them, regardless of whether the defendant launches a complaint. Appropriate administrative or criminal sanctions should be brought against judges who do not adequately pursue allegations of torture in the cases before them. This body should receive adequate funding from the state budget; and

- **Take steps in Mikhailov case.** The Procuracy General should immediately submit the case of Sergei Mikhailov to the Supreme Court to overturn his conviction. It should further bring to justice those officials who tortured Mikhailov, or instigated or tolerated his ill-treatment; investigators and supervising procurators involved also should be held responsible for this miscarriage of justice.

To the International Community
The United Nations
- The High Commissioner for Human Rights should continue to express deep concern to the Russian government about reports of widespread and systematic torture in police custody. She should press the Russian government to implement the recommendations submitted by the U.N. Special Rapporteur on Torture in 1994, and by the Committee against Torture, which considered Russia's second periodic report in November 1996. She should also urge the government to adopt a public and comprehensive government program aimed at combating torture and ill-treatment, based on a thorough expert investigation of the problem;

- The U.N. Special Rapporteur on Torture, Sir Nigel Rodley, should conduct a second visit to Russia specifically to investigate police torture at police stations and IVSs, and to make recommendations on how to improve the situation; and

- Conduct outreach to Russian and international nongovernmental organizations involved in the treatment of, and advocacy for, victims of torture and ill-treatment in Russia and assist these organizations in applying for financial support through the U.N. Voluntary Fund for Victims of Torture.

The Council of Europe
- The Committee for the Prevention of Torture (CPT) should continue to monitor closely torture in Russia, including making at least yearly visits. During these trips, the CPT should carry out unannounced visits to police stations and IVSs, speak to victims, their relatives and lawyers, and to NGOs. The CPT should do everything in its power to encourage the Russian government to publish the Committee's findings;

- The Parliamentary Assembly should continue its monitoring procedure under Order No. 508 of April 25, 1996. Members of the Monitoring Committee should pay particular attention to torture and ill-treatment and the ineffectiveness of remedies against torture, problems which should constitute a significant part of its next report on Russia's compliance with its obligations to the Council of Europe. The Monitoring Committee and the Parliamentary Assembly should strongly encourage Russia to adopt a public and comprehensive government program aimed at combating torture and ill-treatment, based on a thorough expert investigation of the problem. If no visible progress toward solving the torture problem is made within a year of submission of the report, the Monitoring Committee should draft a motion requesting the Parliamentary Assembly to take punitive measures against Russia, which could include suspension of the credentials of the Russian delegation. The Monitoring Committee should furthermore vigorously pursue full implementation of all obligations under Opinion 193 and the withdrawal of all reservations made by Russia to the European Convention for Human Rights;

- The Legal Affairs Directorate should encourage the Russian government and parliament to adequately address the advice on the draft code of criminal procedure provided by experts appointed by the Council of Europe;

- The Council of Europe should offer all necessary technical and other assistance to the Russian government to implement a comprehensive program aimed at bringing an end to police torture and ill-treatment; and

- Law enforcement officials, lawyers, and judges who are selected for training by the Council of Europe should be carefully vetted to ensure no past involvement in police brutality. Any training programs should have an extensive human rights dimension, including instruction on the prohibition of torture and the obligation to investigate. The Council of Europe should also examine whether the ideas put forth in training materials have been implemented.

The Organization for Security and Cooperation in Europe

- The OSCE should continue and increase its focus on combating torture in line with its commitments;

- It should urge the Russian government to invite a mission of OSCE experts with the specific mandate of further investigating torture practices in police stations and detention centers and drafting a set of recommendations for addressing them. The OSCE should stress to the Russian government that, in case of a refusal, OSCE member states are determined to invoke the emergency mechanism of paragraph 12 of the Moscow Document and dispatch a mission of rapporteurs to Russia;

- Law enforcement officials, lawyers, and judges who are selected for training by the OSCE should be carefully vetted to ensure no past involvement in police brutality. Any training programs should have an extensive human rights dimension, including instruction on the prohibition of torture and the obligation to investigate. Any training program should be followed up to ensure implementation of training materials; and

- The OSCE should invite its Advisory Panel of Experts on the Prevention of Torture to scrutinize the findings in the present report and to advise the OSCE and its institutions on how to implement this report's recommendations.

The European Union

- The European Union should demand that the Russian government adopt an effective program to eliminate torture, make specific reference to the human rights provision of its Partnership and Cooperation Agreement;

- The European Parliament should adopt a resolution expressing its grave concern about torture in Russia. This resolution should call on the Russian government to introduce torture as a separate crime and to adopt a new criminal procedure code in line with international standards. The resolution should also call on the European Commission to monitor closely the problem of torture in Russia;

- The Council of Ministers should implement fully the relevant human rights provisions of its June 4, 1999 Common Strategy of the European Union on Russia. These include "providing support for and... encouraging the necessary institutional reforms toward a modern and effective administration within Russia's Executive, Legislature, and Judiciary at federal, regional, and local levels; in particular by developing the capacity of an independent judiciary, public administration and accountable law enforcement structures..." and "supporting Russian efforts to meet its international human rights commitments... giving assistance in safeguarding human rights...." The Council of Ministers is encouraged to report regularly and publicly on the successes of its efforts toward meeting these goals;

- Through the Technical Assistance to the CIS or any other program, the European Union should fulfill its commitment to supporting NGOs by allocating generous funds to those involved in researching torture, and treating, and advocating for victims of torture; and

- Law enforcement officials, lawyers, and judges who are selected for training funded by the European Union should be carefully vetted to ensure no past involvement in police brutality. Any training program should have an extensive human rights dimension, including instruction on the prohibition of torture and the obligation to investigate. The European Union should also examine whether the ideas put forth in training materials have been implemented.

The U.S. Government
- The U.S. government should pay particular attention to documenting instances of torture in Russia in its *Country Report on Human Rights Practices* and raise concern about the problem at every possible opportunity in bilateral relations with Russian authorities;

- It should fully implement the Leahy amendment to the Foreign Operations Appropriations Act to ensure that no U.S. assistance benefits units of security forces that are responsible for gross violations of human rights, unless those responsible have been brought to justice. Implementation should include vetting of all Russian recipients of U.S. security assistance, providing technical assistance to Russian authorities to ensure that abusive police are brought to justice, and negotiating monitoring agreements with Russian government entities that receive assistance. The U.S. government should, as a matter of priority, actively seek information on abuses by law enforcement officials not only from the relevant government agencies, but also from Russia's central and regional media, human rights organizations, and other sources. It should condition any technical assistance programs in law enforcement on the provision of information by the Russian procuracy on criminal investigations against abusive law enforcement officials, and should consider offering financial or technical to in set up a centralized system to gather such information;

- It should conduct outreach to Russian and international nongovernmental organizations involved in the treatment of, and advocacy for, torture victims in Russia. Such outreach should encourage NGOs to apply for funding under the Torture Victims Relief Act of 1998. The U.S. government should also continue to support appropriations to this important program as well as to the U.N. Voluntary Fund for Victims of Torture;

- The U.S. Agency for International Development should allocate considerable funding to NGOs that have a serious commitment to torture research and advocacy; and

- Law enforcement officials, lawyers, and judges who are selected for training by the U.S. government should be carefully vetted to ensure no part in police brutality. Any training program should have an extensive human rights dimension, including instruction on the prohibition of torture and the obligation to investigate. The U.S. government should also examine whether the ideas put forth in training materials have been implemented.

A PERSISTENT PATTERN OF TORTURE AND ILL-TREATMENT

In the past four years, Russian human rights defenders and the media—for the first time since the end of the Soviet era—brought to the fore the issue of police torture and ill-treatment.[1] Throughout the vast expanses of the Russian Federation police torture criminal suspects, routinely and deliberately inflicting severe pain and suffering with the aim of extracting confessions to criminal offenses or other information. Indeed, the practice now appears endemic to Russia's criminal justice system. These abuses range from ill-treatment to unmistakable torture. The victims of this type of police brutality have been ordinary people who are somehow caught up in the criminal justice system as petty offenders, criminal suspects, and even as witnesses who might incriminate others. There is no clear ethnic dimension as to who is subjected to torture—nor are victims likely to be political.[2] Torture and ill-treatment aimed at receiving confessions or other information occur both at the time and place of detention and in the course of the three days police may keep detainees in police custody. The abuse generally stops after transfer to a pretrial detention center, though the atrocious conditions at these detention centers may constitute another form of ill-treatment.

This torture and ill-treatment occurs in the context of a half-reformed criminal justice system that has retained many of the worst aspects of its Soviet predecessor. Accountability is evaded on a large scale and impunity is the norm. Police are under great pressure to produce confessions and statistics showing high numbers of solved crimes; they operate under few constraints, as the system in law and practice offers

---

[1] A major Amnesty International report on torture in Russia contributed significantly to this raised awareness. See, Amnesty International, "Torture in Russia: 'This Man-Made Hell'" (EUR 46/04/97), April 1997.

[2] There is, however, a clear ethnic dimension to a pattern of abuse, including police violence, in the enforcement of residence permit requirements. See, Human Rights Watch, "Russia: Ethnic Discrimination in Southern Russia," *A Human Rights Watch Report*, Vol. 10, No. 8 (D) July 1998; Human Rights Watch, "Moscow: Open Season, Closed City," *A Human Rights Watch Report*, Vol. 9, No. 10 (D) September 1997. Also, during the 1994-1996 war in Chechnya, Russian security forces tortured Chechen men almost exclusively to coerce intelligence information. The torture took place in so-called "filtration camps" in the Northern Caucasus operated in part by the Ministry of Internal Affairs. See, The Memorial Human Rights Center, *Chechnya: Tsep' oshibok i prestuplenii* (Chechnya: A Chain of Mistakes and Crimes) (Moscow, 1998), pp.21-233. Human Rights Watch, "Russia: Three Months of War in Chechnya," *A Human Rights Watch Report*, Vol. 7, No. 6 February 1995; Human Rights Watch, "Russia/Chechnya: A Legacy of Abuse," *A Human Rights Watch Report*, Vol. 9, No. 2(D) January 1997.

The Methodology of Torture

insufficient legal and judicial safeguards against abuse. These issues are discussed elsewhere in this report.

The most widespread method of police torture in Russia is prolonged beating. Asphyxiation, suspension by the arms or legs, and electroshock are also common. In addition, police use trusted prisoners in pretrial cells as proxies to beat and threaten suspects into cooperating with the investigation. Police almost always combine physical torture with threats of further physical harm and other psychological abuse. In some cases, torture has led to the victim's death or permanent disability. Most torture victims interviewed by Human Rights Watch were adult males; we interviewed five victims who were minors when they were tortured, witnesses to the torture of minors, and the parents of the five minors. We examined only four cases of female suspects who were ill-treated, although further research is required to draw significant conclusions about the treatment of women in the course of police investigations.

In a letter to then-Minister of Internal Affairs Sergei Stepashin, Russia's ombudsman, Oleg Mironov, wrote that half of the detainees he had spoken to at detention centers claimed they were tortured.[3] Several judges and former judges have made observations on the endemic nature of torture in criminal cases that characterize the problem as even more severe. According to Moscow City Court Judge Sergei Pashin, an outspoken advocate of judicial reform, four out of five defendants who appear before him claim they were tortured. According to Pashin, there is evidence of torture in about half of these cases.[4] One former judge told Human Rights Watch that, based on her experience as a judge, she believes up to 80 percent of defendants who persistently refuse to confess may have been subjected to torture.[5]

An indication of the frequency of torture is the growing number of torture complaints that almost all human rights organizations in Russia receive on a regular

---

[3] Human Rights Watch interview with Oleg Mironov, Moscow, February 16, 1999. For a copy of the letter and the response of the Ministry of Internal Affairs, see appendices B and C. The office of the ombudsman was created in 1998 to defend citizens against violations of their rights. The ombudsman has far-reaching powers to do so, including unlimited access to penitentiary institutions and police stations. The ombudsman also has access to official information and officials are obliged to answer his inquiries.

[4] Human Rights Watch interview with Sergei Pashin, Moscow, January 28, 1999. It should be noted that the cases Pashin hears involve particular serious crimes and not necessarily representative of all criminal cases.

[5] Human Rights Watch interview with Elena Raskevich, Moscow, July 9, 1998.

basis. National and regional newspapers have printed dozens of articles about torture and other police abuses during the past four years.

The frequency of torture appears to vary among police stations. According to Sergei Pashin, torture methods are used to some extent in all police precincts in Moscow. However, he qualified about 15 percent of the Moscow police stations as "bad," primarily the new ones.[6] According to some observers, a contributing factor is that officers assigned to new police stations are taken from other precincts, which are reluctant to give up their best officers and instead see an opportunity to get rid of, among others, those who are most frequently the subject of complaints. Andrei Babushkin, of the Committee for Civil Rights, believes that the frequency of torture in a particular precinct also depends on the district—what in effect amounts to a class distinction. In older districts with a more settled population made up mainly of white-collar workers and businessmen, torture is usually less frequent than in districts with a low-income population.[7] The level of tolerance toward beatings and other means of coercion on the part of the police chief may play the principal role. According to Mikhail Pashkin of the Union of Police Officers of the City of Moscow, police chiefs usually know which officers torture suspects and could thus prevent it from happening.[8]

Human rights activists have observed an increased frequency in the use of torture to solve minor crimes, such as theft. Because torture is mainly used as a means of coercing a confession, once a satisfactory confession has been secured torture usually stops. Those who confess immediately are unlikely to be tortured, although they may be beaten when detained.

Torture begins at various times after detention. The accounts of former detainees who were arrested at home reveal a consistent pattern of police behavior. Several recounted how, while police behaved politely in homes (in the presence of relatives), their tone suddenly changed in the police car or at the station. There, suspects were no longer addressed with the polite "*vy*" but with the familiar "*ty*" and police made it clear that the detainee had nowhere to turn, that he was "a nobody," that they could "do with him whatever they want," "that nothing and no one could help him," and that he had "better cooperate, or else...." Using a combination of psychological and physical violence, police try to utterly disorient the individual, or reduce him or her to a state of shock so that he or she will provide any

---

[6] Human Rights Watch interview with Sergei Pashin, Moscow, January 28, 1999.
[7] Human Rights Watch interview with Andrei Babushkin, Moscow, February 15, 1999. The Committee for Civil Rights began publishing reports on torture in Russia in 1996.
[8] Human Rights Watch interview with Mikhail Pashkin, chair of the Coordination Council of the Union of Police Officers of the City of Moscow, Moscow, February 25, 1999.

"necessary" information or sign any document. Igor Kaliapin of the Nizhnii Novgorod Society for Human Rights told Human Rights Watch:

> The conversation [at the police station] is not one between a policeman and a citizen [but] a real settling of scores, as bandits settle scores, pulling someone into a dark place, that's exactly what happens here.
>
> The point is not to beat someone up but to bring him into such a state of shock that he realizes that he is nobody here.... Sometimes, alarmed relatives from whom they took him three, four, five hours ago [start phoning]. It's night time. Relatives start phoning and the person who just beat you may pick up the phone in the office and say: "No, you know, we're still talking, phone back later." You hear that and understand that behind you something has slammed shut.[9]

In many cases, police officers first "offer" suspects the chance to sign a confession, or attempt to coerce them into doing so through threats. In others, they beat the suspect even before telling him what he has been accused of or what they want from him. For example, Boris Botvinnik told Human Rights Watch that when police rang the doorbell to his apartment, riot police, who had forced their way into his apartment from the balcony, beat him to the floor even before he was able to open fully the door.[10]

In most cases, police investigators (who are senior police officers with legal training) do not take part in beatings and torture, leaving this to police detectives. They are usually not present during most of the abuse but walk in from time to time to check if any "progress" is being made, encouraging their subordinates using such euphemisms as "continue to work with him," or "continue your conversation." For example, Anton Shamberov told Human Rights Watch that his case investigator, Senior Investigator Alexander Bubnov of the Nizhnii Novgorod City Procuracy, from time to time walked into the office where Shamberov was being tortured to ask about the progress of the interrogation:

> The detectives told him that I am very stubborn.... They said that they were not getting any results. He [Bubnov] told them: "Continue to

---

[9] Human Rights Watch interview with Igor Kaliapin, Nizhnii Novgorod, October 17, 1997.
[10] Human Rights Watch interview with Boris Botvinnik, Moscow, March 14, 1997.

work." He meant to continue the beatings and all sorts of tricks so that I would give testimony.[11]

Numerous torture victims and several procurators told Human Rights Watch that abusive police are careful to avoid leaving visible marks of physical abuse. However, in many cases police inevitably left visible marks, claiming later that the suspect sustained the injury while resisting arrest or as a result of an accident, without police involvement.[12]

Sustained Beatings

The most widespread method of police torture is sustained beating. Police punch, kick, and use nightsticks or other instruments, aiming for the victim's head, back, legs, kidney area, and heels.

Anton Shamberov and his brother Kirill Komlev were detained on September 5, 1996 and accused of having murdered a former police officer. According to Shamberov's testimony, once they arrived at the police station, officers immediately started beating them. Shamberov told Human Rights Watch:

> Popov [a policeman] came in...and said: "I know all about you, that you killed a guy, you killed Berzman." I said that I had no clue what he was talking about. He said: "Well, if you don't, we will talk with you differently now." Seven or eight detectives came in.... They started to beat me: "Tell us, how did it happen...." I didn't know what they were talking about. Then their boss, a big one...about fifty years of age, brought in four nightsticks. They beat me, mainly, on the body, then they lay me down on a bench, took my sneakers off and beat on my heels; they beat my heels for a very long time, I couldn't walk for two days afterwards.... Sometimes they beat me on the head, lay me down on my stomach, not on a couch but on a bench.... I don't remember how long they beat me but it seemed a very long time.
>
> [At the end of the day] they took me to the IVS[13] [police holding center], I rested there overnight, you could say. In the morning...the detectives were there and the "work" continued. As I understood, there were ten

---

[11] Human Rights Watch interview with Anton Shamberov, Nizhnii Novgorod, October 18, 1997.

[12] One of the most common among the latter is the police claim that the injured detainee fell.

[13] Izoliator vremenogo soderzhaniia. These are holding cells, usually in central city police stations.

people [detectives] and they [worked] with all three or four of us [suspects].... Two young detectives were with me constantly...and from time to time others walked in, who, as I understood, were beating in other offices, but came in to me to give me a slap...I was beaten to such an extent—they have stools that are attached to the floor—that I fell over together with the stool. That day they beat mainly on the arms and legs.

On September 8, on Monday, when the detectives arrived, the same started again, only in other offices, but not constantly.... [On the 11th or 12th at around midday] Denisov, the head of the investigative department, came in. He came in and sent all the detectives out of the office, saying he would talk to me. He offered me a seat at the table, he sat down himself and talked fairly politely. He said: "You should understand that we have a serious organization and if you ended up here, you are unlikely to leave. Be a good man." I didn't say anything to him, only listened to what he told me. He said: "O.K., if you don't want to...," and left. The detectives came in again, put me against the wall, encircled me and started to beat.... These beatings continued literally until the 13th [of September].[14]

Police came to the apartment where Andrei Getsko was staying in Bratsk at 1:00 a.m., September 30, 1994, to detain him on suspicion of armed robbery. In a failed attempt to escape, Getsko jumped down from the balcony; he was detained after a police officer shot him in the foot. Police officers beat Getsko on the ride to the hospital, and continued to do so in the hospital elevator. He told Human Rights Watch: "They were beating me, I was on the floor, all covered in blood. The doors opened and the doctors entered the lift and said: 'What are you doing here, who are you beating up? Animals!'"[15] Police replied that they were carrying a "dangerous criminal" and refused to show their ID cards. The doctors took Getsko to an operating room and performed minor surgery on his foot.

Despite a doctor's instructions for Getsko to remain in the hospital, police took him to the police station immediately after the operation. Waiting for a car outside the hospital, officers kicked him in the injured foot. On arrival later that night at GOM 1, the main city police station in Bratsk,[16] they reportedly resumed beating Getsko in an office on the second floor. According to his account, they put

---

[14] Human Rights Watch interview with Anton Shamberov, Nizhnii Novgorod, October 18, 1997.
[15] Human Rights Watch interview with Andrei Getsko, Bratsk, April 5, 1998.
[16] GOM is the Russian acronym for gorodskoe otdelenie militsiia, or city police department.

him on his stomach on a table, laid a thin file on him, and beat him with a crowbar over the file:

> They brought in the crowbar, stretched me out over the table.... One stretched my legs, another my arms, they put a thin file on my back and started to beat me with the crowbar on the back, kidneys, lungs.... Then they started to beat me with a nightstick on the back, now without any files. That was on the table too. Two held me and two beat me.[17]

Fearing that he would die or become crippled, Getsko said he eventually wrote a confession, which police officers dictated to him. He was subsequently sent to the prison hospital and then the SIZO (pretrial detention center) in Bratsk, where he spent three years awaiting trial hearings that were repeatedly suspended. With the help of a local human rights organization, Getsko was released on bail on September 16, 1997. In 1999, the procuracy dropped the criminal charges against Getsko.

On September 25, 1996, a group of Cheremkhovo (Irkutsk province) policemen drove then thirty-one-year-old Andrei Kol'tsov to a forest approximately two kilometers from the local IVS, where, by his account, they beat him and threatened him with being torn apart:

> They pulled me out of the car and started to beat me.... The beating continued, I think, for two hours, it was during the day, right after lunch. They beat me all over my body, only not in my face. They beat me especially on the buttocks. My whole back was bruised. My hands were handcuffed behind my back. They put [me] on the ground and beat me there. The jacket of one of the detectives even ripped under the armpits.
>
> It went so far that they attached one of my legs to a tree [with a rope], and the other to the car.... He [Chernyshev, the head of the local organized crime unit][18] said: "We will blow up and bury you." He also repeated that he had permission from the procurator to shoot me during an escape attempt.... They turned on [the engine], of course, stretched the rope, and he [Chernyshev] stepped on the rope, one [of the police officers] sat behind the steering wheel. What happened was that you do

---

[17] Human Rights Watch interview with Andrei Getsko, Bratsk, April 5, 1998.
[18] In Russian, the organized crime unit is referred to by its acronym, RUOP, raionnoe upravlenie po bor'be s organizovannoi prestupnost'iu, or the district directorate for organized crime.

a split. They stopped because I agreed to their conditions [to write a confession].[19]

Human Rights Watch researchers viewed medical documents from the IVS and the reports of a forensic examination that corroborated the injuries Kol'tsov described, registering numerous large bruises on the chest and a broken rib.

In October 1995, an inhabitant of the city of Bratsk in Irkutsk province was, by his account, beaten both at the police station and in a forest:

> They detained us and brought us in [to the police station], sat us down at a table, gave a us pen, a piece of paper and said: "Write." Write what? He walked up, he had a bottle of vodka and drank from it, he hit me with a nightstick, sat there drunk.
>
> You sit there on a chair, they walk up and beat from two sides.... They beat [me] together or in shifts.... [The beatings continued] [a]ll night and the following morning until lunch. All night they beat without interruption. They maybe calmed down for a minute, sat down [and then started again].
>
> The following day he [one of the detectives] ran in immediately after the roll call [in the IVS], very angry.... [H]e put me in the car and took me to a church.... The church stood some fifty meters [from the forest], close by. They attached me to a tree with handcuffs, reached for a gun and began to threaten me: "We will shoot you now! Answer our questions!" I said that I won't answer. And that was it. They beat me with [their] fists and kicked me in my chest and stomach. That continued for about an hour, then they put me in the car and brought me to the [IVS].[20]

In some cases, police beat detainees on the head through books or criminal case binders to avoid leaving traces. For example, Denis Iuzhnii from Ekaterinburg, who was detained on suspicion of burglary, told Human Rights Watch:

> They sat me down on a chair and put a "Talmud" with [criminal] files on my head and started to beat me on top of it so as to not leave any

---

[19] Human Rights Watch interview with Andrei Kol'tsov, Cheremkhovo, Irkutsk province, April 2, 1998.
[20] Human Rights Watch interview with Sergei Sergeev, Bratsk, Irkutsk province, April 6, 1998. "Sergei Sergeev" is not the man's real name.

> marks.... They kept me under that file for about five hours. [Then] I told them: "O.K., guys, write down whatever you want and I'll sign it."[21]

Andrei Tuzikov, from Bratsk, told Human Rights Watch a similar account:

> They brought me into the office from the KPZ.[22] [A detective] took the handcuffs off one hand and reattached it to a radiator.... I stood [there]. He put a book on my head and hit [me]. I didn't see exactly with what, but I think it was some sort of stick and he hit me several times. The book was thick with a hard cover. I didn't loose consciousness but lost my orientation.[23]

"Slonik" and Plastic Bags

Why would we need to use a gas mask when there are plastic bags?

> —Sasha Sidorov, a police detective, denying that police use gas masks to torture suspects.[24]

Torture by near asphyxiation is used less frequently than sustained beatings but almost always in combination with them. Police officers handcuff their victim to a chair and force an old-fashioned gas mask or plastic bag over the head. Subsequently, the oxygen supply is cut; at this point, in many cases, police beat the suspect, causing him to hyperventilate. Some victims reported losing consciousness; police revived them to demand they write a confession and repeated the procedure if they resisted. This type of torture is called *"slonik"* or elephant in Russian, a reference to the resemblance of the gas mask's hose to an elephant's trunk.[25]

In 1998, the Supreme Court of the Republic of Mordovia convicted seven police officers for torturing several criminal suspects, using asphyxiation in combination with suspension. One of the detainees had died as a result of the

---

[21] Human Rights Watch interview with Denis Iuzhnii, Ekaterinburg, August 13, 1997.
[22] Kamera predvaritel'nogo zakliuchenie, or a temporary holding cell in a police precinct.
[23] Human Rights Watch interview with Andrei Tuzikov, Bratsk, Irkutsk province, April 5, 1998.
[24] Human Rights Watch interview with Sasha Sidorov, Irkutsk, April 9, 1998. "Sasha Sidorov" is not the man's real name.
[25] The Moscow Prison Reform Center reported that police sometimes spray tear gas in the gas mask to make the victim vomit and force the victim to look at himself in the mirror as a form of humiliation. Human Rights Watch research could not confirm this practice.

torture. Presiding Judge Vasilii Martyshkin issued a statement supplementing the verdict (*chastnoe opredelenie*[26]) in which he described the torture:

> Thus, as the court established, in April 1994 in an MVD building,[27] in office no. 343, [police officers] Daev, Sazonov, Antonov used force during a so-called "informal questioning" before the interrogation of [criminal suspects] Derkaev A.A., Abramov V.V., Abramov N.A., and others by investigator of the Investigative Department of the MVD Ushakov V.P. In doing so, they put a gas mask on their heads, cutting the oxygen with the aim of receiving confessions from the suspects to stealing a MTZ-80 tractor from the collective farm "Kalinin" in the Bol'shebereznikovskii district of Mordovia. [The policemen] handcuffed [the brothers] Abramov, Derkaev, and the other victims, tied their legs to the floor, pulled their head toward the legs with the belt of a kimono, and beat them. One victim in the case, police major and chief of the B. Bereznikovskii GAI, Abramov N.A., lost consciousness.
>
> As [suspect] Abramov V.V. testified in court, he was tied in the "konvertik" position and put on his back, [police officer] Antonov and the other MVD employees beat him with the strap of the gas mask on the scrotum. Derkaev, who sustained a broken rib during the "informal questioning," told the court that [police officer] Frolkin, after putting his foot on [Derkaev's] genitals, demanded a confession, saying that he will not need them [his genitals] anymore in life.
>
> On July 25, 1995, [police officers] Daev, Sazonov, Guliaikin demanded a confession to armed robbery from minor Lavrent'ev A.S. in office no. 306 of the Lenin ROVD[28] and demanded that he name accomplices. They asphyxiated the minor several times with a type RSh-4 gas mask.

---

[26] Under article 21(2) of the Russian criminal procedure code, a judge can issue a separate statement, or *chastnoe opredelenie*, to state agencies, public organizations, or officials whenever he or she has established in court that violations of the law and human rights, reasons for the commission of the crime, or circumstances that promoted its commission demand appropriate measures from these agencies. See Appendix F for the full text of the separate statement.

[27] MVD is the Russian acronym for Ministerstvo Vnutrennikh Del, or Ministry of Internal Affairs.

[28] ROVD is the Russian acronym for raionoe otdeleniie vnutrennykh del, or district police station.

During the torture, which lasted for a long time, Lavrent'ev twice urinated on himself, and was beaten.

Unable to withstand the violence, the minor implicated his acquaintance Igonin O.V., assuming that the latter was serving in the army. However, Lavrent'ev was mistaken, because Igonin was a student.

During the night of July 25, 1995, [police officers] Daev, Sazonov, Kuflin, Guliaikin, on the instruction of former heads of the Lenin ROVD in Saransk—Golov Iu.I., Chekhonin V.A.—detained Igonin O.V. in the presence of his parents at his home.

Without submitting the detained Igonin O.V. to the duty officer's department [for registration], without writing a detention report, during night time—at 2:00 a.m.—Daev, Sazonov, Guliaikin, Kuflin, began to force Igonin into confessing to armed robbery...after they handcuffed him and bound his legs. To that end, they all together put a gas mask [on Igonin] and cut the oxygen. When Igonin choked, they brought him to his senses and the torture session was repeated. At around 4:00 a.m. of July 26, 1995, Igonin died, unable to stand the "informal questioning," as the defendants [the policemen] called their actions with respect to the victims.[29]

Although torture cases that do not result in deaths in custody are rarely prosecuted, an apparently similar case in Ekaterinburg was prosecuted in 1997, but did not result in a conviction. Procurator Evgenii Ergashev told Human Rights Watch that the deputy head of criminal investigation of the Kirov district police department, Sergei Kolosovskii, and two of his subordinates had beaten a young man by the name of Paivin for hours at the Kirov station, and had asphyxiated him by forcing a gas mask over his head and spraying alcohol or ammonia into it.[30]

Police reportedly used near suffocation on fifteen-year-old Oleg Fetisov from Ekaterinburg in 1996. Fetisov told Human Rights Watch:

At first they just beat [me], then they handcuffed my hands behind my back, sat me down on a chair and put a gas mask on my head and cut off the pipe. That was repeated about four times.... The first and second time

---

[29] *Chastnoe opredelenie* by Judge Vasilii Martyshkin of the Supreme Court of the Republic of Mordovia, case 2-4/98, February 12, 1998.
[30] Human Rights Watch interview with Evgenii Ergashev, Ekaterinburg, August 12, 1997.

I almost lost consciousness, they took off the gas mask and I sat down on the chair, they allowed me to rest. They kept me without air for about a minute, maybe a bit longer.[31]

Boris Botvinnik, a mathematics Ph.D. candidate studying in Moscow, told Human Rights Watch of his interrogation in September 1996:

While they were carrying out the house search there, they found a gas mask. That was still without the witnesses [who were called in for the house search] and they put the gas mask on me, closed the breathing valve, and asked me some things. Then they decided to interrupt [the session] and called in the witnesses.[32]

Botvinnik told Human Rights Watch that the witnesses stayed for only ten minutes, after which police took him outside and beat him in the courtyard for half an hour. He was then taken back into the building:

The riot police officer started to pick a plastic bag from my bag. He said that he wasn't going to waste his own, and methodically took bags out of my bag and blew into them. I think the third one he picked was a red LEGO bag. I had bought Sashka [Botvinnik's daughter] a present for her first half-a-year, the bag turned out to be intact. They put the bag over my head. From time to time the detective came in. As I understood, he clarified some details because the riot police did not know what was needed.... The bag on my head, they beat on my forehead and ears. Sometimes, when I held my breath for a long time, they punched my solar plexus.[33]

Andrei Kol'tsov, from Irkutsk province, told Human Rights Watch that after he had signed a forced confession in 1996, police demanded material evidence from him and torture resumed. They wanted to know what car Kol'tsov had used to take away the televisions he had allegedly stolen and where those televisions could be found. When Kol'tsov said that he did not know, police turned to the gas mask:

---

[31] Human Rights Watch interview with Oleg Fetisov, Ekaterinburg, August 11, 1997.
[32] Human Rights Watch interview with Boris Botvinnik, Moscow, March 14, 1997. In Soviet times, the civil defense (*grazhdanskaia oborona*) handed out gas masks to all households as a precaution for possible chemical weapons attacks. These gas masks remain in many Russian apartments.
[33] Human Rights Watch interview with Boris Botvinnik, Moscow, March 14, 1997.

He [the investigator] said to me: "In what car did you take away those televisions?" I said: "I don't know about any car, I didn't touch those televisions." I continued to deny [it] after [signing] that confession. He said: "Well, maybe we shall force you to remember?" He took a gas mask out of the cupboard.... [They cut the oxygen] until I started to choke and to fall. They didn't spray anything into it, just held my breath, did that two or three times. After the gas mask they didn't do anything more, they stopped for some reason, they maybe got scared: my condition was so [bad].[34]

Alexander Volod'ko, who was detained and interrogated in 1996 in Aleksin (Tula province), wrote in a diary that on two occasions, police had asphyxiated him by dunking his head in a puddle, somewhere out in the forest by a river not far from Aleksin:

[T]hey grabbed my legs and put my head in the water, mud, and stones. It wasn't deep there, only my face and ears were under water, not more. I was turned over, and the water gushed into my nostrils, causing severe pain. I started to choke and twitch, swallowing the mud and water with my mouth, mentally already saying goodbye to my loved ones—the horrible moment of transition into nothing—but then they pulled me out. They didn't give me time to recover my breath and, beating me, threw me in the car...[35]

Electroshock
Human Rights Watch interviewed only three persons from three different regions who said that they were tortured by electroshock. However, human rights activists in a number of regions report that police use electroshock frequently. Andrei Babushkin, of the Committee for Civil Rights, stated that electroshock is used quite regularly in Moscow because it leaves only few marks that pass quickly.[36] The Nizhnii Novgorod Society for Human Rights has also received various reports on the use of electroshock.

---

[34] Human Rights Watch interview with Andrei Kol'tsov, Cheremkhovo, Irkutsk province, April 2, 1998.
[35] Alexander Volod'ko wrote *Diary of Torture* about his experience in detention. The diary was smuggled out of prison and excerpts were published. See, Moscow Center for Prison Reform, *Nasilie v organakh MVD* (Moscow, 1998), pp. 5-18.
[36] Human Rights Watch interview with Andrei Babushkin, Moscow, February 15, 1999.

Igor Akhrimenko told Human Rights Watch that he was subjected to electroshock in April 1994 and described a small machine through which he said it was applied:

> They took me into a room for the first time.... Immediately Veber [a detective] hit [me]from the side, nobody said anything, he punched me in the temple.... Yes, I lost consciousness for maybe two minutes. Then they put handcuffs on me and attached me to a radiator. They have an electric "cranking machine," they attached it to my ears and turned on the current. It's impossible to stand that!
>
> It's such a small machine, with a handle. From the "cranking machine" to the ears went two electric wires with clamps, they were attached to the ear lobe. I was attached to the radiator, and one [policeman] still held me by the legs, another by the head. They asked me questions and turned the handle around. At first they turned slowly, then faster. When they turned [it] quickly, I just lost consciousness. I lost consciousness five times...[37]

Dmitrii Koriagin from Pereslavl'-Zalesski, a city about one hundred kilometers from Moscow, wrote a complaint to the procuracy in which he said that police officers in Pereslavl'-Zalesskii tortured him by suspension until he lost consciousness. When he came to, he reported, police subjected him to electroshock:

> [After I regained consciousness] I started to scream again and demanded that they untie me and stop the torture. Suddenly I felt an electroshock and lost consciousness again. When I woke up, I felt a change in my consciousness. My whole body ached from pain. It seemed like everything was moving, as in slow motion, up-down.[38]

Suspension and Trussing

Russian police use a variety of positions for torture involving suspension or painful binding of a prisoner. For the *"lastochka"* (the swallow) position, the victim's hands may be cuffed behind his back and attached to an iron bar or pipe; he thus hangs, without his legs touching the ground, while police beat him with

---

[37] Human Rights Watch interview with Igor Akhrimenko, Irkutsk, Sizo 1, April 8, 1998.
[38] Complaint to the procuracy in Pereslavl'-Zalesskii concerning the detention of Dmitrii Koriagin on August 3, 1997, written March 3, 1998.

nightsticks.³⁹ In a variation on "lastochka," the detainee is forced face down on the ground and his legs are tied tightly with a rope to the handcuffed hands. These positions cause grave pain in the joints, cut off blood supply to the wrists, and dislocate arms or shoulders. In the *"konvertik"* (the envelope) position, the detainee is forced to sit with his head between his bent knees while his hands are tied to his feet. In Nizhnii Novgorod, a detainee died in the mid-1990s after being held in this position for a long period and subjected to sustained beatings. A forensic medical examination found forty bruises on his body, which had been inflicted by nightsticks.⁴⁰

Dmitrii Koriagin wrote in a complaint to the procuracy that he and his brothers, Ivan and Alexander, were detained in a state of intoxication on August 3, 1997 in Pereslavl'-Zalesskii. The three men had complained about their arrest, he said, and in response police beat them at the precinct with nightsticks and sprayed tear gas in their eyes. Dmitrii Koriagin was taken into a separate room and made to undress:

> They twisted my arms behind my back, put on handcuffs so that I could not move my wrists. Then they threw me on a torture mattress head down. This is a mattress that is covered in leather. It is attached to an iron bench, the legs of which are attached to the floor. At the end of the mattress my legs were tied by the ankle. Then they put a rope under the chain of the handcuffs so that it wound around it and both ends of the rope strongly stretched over my back so that, as it seemed to me, they will break my hands in the joints.⁴¹

---

[39] In the case of *Aksoy* v. *Turkey* (December 18, 1996), the European Court of Human Rights ruled that the treatment to which Mr. Aksoy had been subjected ("Palestinian hanging": he was stripped naked, with his arms tied together behind his back, and suspended by his arms) constitutes torture. The court held that:

> this treatment could only have been deliberately inflicted; indeed, a certain amount of preparation and exertion would have been required to carry it out. It would appear to have been administered with the aim of obtaining admissions or information from the applicant. In addition to the severe pain which it must have caused at the time, the medical evidence shows that it led to a paralysis of both arms which lasted for some time (...). The Court considers that this treatment was of such a serious and cruel nature that it can only be described as torture. (Para. 64)

[40] See, Nizhnii Novgorod Society for Human Rights, "The Use of Torture on the Territory of the Nizhnii Novgorod Province, 1997," p. 13, the case of Mr. Chistiakov.

[41] Complaint to the procuracy in Pereslavl'-Zalesskii concerning detention of Dmitrii Koriagin on August 3, 1997, written March 3, 1998.

After the brothers' administrative court hearing for public drunkenness, Dmitrii Koriagin was allowed to speak with his brother Alexander, who, he said, told him he had been hung from a roofbeam:

> Alexander told me that they had hung him down from a rafter twice with his arms twisted in handcuffs [so that his feet didn't touch the ground], while they beat him up, and that he had spat blood in the face of police chief Mukhin when he [Mukhin] had lifted his head by [his] hair as he was hanging down from the rafter.[42]

Anatolii Koriagin, the father of the three men, told Human Rights Watch that police hung Alexander until he lost consciousness, took him down, and then put up Koriagin's eldest son, Ivan. When Alexander again complained about the treatment, police hung him from the rafter once more.[43] Police charged Ivan Koriagin with extortion, and released Dmitrii and Alexander.

German Il'in of Irkutsk province told Human Rights Watch that police had suspended him from a pipe in November 1995:

> Well, they handcuffed me over a pipe, the pipe's between the hands, it was a warm pipe. They lifted [me] up just a bit and I hung, my feet were just barely above the ground.... I hung there for twenty to thirty minutes, I don't remember exactly. There ten minutes seem like a century. [While I was hanging] he beat me in the liver and kidney areas unexpectedly.[44]

Torture by Proxy
When someone doesn't confess and the police officer thinks he is guilty, they just lock him up under article 122 of the criminal procedure code[45].... A protocol is written and he's taken to the IVS, where they put him [in a cell] with criminals and they [the criminals] not only start to beat him but possibly even torture him.

---

[42] Ibid.
[43] Human Rights Watch interview with Anatolii Koriagin, Moscow, April 13, 1998.
[44] Human Rights Watch interview with German Il'in, Ikei, Tununsk district, Irkutsk province, April 3, 1998.
[45] Article 122 of the criminal procedure code sets out circumstances under which police may detain people on suspicion of having committed of a criminal offense for up to seventy-two hours without a prior warrant from the procuracy.

> *I, for example, would myself never beat someone to leave visible marks. Why would you risk yourself, your freedom? It's better to send [the person] to the SIZO and let them work on him over there.*
>
> —Sasha Sidorov, a police detective from Irkutsk, April 9, 1998.[46]

Police detectives use criminal suspects and defendants who are trusted and given special privileges in SIZOs and IVSs to beat, rape, or otherwise force suspects and defendants into confessing or providing needed testimony. This widespread practice is called the "pressing room" or "press hut" (*press-khata* in Russian) because police trustees "press" the detainee within the confines of the pretrial cell. In exchange for their services, these prisoners—who serve both as police enforcers and informers—receive privileges, such as access to narcotics and women. Elena Zheletskaia, a lawyer with regular access to the SIZO in Ekaterinburg, told Human Rights Watch:

> [T]here are cells that work for the detectives, they're called "red cells." The person there is not held as everywhere else, there [they have] all privileges: a television, a tape player...and, most importantly, seven beds for seven people.... Say, the head of the criminal police or police chief tells the detectives in the prison that this or that person is on his way and that certain information needs to be received from that person, and they put him in a "red cell," and there they [the informers] extract [the information] gradually.... The cell mates organize beatings, strangling sessions, don't allow them to leave the cell, don't give them water.... They don't necessary beat, they can morally trample on them.[47]

Torture by proxy was highlighted in the 1994 report by the U.N. Special Rapporteur on Torture, Nigel Rodley. The Special Rapporteur wrote that during his twelve-day visit to Russia, he received "persistent reports from reliable sources that violent inmates are intentionally placed in cells to brutalize other inmates and to break their wills by creating an atmosphere of fear and repression, with a view to securing confessions or other information."

In late 1993, Mikhail Iurochko, a man in his early twenties from Arkhangel'sk, was detained in his home town on suspicion of the murder of his two nieces, and

---

[46] Human Rights Watch interview with Sasha Sidorov, Irkutsk, April 9, 1998. "Sasha Sidorov" is not the man's real name.
[47] Human Rights Watch interview with Vera Strebizh and Elena Zheletskaia, of Shans, a children's rights organization, Ekaterinburg, August 10, 1997.

confessed after police placed him in a "pressing room." Although courts found him guilty of the crimes on two occasions on the basis of confessions, Russia's Supreme Court overturned his own and his "accomplices" convictions—and his death sentence—on both occasions pointing to a lack of evidence. In 1999, the procuracy in Arkhangel'sk dropped the criminal charges against Iurochko and his codefendants.

In October 1993, Iurochko's cell mate in the pressing room at first put mainly psychological pressure on him, but eventually raped him to compel him to testify against his friends. At the same time, the investigator tried to force him to confess to the crime as well:

> [W]hen I was in the IVS, my cell mate started to "convince" me more categorically, saying that they could beat me up, rape me.... The detectives questioned me the whole day, sometimes until 2:00 a.m.... [He] laid hands on me. He didn't beat me up but punched me, [giving] slaps on the back of the head. He disturbed the rhythm of my thoughts, so to say, so that I didn't feel comfortable.[48]

After three days, Iurochko confessed to the murder and police pressured him to implicate some of his friends:

> They put [another] cell mate with me, one with experience [in the prison system]. He started to coach me, saying: "Let's have more people, especially those who were close, who maintained contact with you, your friends."...[49]

> He kept leading me on and leading me on, detectives visited me, talked, threatened: "we'll show you your place, we'll rape you, we'll break you, nobody and nothing can help you." They would send me back to the cell, say horrible things about my mother, sister, and the rest was done by my cell mate, he was a direct participant, very direct.[50]

> He, so to speak, humiliated me the entire time I was in that place. I felt like my life had come to an end. That was October 17. I had already lost

---

[48] Human Rights Watch interview with Mikhail Iurochko, Arkhangel'sk, July 21, 1998.
[49] Ibid. When Iurochko confessed to the murder, police coerced him also into confessing to having taken goods stolen from the victim's house to a cemetery.
[50] Ibid.

my life potential and in the end my cell mate raped me.... After that, I included Evgenii and Dima [two close friends] in my testimony.[51]

One of the two men implicated, Dmitrii El'sakov, told Human Rights Watch how one police trustee cellmate beat him and burned him with hot water, with obvious police complicity. El'sakov said his ordeal began with police threats:

> It started with threats, slaps on the head [from detectives at the police station]: "You must confess, others are testifying against you, write a confession that you participated in the crime." I said that I didn't commit the crime and wouldn't write anything. "You will write it anyway, you will confess and do what we want. Do you want to be raped? Do you want to be humiliated? With such a crime.... We'll organize that for you right away, we'll fix it."
>
> I was thrown into a cell [at the IVS], as it became clear later, where their agent was sitting. A big one, with tattoos all over. He started to work on me, at first only with words, some sort of screams, attacks: "even if you didn't do it, they [the codefendants] are hanging it on you, you should answer and hang it on him." That went on for three days, then, as they noticed it didn't have an effect, when I came in from the investigator...he [the cell mate] told me straight out that I had to write a confession. I said that I wouldn't write anything. He punched me hard several times in the kidney area—I have problems with my kidneys—I had told him.... I fell on my knees. He choked me a little bit, hit me over the head, and put a piece of paper [in my hand] with a pen and that is how my first so-called repentance appeared, under his dictation.

El'sakov changed his testimony after he was granted access to a lawyer. He was subsequently again put in a "pressing room":

> I walked down from the investigator's office. In half an hour, they literally called in that Misha [the police trustee] from his cell. The detective said that I had withdrawn my confession and that that doesn't fit their plans. Misha came in drunk, after a few minutes with a bottle of vodka, he sat down and started to drink. While he drank, he said all sorts of insults, that he will rape me now, etc.... [H]e hit me over the head and

---

[51] Ibid.

I fell back on the cot, then he threw hot water over me from a tea kettle, it fell on my hand, my back.... I had serious burns. Then they [Misha and two other prison trustees] hit me in the kidney area yet a few more times. Two of his guys were holding me, he hit [me]....[52]

In May 1995, the Arkhangel'sk Province Court sentenced Mikhail Iurochko and codefendant Evgenii Mednikov to death, and Dmitrii El'sakov to fifteen years' imprisonment. On appeal, the Supreme Court overturned the sentence and sent the case back to the procuracy for further investigation. On November 5, 1997, the Arkhangel'sk Province Court once again convicted the men, sentencing Mednikov to death, and Iurochko and El'sakov to fifteen and twelve years respectively. In 1998, the Supreme Court again overturned the sentence and remanded the case to the procuracy, which finally closed the case for "insufficient evidence" on May 31, 1999.[53] All three men have been released.

Threats of Violence

Police combine physical torture with psychological abuse to utterly disorient the individual. This abuse consists primarily of threats of continued physical violence, or threats to the suspect's family. As Aleksandr Turabaev from Irkutsk, himself a torture victim, told Human Rights Watch:

> The term "interrogation" here does not mean that they take a police report and ask you questions. Here, an interrogation [is] when five or six people come together and start to scream insults at you: "you're a horse," "a pig," other insults; "who did you contact!?," "we'll break you," "confess!," "you drunk!"[54]

These insults are usually accompanied by a standard series of threats. These may include threats to "do with you whatever we like"; to kill, rape, or otherwise physically injure the person; to have the person sentenced to death, even if not charged with a crime that carries the death penalty; to throw the person into a "pressing room" where "criminals will take care of you"; and to harm the person's family. Threats against family members are particularly effective, as the individual is isolated from the outside world and has no way of knowing what is happening to them.

---

[52] Human Rights Watch interview with Dmitrii El'sakov, Arkhangel'sk, July 21, 1998.
[53] Decision of the Arkhangel'sk province procuracy of May 31, 1999.
[54] Human Rights Watch interview with Alexander Turabaev, Cheremkhovo, Irkutsk province, April 2, 1998.

For example, in 1996, as described above, police in Nizhnii Novgorod used extensive psychological pressure against Anton Shamberov and his brother, Kirill Komlev, whom they accused of killing a friend of the city police department's chief detective. Shamberov told Human Rights Watch:

> [The detective said:] "Berzman was my friend. Why did you [kill him]?" And to the detectives: "Don't write up a detention report yet. Why did you bring him here? He should have been taken to the forest, as I told you, to shoot him there." One detective, who had detained me, then took a pen knife, unfolded it and said: "I will cut your ears off now." He approached my ears and started to poke a bit there.[55]

Shamberov and Komlev were both told that Mark Berzman, the brother of the murder victim, had mafia links and that he wanted them dead. Police told them they should consider themselves lucky to be at the police station. Shamberov told Human Rights Watch: "They said that Berzman was somehow connected with the mafia, that I'd better confess so that I would go to jail because [then] they wouldn't shoot me in the street, and "you have a family, and a young child."[56]

Police also are said to attempt to lure suspects into escape scenarios, then threaten to kill them should they escape. In such cases, police create the circumstances for an escape, taunt the detainee about escaping, and warn that police officers will shoot him if he tries. As described above, the head of the organized crime department of a local police precinct in Irkutsk province reportedly took Andrei Kol'tsov to a forest:

> They drove me into the forest, opened the door.... They told me: "We have permission to shoot you." Well, they opened the door and offered me the chance to run, saying that the procurator gave permission to shoot me. I said: "Why should I run?" He says: "Well, if you don't want to...." They pulled me out of the car and started to beat me up.[57]

In July 1996, according to Alexander Volodko's published diary, police staged his mock execution near the city of Aleksin in Tula province. Volod'ko wrote:

---

[55] Human Rights Watch interview with Anton Shamberov, Nizhnii Novgorod, October 18, 1997.
[56] Ibid.
[57] Human Rights Watch interview with Andrei Kol'tsov, Cheremkhovo, Irkutsk province, April 2, 1998.

> They said that they knew everything and would shoot me under the guise of an escape attempt. They dragged me via a little path down a slope and placed me by a tree. The "goblin" [masked riot police officer] cocked the gun. "Say your last word!"— "I don't know anything, I'm not guilty of anything, you're killing an innocent person!" Instead of a bullet, [I received] a kick in the chest.[58]

Boris Botvinnik said he was subjected to other methods of psychological pressure, including threats to take revenge on his family if he would not confess.

> In the first report I said that I didn't know anything... .Then they put me in the corridor and fastened me to a pipe and I sat there. While I was sitting there, a detective came up to me and said: "Believe me, you will go to prison anyway, you're either going to go to prison or we give you back [to the riot police, who beat Botvinnik at his apartment]. The question is where you will serve and for how long. If you start to deny it, we have "pressing rooms," and we have more, in the end we hand you over to those detectives, and, besides, we can arrange for the same thing to happen at your home in Volgograd. Whatever you want, take your pick."[59]

Police in Tulunsk district threatened German Il'in that as long as he refused to write a confession his wife, Lida, would be held in detention, and further threatened to put his children in an orphanage. Il'in told Human Rights Watch:

> They said that they will put her in jail...for such a long time that she'll die on the potty et cetera. "The children will remain like that [without parental supervision], and by the time you are released, there won't be anyone left. So, if you sign, your wife will go home." They told me that "they'll rape her now, there are women who are good at doing whatever you want, butch and femme lesbians." That was horrible, I got sick, suffered, let them at least allow Lida to go to the children.... I will give testimony, I will give [it] against myself, as they wish. I wrote what Sveshnikov dictated and gave him the piece of paper.[60]

---

[58] Alexander Volod'ko, *Diary of Torture*.
[59] Human Rights Watch interview with Boris Botvinnik, Moscow, March 14, 1997.
[60] Human Rights Watch interview with German Il'in, Ikei, Tulunsk district, Irkutsk province, April 3, 1998.

Like many others, Il'in told Human Rights Watch that police threatened to send him to a "pressing room:"

> "Well, what?! Did you get it or not, farmer?! Look, you'll get the pressing room and you'll have everything, what do you think? We've broken better ones! Ones like you we'll break—when necessary.
>
> We'll put you in a cell, there they will give it to you...they will kill you, they will hang you...."[61]

Police, according to her account, threatened to send Tatiana Popkova to a "pressing room" when she refused to sign a statement that she had not been allowed to read:

> They told me that "if you don't sign now, we will put you in the KPZ, there are female criminals there, they will straighten things out with you quickly. They will undress you, take your good things away and they will humiliate you, because they are all hardened girls there."[62]

Alexander Turabaev, also from Irkutsk province, said he was told that he would be "thrown to bad people" who would strip him of his male dignity.[63]

---

[61] Ibid.
[62] Human Rights Watch interview with Tatiana Popkova, Usol'e-Sibirskoe, Irkutsk province, April 9, 1998.
[63] Human Rights Watch interview with Alexander Turabaev, Cheremkhovo, Irkutsk province, April 2.

MEDICAL EVIDENCE OF TORTURE

Because torture generally occurs in the absence of eyewitnesses willing to testify, medical evidence is important proof in substantiating a victim's torture claim.[64] It is critical not only for holding accountable the abusive police officer but also for eventually excluding from evidence a confession that has been extracted under duress.

It is vital for the torture victim to be examined by a physician or forensic doctor as soon as possible after the ordeal. Immediately after the abuse, a doctor can often determine with a degree of certainty when the injury was sustained and what caused it. For example, scorch marks on the skin can be linked to electroshock, and long bruises to blows inflicted with a nightstick. In combination with documents on the date and time of arrest and on the detainee's condition upon arrival at the detention center, the abuse can sometimes be proven beyond a reasonable doubt. However, with every day that passes, the level of certainty with which a medical doctor can link the injuries to torture decreases, and within a month most medical evidence will have disappeared, unless injuries leave a scar or have become chronic.[65]

Authoritative international standards, such as the Body of Principles for the Protection of All Persons under Any Form of Detention or Imprisonment (Principles on Detention), recognize the importance of prompt access to medical professionals. The Principles on Detention require that detainees have access to a medical examination "as promptly as possible after his admission to the place of detention

---

[64] Although physical signs of torture may disappear fairly quickly, psychological damage may last for many years. A study by Danish torture specialist Ole Vedel Rasmussen concluded that long-lasting symptoms were present in approximately two-thirds of the torture victims examined. The most frequently recorded symptoms were sleep disturbances, irritability, anxiety, and depression. Psychological examinations of torture victims could provide important evidence of torture. However, during our research in Russia, we did not find a single case in which the procuracy had appointed a psychological expert to provide an assessment. See, Ole Vedel Rasmussen, "Medical Aspects of Torture," *Danish Medical Bulletin,* vol. 37, supplement 1, January 1990, pp. 28-33.

[65] It is often not easy to link scars (from kicks, blows, or burning cigarette butts), damage to the nervous system (which may result from suspension and blows to the head), loss of eyesight (which may result from blows to the head) or brain damage (which may result from asphyxiation) to torture because similar injuries can be sustained otherwise as well. Medical doctors can positively link them to torture only in exceptional cases.

or imprisonment."[66] Further medical care or treatment should be provided whenever necessary, and detainees should in most cases have the right to request a second opinion.[67] All medical examinations should be duly recorded.[68] The U.N. Standard Minimum Rules for the Treatment of Prisoners require that untried detainees have the right to visits by their doctor.[69]

In Russia, however, torture victims are rarely able to obtain a prompt medical visit. Russian criminal procedure, physicians' reluctance to have anything to do with the police, and simple financial constraints combine to make it unlikely that the torture victim will obtain medical documentation of torture.

Access to a Forensic Expert

Law enforcement officials and courts regard conclusions of forensic experts from state-run forensic medical evidence centers as the most authoritative and often refuse to take into serious consideration other medical evidence. However, state forensic experts can examine people only at the request of certain law enforcement officials and judges, and only in the context of a criminal investigation. Thus, a forensic examination cannot generally be ordered as part of the initial, informal inquiry into a torture complaint. Torture victims and their lawyers cannot approach these forensic experts directly. They can, of course, request the investigator or judge in the case to order a forensic examination, but the latter can simply dismiss the

---

[66] Principle 24 states:
> A proper medical examination shall be offered to a detained or imprisoned person as promptly as possible after his admission to the place of detention or imprisonment, and thereafter medical care and treatment shall be provided whenever necessary. This care and treatment shall be provided free of charge.

[67] Principle 25 states:
> A detained or imprisoned person or his counsel shall, subject only to reasonable conditions to ensure security and good order in the place of detention or imprisonment, have the right to request or petition a judicial or other authority for a second medical examination or opinion.

[68] Principle 26 states:
> The fact that a detained or imprisoned person underwent a medical examination, the name of the physician and the results of such an examination shall be duly recorded. Access to such records shall be ensured. Modalities therefore shall be in accordance with relevant rules of domestic law.

[69] Rule 91 of the U.N. Standard Minimum Rules for the Treatment of Prisoners reads: "An untried prisoner shall be allowed to be visited and treated by his own doctor or dentist if there is reasonable ground for his application and he is able to pay any expenses incurred."

request, claiming it is not germane to the criminal case.[70] A vicious circle ensues: Investigators often refuse to institute a criminal investigation against alleged torturers for a lack of sufficient grounds, and without having opened a criminal investigation involving the alleged torturers, the medical examination, which could provide sufficient grounds, cannot be carried out.

Investigators may also order forensic medical examinations of injuries allegedly sustained as a result of police torture in the context of the criminal case against the torture victim. However, they do not usually do so and most requests from lawyers and defendants for such medical assessments are reportedly turned down. For example, in the case discussed above, Boris Botvinnik and his lawyer asked investigators, and later a judge, numerous times to order a forensic examination. Despite the fact that a hospital in Volgograd had diagnosed Botvinnik with head trauma, both investigators and judge refused these repeated requests.

Irkutsk lawyer Robert Sheptalin told Human Rights Watch that it is very difficult to have a forensic expert appointed to examine police torture victims, although deception of the police sometimes allows this:

> The investigator...used physical force against the wife of Chernykh [Sheptalin's client], that is, they started to beat her up so that she would give testimony against her husband.... [After they let her go] I tricked the police officers.... She went to [another] police precinct and said: "I've been beaten up." She didn't say who beat her up. The police officer gave her the referral for a [forensic] examination.[71]

In a rare example, the procuracy investigator on Andrei Kol'tsov's case ordered a forensic examination when Kol'tsov requested one. Medical personnel at the IVS facilities both in Angarsk (September 26, 1996) and in Cheremkhovo (October 8, 1996) had recorded Andrei Kol'tsov's injuries. When Kol'tsov was able to contact his lawyer on October 8, the latter immediately demanded that the case investigator order a forensic examination. The investigator agreed, probably due to the still visible injuries and the examinations by IVS personnel, and a forensic expert examined Kol'tsov on October 23, 1996. Kol'tsov told Human Rights Watch:

> I was called in, taken to the interrogation room [sic] and told: "What kind of complaints do you have. You did complain, right?" I said: "I have a broken rib." The forensic expert asks: "Where is it?" I showed

---

[70] Article 184 of the criminal procedure code states that the investigator can decide to order an expert examination if he "recognizes the necessity of carrying out an expert assessment."
[71] Human Rights Watch interview with Robert Sheptalin, Irkutsk, April 1, 1998.

him. He wrote it down after touching with his hands. We had requested that I be taken to the polyclinic of the city of Cheremkhovo and be examined completely there. The expert recorded only part of the bruises and left.[72]

Access to a Medical Doctor for Former Detainees

When they cannot be examined by a forensic expert, torture victims who have been released have other options to treat and document their injuries. Torture victims who have been released can turn to *travmapunkty*, or emergency rooms, or visit their general practitioner. *Travmapunkty* exist at the district level in every city or village and are equipped to provide first aid, run simple medical tests, and take X-rays. For more complicated examinations, the doctor at the emergency room can direct the individual to a specialist at a polyclinic. Victims can also call in the *skoraia pomoshch*, the ambulance service. If the individual indicates the nature of his injuries, ambulance personnel can bring portable equipment with them to run simple tests on the spot. As with emergency rooms, for more complicated tests the individual will be directed to a specialist at the polyclinic. Also, ambulances are usually manned by doctor's assistants (*fel'dsher*) who do not have a full medical education. *Uchastkovye vrachi*, or general practitioners, are not equipped to run any kind of tests more complicated than measuring blood pressure or checking reflexes and will direct the individual to a specialist if deemed necessary.

These non-forensic doctors are supposed to list the patient's complaints, describe the injuries in detail (including color, shape, length of bruises and wounds, etc.), and note the patient's story about their origin. Forensic doctors can later use these descriptions to establish the approximate time the injury was sustained, the object that caused the injury, and other factors that can play a key role in prosecuting abusers. However, medical examinations performed by emergency rooms, ambulance services, or general practitioners are often not sufficiently thorough or their diagnoses lack the necessary detail for forensic experts to draw categorical conclusions about the cause of injuries. There appears to be a tendency to focus on visible injuries, such as bruises, and ignore internal ones, unless there are specific and unsolicited complaints about organs or senses. For example, if the victim complains of pain resulting from blows to his heels with a club, the doctor may diagnose the heel as being bruised but not take an X-ray, which could confirm damage to the heel bone.

---

[72] Human Rights Watch interview with Andrei Kol'tsov, Cheremkhovo, Irkutsk province, April 2, 1998.

Two forensic experts told Human Rights Watch that the quality and level of detail of medical documents issued by non-forensic doctors are not always sufficient for categorical conclusions.

> These medical documents are by far not always exhaustive in terms of the description [of the injury]. [Regular] doctors are concerned with treatment and their attitude toward description of details—the size of the injuries, their color, in other words the matters that interest us—is such that they often miss them.... Therefore, we can often not answer concrete questions about the time and manner [of the injury].[73]

An additional problem is that doctors become reluctant to examine a torture victim as soon as they learn how the patient sustained his injuries. Doctors are obliged to report any examination of injuries that may be related to a criminal offense to the police and, like most people in Russia, medical professionals prefer to avoid all contact with the police. Such examinations may lead to questioning by a prosecutor, having to testify in court, and possible unpleasant encounters with police officers, who could put the doctor under pressure to change his conclusions. Valerii Abramkin, of the Moscow Center for Prison Reform, told Human Rights Watch:

> [T]hey are just afraid because they are unprotected. Nobody seems to take that into consideration and they say: "why do they [doctors] not issue [medical documents]? Aren't they independent of the police, these emergency rooms?" If you talk to him [a doctor], he will tell you: "Ok, and what will they do with me then, I [have to] live here!" Especially, if [they live] not in Moscow but in a small town.... In any case, it's much easier not to issue [a medical document].[74]

While most medical care is officially free of charge, any medical assistance beyond the most basic has to be paid for in today's Russia. Emergency rooms will still issue, free of charge, medical certificates superficially documenting the state of health of the individual, but they charge for in-depth examinations. This is a financial hardship for victims of police abuse, many of whom are poor.

---

[73] Human Rights Watch interview with Larisa Romanova and Yuri Solntsev, Moscow, February 11, 1999.
[74] Human Rights Watch interview with Valerii Abramkin, July 15, 1998, Moscow.

Detainees' Access to Medical Doctors

The vast majority of victims of torture and ill-treatment remain in detention for many months after their ordeal and face overwhelming difficulties in obtaining medical documentation of torture and ill-treatment. Russian law does not grant untried detainees the right to be examined by their own doctors or a doctor of their own choice, as called for under international standards (see above). Detainees thus depend on the medical personnel at prison and detention centers.

As a rule, police stations and most IVS facilities do not have medical personnel on duty.[75] This means that a detainee must first complain to the duty officer at the detention center or police station, who then decides whether to call an ambulance or provide the detainee with first aid using an emergency kit.

Ex-detainee German Il'in, from the village of Ikei in Irkutsk province, told Human Rights Watch that the duty officer refused him access to a medical professional after he was detained and beaten severely at his farm on November 20, 1995. When police brought him, his wife, his child, and his neighbor to the IVS at the Tulun police station, he demanded a medical examination:

> They took us past the duty officer, kept us in his office and registered us, then they took Lida and myself to a cell. I asked them to record my injuries but they refused. I asked the duty officer, I asked our [local] policemen, Gurikov, Sveshnikov.... They answered: "What expert?! You will have an expert now! One more sound and we'll put you in the punishment cell."[76]

It took approximately one month of constantly demanding access to a doctor by both Il'in and his wife (who had been released) before the police and the procuracy finally agreed to call in a doctor to examine him. In contrast, a former police investigator from Moscow asserted that duty officers do not obstruct access to

---

[75] There appear to be several exceptions to the rule that IVS do not have medical personnel on duty. One torture victim told Human Rights Watch that the IVS in Angarsk and Cheremkhovo (both Irkutsk province) do have medical personnel. Also, the deputy head of Irkutsk province police, Vitalii Bartoshevich, told Human Rights Watch that a nurse is present in the IVS twenty-four hours per day and it is her duty to "record the status [detainees'] health" and possible injuries (Human Rights Watch interview with Vitalii Bartoshevich, Irkutsk, April 9, 1998). On the other hand, the acting head of IVS No. 1 in Novgorod, Mr. Isachenko, told Human Rights Watch that there are no medical personnel at that IVS (Human Rights Watch interview, Novgorod, July 17, 1998).

[76] Human Rights Watch interview with German Il'in, Okei, Tulun district, Irkutsk province, April 3, 1998.

Medical Evidence of Torture

physicians, "Duty officers have a strong incentive not to turn down requests for medical assistance: They will be held responsible if the detainee's condition further deteriorates or he dies."[77] But in practice, access to medical attention in police custody appears to depend solely on the attitude of the officers in charge of the particular detention center.

Another former detainee Human Rights Watch interviewed, Valerii Shapochnikov, complained that when a medical doctor visited him in the IVS in Irkutsk province on November 25, 1997, two days after he was detained and beaten, the examination was only cursory:

> They brought him to me in the KPZ, he examined me in the cell. I undressed to my waist, where everything was swollen, it hurt, my jaw was swollen, I showed him, he looked and says: "Well, you don't have anything there!" I showed him that I urinated with blood and that everything hurt. He said: "No, maybe you have a small internal blood blister and that's it." He turned around and left.[78]

Within three days of the moment of detention, detainees must be transferred to SIZOs from police stations and IVSs.[79] SIZOs have permanent medical staff and every new detainee is examined. Detainees are routinely checked for a series of illnesses, including HIV infection and syphilis. According to the head doctor at the Arkhangel'sk SIZO No. 1, Dr. Alexander Mazanov, other aspects of the detainee's health are checked if he or she has complaints or if there is another reason to do so. He also said that any complaints about beatings or other forms of ill-treatment are entered on the inmate's medical card, including details on the identity of the perpetrator(s), the place, time, and method of ill-treatment. He further said that when a detainee does not have any visible injuries but complains about headaches or pain in the kidneys, doctors can run only elementary tests to establish possible internal damage.[80]

---

[77] Human Rights Watch interview with Vladimir Federov., Moscow, June 8, 1999. "Vladimir Federov" is not the man's real name.

[78] Human Rights Watch interview with Valerii Shapochnikov, Tulun, Irkutsk province, April 4, 1998.

[79] Article 96-2 of the criminal procedure code prohibits police from keeping suspects in IVSs for more than three days. Under presidential decree 1226 of 1994, police could hold criminal suspects believed to be linked to organized crime for thirty days in IVSs. However, this decree was rescinded in 1997.

[80] Human Rights Watch interview with Dr. Alexander Mazanov, chief doctor of SIZO No. 1 in Arkhangel'sk, July 24, 1998.

While access to medical personnel at SIZOs is better than at IVSs or police stations, detainees may mistrust prison doctors. Until September 1998, SIZOs were under the authority of the same ministry as the police. Although they are now part of the Ministry of Justice, many inmates see prison authorities, investigators, and police as belonging to one and the same system.[81] Inmates may therefore decide not to ask for a doctor or not to inform him or her of the real origin of their injuries for fear of repercussions.

Death in Custody or Permanent Physical Damage

Torture causes lasting emotional and physical harm to the victim. It sometimes leads to the death of the suspect, during or subsequent to this treatment. Some deaths in custody have resulted in legal proceedings in Russia and received publicity in the local media, but these cases may represent only a small minority of the total. Public exposure of torture, and prosecutions in turn, seem to be limited largely to cases in which the detainee dies in custody—or is seriously injured—in circumstances that cannot entirely be concealed.

Oleg Igonin from the city of Saransk in the Republic of Mordovia died in 1995 after police tortured him by asphyxiation (see above, "Slonik"). On July 25, 1995, three police detectives from the Lenin police precinct in Saransk detained a minor, A. Lavrent'ev, on suspicion of a robbery. They asphyxiated and beat him, and demanded that he confess to armed robbery and name his accomplices. Lavrent'ev named Oleg Igonin as his alleged co-offender, after which the Saransk precinct chiefs instructed their subordinates to detain Igonin. The three detectives and a colleague detained Igonin at his home at 2:00 a.m., brought him to the police station, did not register him with the duty officer or write a detention report, and forced him to write a confession. Police asphyxiated Igonin on various occasions, until Igonin died at around 4:00 a.m. at the station. All four police officers were found guilty of torture and sentenced to prison terms ranging from three to nine and a half years.

During a hearing at a Nizhnii Novgorod court, it was established that several years earlier Nizhnii Novgorod police had beaten and bound a detainee, who died as a consequence. An officer had beaten Chistiakov and thrown him in a punishment cell, apparently as a form of punishment for demanding that police release him. The officer reportedly took Chistiakov out of the cell, beat him and, after tying him up in the "konvertik" position, threw him in a punishment cell, where he died. A forensic expert examination found forty bruises from night sticks on his body.[82]

---

[81] IVSs, by contrast, continue to be under the MVD's control.
[82] Nizhnii Novgorod Society for Human Rights, "The Use of Torture on the Territory of the Nizhnii Novgorod Province, 1997," p. 13.

Medical Evidence of Torture

Two police officers were found guilty of this crime but received suspended sentences.

In 1997, the Voronezh Province Court sentenced three police officers to eight, nine, and ten years of imprisonment for torturing to death a criminal suspect and burning his body. The officers tortured the detainee and his brother for several hours, beating and asphyxiating him. When they realized one of them had died, they tried to dispose of the body by burning it and dumping it in a sewer.[83]

Boris Botvinnik, whose treatment has already been noted, lost most of his eyesight after police beat and asphyxiated him at his Moscow apartment in September 1996. About ten days after his detention Botvinnik, noticed that his vision, which had previously not given him any problems, was deteriorating, at first very rapidly, later more gradually. Approximately three weeks after his detention, Botvinnik requested in writing to see a doctor. It took another several weeks before Botvinnik was examined by an eye specialist, who concluded that only about 10 percent of Botrinnik's eyesight remained and recommended a more thorough examination at an eye clinic. In mid-December, specialists of the Gel'mgol'ts Institute, Russia's leading eye clinic, found that he had suffered from descending atrophy. On the basis of this diagnosis, Botvinnik was released from pretrial detention on January 17, 1997. A medical examination conducted after his release at a Volgograd hospital diagnosed Botvinnik with post-traumatic basal arachnoiditis—a low-grade chronic inflammation of a layer of membranes covering the brain and spinal cord. This chronic inflammation was said to have caused the damage to Botvinnik's eyesight. According to a British neurologist, who was unable to examine Botvinnik in person, Botvinnik condition as diagnosed by Russian medical doctors may have been caused by beatings to the head.[84]

Human Rights Watch learned of four cases of detainees in three different Russian cities (including Arkhangel'sk, Ekaterinburg, and Nizhnii Novgorod), who jumped out of high police interrogation room windows to escape torture—too many to be a coincidence. Two of the detainees sustained severe permanent injury, and one died. While torture did not directly cause these injuries, the terror, disorientation, and despair in each case prompted suicidal leaps that were a consequence of the torture.

Twenty-four-year-old Dmitrii Ivanov, from a town in Central Russia, leapt from the window of an investigation room in August 1997 and was crippled for life. Police detained Ivanov on August 5, 1997 at a car park where he was waiting for a friend. Ivanov, who had had his jaw broken by police officers during an arrest

---

[83] Gennadii Litvintsev, "Samosud v militseiskom zastenke," *Rossiiskaia gazeta*, April 8, 1997, p. 8

[84] Human Rights Watch interview with Dr. Christopher Hawkes, October 6, 1999.

several years earlier, tried to run but was apprehended. At the police station, Ivanov was taken to the third floor and ordered to confess to being among a group of people who robbed a computer firm. Police officers announced they would "play soccer" with him until he would "remember" how everything happened.

Police subsequently beat Ivanov and subjected him to electroshock. In his words, he "flew through the room, like a soccer ball." The detectives in the meantime told Ivanov to confess to a series of crimes, including robbery and dealing in stolen goods. Police suggested people he should name as his "clients." Unable to stand the pain any longer, Ivanov noticed the open window and jumped.

He fell fifteen meters and landed on his back on a parked car. Police phoned an ambulance and apparently removed his handcuffs before the ambulance arrived. At the hospital, doctors determined that Ivanov's spine had been fractured in four places and operated on August 7. According to Ivanov, a police officer named Zhenia (who had participated in his torture) visited him before the operation and suggested that since Ivanov would possibly not survive the operation, he might as well write a confession. Police did not inform Ivanov's family of his arrest or injury, although on August 10 a nurse at the hospital phoned at Ivanov's request. Investigators changed Ivanov's status from suspect to "witness" after the accident.

Ivanov was discharged from the hospital in late September 1997, disabled for life. When Human Rights Watch representatives visited Ivanov in October 1997, he was not able even to sit up. The life of his family has been turned upside down, as he needs constant outside care and a variety of expensive drugs, on which his mother spends the majority of her income.[85]

On November 21, 1996 in Ekaterinburg, then fifteen-year-old Oleg Fetisov jumped out of a window of the Verkh Isetskii police station, where three police officers questioned, beat, and asphyxiated him. Fetisov noticed an open window and jumped. Fetisov was taken to the hospital with a fractured skull, pelvic bone, and arm, a small cerebral hemorrhage, a damaged knee, and a concussion. Fetisov spent twenty-one days in the hospital and several more months at home recovering.

In 1996 a twenty-year-old man from Arkhangel'sk threw himself out of a police precinct window and fell to his death on the street in front of the precinct building. Blood stains in the office where he was questioned and reported injuries on the man's body that apparently were not caused by the fall gave reason to believe

---

[85] Human Rights Watch interview with Dmitrii Ivanov. "Dmitrii Ivanov" is not the man's real name, and at his request we do not reveal his home town.

that he may have been tortured. Criminal proceedings against the officers in charge were initially instituted but dropped three months later.[86]

A representative of the Nizhnii Novgorod Society for Human Rights recently reported another such case: twenty-three year old Aleksei Mikheev reportedly jumped out of a police station's upper window after he was tortured with electroshock, landing on a parked motorcycle. He is currently described as paralyzed from the waist down and recovery prospects are uncertain.[87]

---

[86] Igor Lymar', "Chelovekopad," *Pravda severa* [Truth of the North] (Arkhangel'sk), February 22, 1996, p. 1; Igor Lymar', "Pytka smert'iu syna," *Pravda severa*, May 28, 1996, p. 6.

[87] Human Rights Watch telephone interview with Igor Koliapin, Moscow, August 1, 1999.

THE DETENTION PROCESS

The thing is that detention is close to being the main way of solving a crime.

—Yuri Sinel'shchikov, deputy procurator for the city of Moscow[88]

It's very convenient when the person is in a cell. A person at liberty behaves completely differently. A person who is in conditions of isolation is stripped, I think, of something that is of the greatest importance.... At liberty there is a right to chose, and here there isn't, that alone breaks [him].

—Valentina Lutsyshina, lawyer for Dmitry El'sakov[89]

Police use the detention process and the initial period in custody to isolate and disorient criminal suspects, sometimes beginning with the use of extreme violence at the time of detention. Once in custody, detainees rarely have prompt access to a lawyer, and when they do the attorney is often not one of their own choosing.

Under Russian law, police can detain a person in four general sets of circumstances. Article 11(2) of the law on the police allows a police officer to detain an individual for up to three hours to establish his or her identity, but only if the officer has sufficient grounds to suspect that the individual has committed an administrative or criminal offense. The law on administrative offenses allows police officers to detain persons for committing administrative offenses, or misdemeanors, in a limited number of cases.[90] Article 122 of the criminal procedure code allows

---

[88] Yuri Sinel'shchikov, "Nezakonnoe zaderzhanie," *Zakonnost'* [Lawfulness] (Moscow), no. 2, 1999, p. 9.
[89] Human Rights Watch interview with Liubov' Korosteleva and Valentina Lutsyshina, Arkhangel'sk, July 20, 1998.
[90] Article 239 of the Code of the RSFSR on Administrative Offenses states:
   Detention of a person on administrative charges, a body search or a search of a person's belongings, his means of transportation and confiscation of his belongings or documents are permissible in cases directly provided for in legislative acts of the U.S.S.R. and the R.S.F.S.R. in order to stop administrative offenses, when all other measures of pressure have been exhausted, to establish a person's identity, to write a report on an administrative offense, if this is obligatory, to ensure the timely and correct review of cases regarding administrative offenses or execution of such sentences.

The Detention Process

police to detain a criminal suspect without a procurator's warrant for three days in certain specified circumstances.[91] In such cases, police are obliged to inform the procuracy of the detention within twenty-four hours. The procuracy must decide within forty-eight hours after receiving this information whether to sanction the arrest. Article 22(2) of the Russian constitution now provides for arrests to be reported to the courts for judicial sanctioning within forty-eight hours of detention. However, this provision has not yet taken effect due to delays in the adoption of a new criminal procedure code. Police can also arrest an individual after the procuracy has issued an arrest warrant in accordance with articles 89 and 90 of the criminal procedure code.[92]

---

[91] Article 122 states:
   1. The organ of investigation has the right to detain an individual, suspected of committing a crime for which the punishment could be imprisonment, only if one of the following criteria is met: 1) the individual is caught in the act of committing the crime, or immediately following; 2) witnesses, including victims, directly identify the individual as the one who committed the crime; 3) on the body of the suspect, on his clothing, in his possession, or in his place of residence, are found clear traces of the committed crime.
   2. In the presence of other information that gives grounds to suspect the individual of committing the crime, he can be detained only when the individual has attempted to escape, he does not have a permanent place of residence, or the identity of the suspect has not been established.
   3. In all cases of the detention of a person suspected of having committed a crime, the investigative agency is required to write a detention report indicating the grounds, motive, day and hour, year and month, place of detention, explanation of the suspect, time of writing of the detention report, and to report in writing to the procurator. The detention report is signed by its author, as well as the suspect. Within forty-eight hours from the moment of receiving the detention report, the procurator must give sanction for either taking of the person into custody, or his release.

[92] Article 89 of the criminal procedure code states:
   1. When there are sufficient grounds for believing that the accused would evade an inquiry, preliminary investigation or trial or will obstruct the establishment of the truth in a criminal case or will engage in criminal activity, as well as in order to ensure execution of a sentence, the person conducting the inquiry, the investigator, the prosecutor and the court may apply one of the following preventive measures in respect of the accused: a written undertaking not to leave a specified place; a personal guarantee or a guarantee by a public organization; detention in custody.
   2. Bail shall be permitted as a preventive measure if sanctioned by a procurator or if a court so decides.

Police are obliged to identify themselves and to inform the detainee of his or her rights.[93] These rights include the right not to testify against oneself or a close relative, and the right to a lawyer from the moment of detention.[94]

Our research shows that police routinely disregard the above-mentioned procedures. Many of the torture victims we interviewed were taken to police stations for what police portrayed as voluntary visits, often late in the evening. Several others were detained for administrative violations, and, once in detention, questioned about criminal offenses. Police often hold detainees who are detained without sufficient grounds outside the normal detention areas as a way of avoiding their registration.

In an article in *Zakonnost'*, the monthly publication of the procuracy, the deputy procurator for Moscow, Yuri Sinel'shchikov, confirmed that investigations by the Moscow procuracy found that so-called "non-procedural" detentions are very frequent:[95]

---

3. Army personnel, as a preventive measure, may be placed under supervision of the commanders of their respective units.

4. Should there be no grounds which necessitate a preventive measure the accused shall sign the statement pledging to appear upon summons and inform about change of residence.

Article 90 of the criminal procedure code states:

In exceptional cases a preventive measure may be applied to a person suspected of having committed a criminal offense even before a charge is brought against him. In such a case the charge shall be brought not later than ten days from the time of the application of the preventive measure. If no charge is brought within this period, the preventive measure shall be canceled.

[93] According to Mikhail Pashkin of the Moscow police union, this obligation is contained in MVD internal regulations. Human Rights Watch interview, Moscow, February 25, 1999.

[94] Article 48 of the constitution states that:

1. The right to receive qualified legal assistance shall be guaranteed to everyone. In cases provided for by law, legal assistance is provided free of charge.

2. Everyone who is detained, taken into custody or accused of committing a crime shall have the right to make use of the assistance of a lawyer from the moment he was detained, taken into custody or presented the accusation respectively.

Article 51 of the constitution states:

1. No one is obliged to testify against himself, his spouse and close relatives, the range of which shall be defined by a federal law.

[95] Police officers are almost never prosecuted for unlawfully detaining criminal suspects. According to Sinel'shchikov, this happens only in a few dozen cases per year.

The most widespread non-procedural detention is the detention of persons who are suspected of having committed a crime without formalizing that fact on the basis of article 122 of the criminal procedure code.... Besides, the suspects are frequently detained without a [police] detention report because there are no grounds for detention under article 122 of the criminal procedure code.

Police officers use various methods to cover up such facts. In particular, they keep the suspect outside the IVS [temporary holding center at police stations], placing him in offices, the room of the duty officer, and other places where there is no strict registration of such persons. (In one police precinct, detainees were handcuffed to a pipe that had been installed throughout the corridor especially for that purpose).

An inspection at the precincts under the jurisdiction of one of the district procuracies found 130 cases of such [unlawful] detentions [on administrative charges] of citizens. They were taken to the precincts on suspicion of having committed a crime but the detention reports were...written not based on article 122 of the criminal procedure code but on the basis of the Code of Administrative Offences.[96]

Police use these methods apparently when they lack sufficient grounds to detain a suspect under article 122 of the criminal procedure code. For example, a number of torture victims and their relatives told Human Rights Watch that police justified their detentions by referring to their conformity to racial stereotypes or "profiles" identifying them as suspects, even though this cannot alone be considered sufficient grounds for arrest or detention.

Informal Detentions
When police request an individual to make a voluntary visit to the police station, he or she is under no formal obligation to go. The individual has technically not been detained and theoretically can leave at any time. The ostensibly voluntary nature of questioning under such auspices is advantageous for police as it leaves the procedural status of an individual unclear and relieves police officers of the obligation to process any detention or arrest report or to inform an individual of his or her rights.

---

[96] Yuri Sinel'shchikov, "Nezakonnoe zaderzhanie," *Zakonnost'*, no. 2, 1999, p. 8.

When police detain a suspect without a warrant, they can be fairly polite so as to avoid alarming relatives or bystanders. They mislead the suspect and his relatives, saying the matter is not serious and that the person will return within a few hours. Abuse starts only when the individual gets into the police car or arrives at the station.

Igor Kaliapin, a specialist on torture and criminal justice for the Nizhnii Novgorod Society for Human Rights,[97] sketched what he called the "standard situation" in Nizhnii Novgorod:

> The person is taken at home, and [police] behave fairly correctly.... The doorbell rings. The door opens. Two or three people walk in: "We need this and this person." They introduce themselves.... They show their ID cards and possibly a detention decision under article 122 [of the criminal procedure code]. But they don't always do that, it's often not done. They often come without a decision and just [say]: "We are such and such. We need to talk to you. We'll tell you later about what matter. Let's go."... Relatives, especially, are misled.[98]

If police have no arrest warrant, and fail to induce the suspect to come along voluntarily, they may resort to forcible detention. The 1995 case of Tatiana Popkova is illustrative:

> Officers from the crime police...came to me, they came late in the evening.... They did not show any ID, just told me: "We are officers from the crime police, please come with us." When I refused, they forcibly put me in the [police] car and took me to the city police department.... They were waiting for me on the street when I arrived in a taxi.[99]

---

[97] The Nizhnii Novgorod Society for Human Rights has closely monitored torture and ill-treatment in police lockups and other detention facilities for several years and issued several reports documenting dozens of torture cases in 1997 and 1998. See the organization's website for its reports on torture and other human rights problems: http://www.uic.nnov.ru/hrnnov/rus/nnshr/index.htm. Igor Kaliapin has worked for the organization on criminal justice issues since 1993.
[98] Human Rights Watch interview with Igor Kaliapin, Nizhnii Novgorod, October 17, 1997.
[99] Human Rights Watch interview with Tatiana Popkova, Usol'e-Sibirskoe, Irkutsk province, April 8, 1998.

The majority of those whom Human Rights Watch interviewed agreed to go to the police station. Most of them apparently realized that the offer to come to the police station is nothing less than an order and that any form of protest or insubordination would result in violence. Many might not have realized that the law does not oblige them to go to the police station without a summons. At the station, police held what they have sometimes called an *"operativnaia beseda"* or "informal questioning" with the person. These "informal questionings" are not regulated in the criminal procedure code in any way.

Vladislav Seregin from Cheremkhovo, Irkutsk province, told Human Rights Watch about his detention:

> I was sitting at home on January 21, [1996.] I was on vacation. At around 9:00 a.m. the doorbell rang, my wife gets up, walks out and he says: "Open up, police." She opens the door, he walks in: "Where is your husband?"—"He's still sleeping."— "Wake him up, please." I get up and walk out, he says: "Let's go to the city police department for your testimony on this case." I got dressed without thinking anything of it and went to the city police department.... He said that it would take only half an hour, maximum an hour.[100]

At the police station, Seregin was threatened with physical violence if he would not confess. With a pregnant wife who was about to give birth, Seregin signed a confession that he had stolen meat from the factory where he worked and was allowed to go home. The trial formally started in September 1997 but the judge continually postponed the hearing. Eventually, in January 1998 she heard the case, disregarded Seregin's allegations that he had been threatened, and sentenced him to an eighteen-month suspended prison term.

Detention on Administrative Charges

Although persons detained for administrative offenses have some procedural rights—such as the right to counsel during court hearings and the mandatory presence of the defendant at trial—these safeguards are observed even less strictly than in criminal proceedings. Police frequently detain individuals whom they in fact consider to be criminal suspects on administrative offenses and hold them in detention for up to fifteen days, without granting them access to a lawyer, on the

---

[100] Human Rights Watch interview with Vladislav Seregin, Cheremkhovo, Irkutsk province, April 2, 1998.

basis of court decisions that are issued in their absence.[101] During this period, police officers have ample time to force a confession to more serious, criminal offenses. A lawyer from the city of Arkhangel'sk explained:

> [I]n a case of detention for administrative offenses, a procurator does not take any part at all, there's no need to convince anyone, no need to present conclusions and [police officers can] work quietly, there's no need to engage a lawyer. During that period, the person is stripped of the right to a defense. It's almost impossible for a lawyer to be granted access in a case of petty hooliganism.[102]

In such cases, police officers, sometimes unbeknownst to the "suspect," request a judge to sentence the individual to imprisonment on administrative charges such as public drunkenness, swearing in public, or insulting a police officer. The administrative hearings in the cases researched by Human Rights Watch were held in the absence of the alleged offenders, who thus had no means of defending themselves against the charges. In fact, some of the torture victims said they learned they had been detained on administrative charges only when they gained access to their case materials against them at the end of the preliminary investigation, sometimes more than a year later. This practice violates article 247 of the law on administrative offences, which states that a person accused of an administrative offense must be present during the court hearing and has a right to legal assistance. Administrative court cases can be heard in absentia only if the individual has been informed well in advance of the time of the hearing, does not appear, and fails to request a postponement. In other words, there is no apparent excuse for a trial in absentia when the accused is already in custody.

Mikhail Iurochko and his codefendants, Dmitrii El'sakov and Evgenii Mednikov, were detained first for an alleged administrative offense before they

---

[101] Article 247(1) of the law on administrative offenses grants a person accused of an administrative offense the right to a lawyer only during the court hearing on the offense. A commentary to the code on administrative offenses (I.I. Veremeenko, I.G. Salishcheva, M.S. Studenikina, *Kommentarii k Kodeksu RSFSR ob administrativnykh pravonarusheniiakh*, Moscow 1998), however, notes that this provision no longer conforms to obligations under Russia's constitution, which grants everyone the right to an attorney from the moment of detention, regardless of the nature of the charge. The authors argue that detainees held for administrative offenses should now have access to a lawyer at any time during the proceedings against him. However, this is not yet established practice.
[102] Human Rights Watch interview with Liubov' Korosteliova and Valentina Lutsyshina, Arkhangel'sk, July 20, 1998.

were accused of a double murder and tortured. As noted above, they were tortured, confessed to the crime, and sentenced: Iurachko and Mednikov to death, and El'sakov to fifteen years imprisonment. In 1999, the Supreme Court overturned the conviction, and the three were released. Dmitrii El'sakov told Human Rights Watch about his detention in 1993:

> I came out of the building where I work, in town, and sat in my car. Two detectives came up to me.... They simply told me: "Let's go and talk for ten minutes at the police station, you'll be back in ten minutes." They took me [to the station] and literally pushed me into a cell.
>
> About an hour later, they took me out and showed me a decision of Judge Zakharov for my arrest, that he [sentenced me to ten days of detention] for some sort of petty hooliganism, which a police detective had witnessed a week earlier.
>
> I wasn't taken to the judge, just shown the decision. The judge believed the detective that I had committed hooliganism.[103]

El'sakov was accused of swearing at a police officer whom he said had been harassing him for weeks, telling him to come to the police station to confess to a double murder. He spent the next four and a half years in a SIZO.

The lawyer for Mikhail Iurochko told Human Rights Watch that her client was also detained for hooliganism:

> He was detained on October 8, 1993. The reason: petty hooliganism, which he denies.... [H]e came up to a kiosk, where another man was standing, and they had an argument, and Iurochko was said to have started a fight. The judge gave him fifteen days. He spent [them] in the IVS, where criminal suspects are held. In the case dossier, there is information, specifically a decision to seize his correspondence, which shows that at that moment he was already a suspect in the [criminal] case.[104]

On March 5, 1998, Sergei Samsonov was approached on the street in Sergiev Posad (Moscow province) by two policemen who asked him to come with them to

---

[103] Human Rights Watch interview with Dmitrii El'sakov, Arkhangel'sk, July 21, 1998.
[104] Human Rights Watch interview with Liubov' Korosteleva and Valentina Lutsyshina, Arkhangel'sk, July 20, 1998.

the police station as "their boss wanted to ask him some questions." They held him at the station overnight and took him to court the next day, when he was sentenced to ten days of detention for petty hooliganism. After ten days, during which he was allegedly tortured, he was taken to the IVS on suspicion of murder.[105]

Torture and Ill-treatment at the Time of Detention

As noted above, detainees are often seized in violent police raids on their homes and are subjected to serious physical abuse inside their homes or on the street, and in the presence of their families. Sometimes family members present during these raids are themselves seriously assaulted. In cases described to Human Rights Watch by former detainees and their relatives, police generally either did not identify themselves or flashed their identification too quickly to allow one to read it. Treatment described ranged from systematic beatings to near suffocation.

Mikhail Sobolev was severely beaten at his home on the night of November 28, 1995. Sobolev told Human Rights Watch that plain clothed police officers forced their way into his apartment at about 11:30 p.m., did not identify themselves, and:

> They immediately started to beat me, they didn't listen to my questions. Swear words, blows with the handle of the guns about my head.... They screamed: "On the floor, we're going to shoot, we'll kill you!"... One of them started to kick me, then took a stool, which stood next to him, they beat me with guns about the head, my back.... He took the stool and hit me over the head, my back. The stool fell apart.[106]

The father of Andrei Potanin told Human Rights Watch that police had forced their way into his tenth-floor apartment on the early morning of May 11, 1995 to arrest his son, whom they beat senseless in front of him. He said the raid was led by a deputy head of the crime police named Sergei Kolosovskii:

> When I heard the slamming of metal doors and noise in the apartment I came out of the bathroom and saw Kolosovskii beating my son.... My son fell and lost consciousness.... I started to scream. They were in plain clothes and I didn't know at first who they were: maybe bandits. He [Kolosovskii] pointed a gun at me.... I said: "What are you doing." He answered: "We're from the police."[107]

---

[105] Human Rights Watch interview with Svetlana Samsonova, Moscow, August 6, 1998.
[106] Human Rights Watch interview with Mikhail Sobolev, Ekaterinburg, August 11, 1997.
[107] Human Rights Watch interview with Mr. Potanin, Ekaterinburg, August 8, 1997.

Kolosovskii took Potanin's son to the police station, despite the fact that he did not have an arrest or search warrant.

In 1996, Moscow police detained Boris Botvinnik in a joint operation with riot troops (OMON).[108] Botvinnik said police came to his apartment late on the night of September 18, 1996 and immediately knocked him to the floor. As explained above, police tortured him as they "interrogated" him at his apartment. "They came in, carried out a superficial search, let me get dressed—I had already gone to bed—put on handcuffs and after that some thing like an interrogation started."[109] At trial, two police detectives contradicted each other as to whether Botvinnik had voluntarily come to the police station or was brought in following an arrest warrant.

Access to Lawyers

Under Russian law, criminal suspects have the right to an attorney from the moment of detention,[110] and police are obligated to inform them of this right.[111] Police reportedly rarely respect these obligations, and the more than fifty torture victims we interviewed all said they had not had access to a lawyer immediately following their detention. A former police investigator told Human Rights Watch:

> Lawyers are the worst enemy of any investigator. And I can tell you that, although it may not be right, we always tried to do everything to avoid having a lawyer getting involved in the case, with all truths and untruths.[112]

Some torture victims related how their requests for a lawyer provoked violent reactions from the police. Igor Kaliapin told Human Rights Watch:

> As a rule, [bringing up] the matter of a lawyer is risky. If a detainee asks for a lawyer, they laugh in his face: "What lawyer? We'll show you a lawyer!" "Who do you think you are? Who? What article 51?"[113] Have

---

[108] Otriad militsii osobogo naznacheniia (literally, Special Task Militia Force).
[109] Human Rights Watch interview with Boris Botvinnik, Moscow, March 14, 1997.
[110] Article 48(2) of the constitution.
[111] Article 58 of the criminal procedure code.
[112] Human Rights Watch telephone interview with Vladimir Fedorov, Moscow, June 8, 1999. "Vladimir Fedorov" is not the man's real name.
[113] Article 51 of the constitution establishes the right not to testify against oneself.

you gone out of your mind? Do you know where you are?! What lawyer do you want?!"[114]

Andrei Getsko told Human Rights Watch: "I asked for a lawyer all the time, [and said] that I wouldn't give testimony without a lawyer. But when you start to talk about the law, it makes them even more angry. They became infuriated and started to beat even more." Andrei Kol'tsov demanded to be given a lawyer after he was detained on September 11, 1996 and beaten up in a forest: "I once again started to say: 'What do you want? Give me a lawyer.' They [answered]: 'We'll give you a lawyer right now,' and started to beat me up."[115]

Police have various ways of denying detainees access to a lawyer. When the detainee simply does not ask for a lawyer out of ignorance or fear, police do not inform him or her of this right. When detainees do ask for a lawyer, police may blatantly deny the detainee the right to a lawyer, disregarding whatever effect on the outcome of the case such a procedural violation may entail; or police will try to legitimize the absence of a lawyer by forcing the detainee to sign a statement declining counsel.

The father of Andrei Potanin told Human Rights Watch that his son was beaten during his first interrogation on May 11, 1995, while his demands for a lawyer were ignored:

> They didn't even pay attention to his demands that he should be given a lawyer and he wasn't given one until I found a lawyer. I couldn't immediately find a lawyer.... By that time, twenty-four hours later, I found one, they had already done it all.... During the following interrogations they didn't beat him, then there was a lawyer [present].[116]

Kirill Komlev from Nizhnii Novgorod was detained on September 5, 1996. He immediately demanded a lawyer, but was told that he had no such right.[117] Later that day, police called in a duty lawyer to see Komlev. This lawyer confirmed to Human Rights Watch that he had seen Komlev on September 5 after he had obviously been

---

[114] Human Rights Watch interview with Igor Kaliapin, Niznhnii Novgorod Society for Human Rights, Nizhnii Novgorod, October 17, 1997.

[115] Human Rights Watch interview with Andrei Kol'tsov, Cheremkhovo, Irkutsk province, April 2, 1998.

[116] Human Rights Watch interview with the father of Andrei Potanin, Ekaterinburg, August 8, 1997.

[117] Complaint submitted by Kirill Komlev to the procuracy in September 1996.

beaten. The following day, police apparently forced Komlev to decline the service of his lawyer. Komlev's mother told Human Rights Watch:

> When they detained him [Kirill] on September 5 and started to beat him, he immediately demanded a lawyer.... Despite the fact that, on September 6, I officially hired a lawyer and informed investigator Bubnov, who was in charge of the case, about that on September 6.... Still, they ignored it all and all that torture was used without lawyers. The lawyers were allowed access to them [Kirill and his brother] only on September 13, 1996.[118]

Boris Botvinnik told Human Rights Watch:

> They brought me to Petrovka [the central police station in Moscow]. I was forced to decline legal counsel. They [police officers] promised me that if I would insist on a lawyer, they would give me back to the riot police. I...wrote [a statement declining counsel] because of the phrase: "You won't live to see a lawyer!"[119]

During Botvinnik's first interrogation, as well as during an investigative reconstruction at the crime scene, he had no legal counsel. After he was allowed to have a lawyer, he changed his testimony, as did both his codefendants, who had also "voluntarily" declined the assistance of a lawyer and had previously confessed under duress.

Police frequently detain their victims at a time when it is practically impossible to engage an attorney. Il'ia Berlin, a lawyer in Arkhangel'sk, told Human Rights Watch:

> [U]sually detention is unexpected for the individual. In Russia...people don't have personal lawyers. In order for a lawyer to start working on a case, the relatives [of the detainee] must be informed. They must take the decision to hire a lawyer.

---

[118] Human Rights Watch interview with Liubov' Shamberova, Nizhnii Novgorod, October 17, 1997.
[119] Human Rights Watch interview with Boris Botvinnik, Moscow, March 14, 1997; telephone conversation with Boris Botvinnik, August 17, 1998.

What happens in practice? An amazingly large number of detentions take place Friday afternoon. According to the law, [police] must inform relatives or the person indicated by the detainee about the detention. But on Friday afternoon an individual without personal contacts won't have anywhere to turn: lawyer's collegia are closed.... Thus, it is practically impossible to hire a lawyer until Monday.[120]

Once police elicit a first confession (which is usually enough for a conviction, see below "Torture and Confession Evidence"), the victim's complete isolation becomes unnecessary. In fact, police sometimes call a "friendly" lawyer themselves at that point to frustrate any possible future torture complaints. In such cases, police tell the detainee, who is still disoriented, to repeat his confession in the presence of the "friendly" lawyer and threaten him if he retracts it. Igor Koliapin summarized what many other victims and human rights activists told us: "As a rule, [the police] invite a so-called 'pocket lawyer' in such a situation...that is, a lawyer who doesn't work completely conscientiously."[121] When they realize that it is time to charge the suspect:

> they immediately phone a lawyer. There's no reason to phone the lawyer on duty at the lawyers' collegium. They can phone their "own" lawyer at home...: "Come immediately, we need to charge someone." The lawyer comes and fulfills his formal obligations. He remains present: "I am your lawyer, if you want you can pass on something for your mother...." The lawyer usually understands [how the police received the confession] when he reads the report and the suspect sits there with a beaten-up face or moans. The lawyer...must ask the question: "Don't you want to make a statement about the circumstances under which you gave this testimony? Did they beat you or not?"... A lawyer who is invited by the police usually doesn't do that.... He thinks: "Well, he is a criminal, why should I protect him especially?"[122]

One torture victim told Human Rights Watch how in 1994 a police investigator manipulated his statement declining the police-appointed lawyer into a statement declining all services of an attorney:

---

[120] Human Rights Watch interview with Il'ia Berlin, Arkhangel'sk, July 20, 1998. Lawyers' collegia are law offices.
[121] Human Rights Watch interview with Igor Koliapin, Nizhnii Novgorod, October 17, 1997.
[122] Ibid.

The investigator brought in a lawyer, his friend, sat him down with me and said: "Go with him into the room and tell him for half an hour what you want to tell him." I told him: "Why would I tell your friend anything? I don't trust him." [Another day], the investigator brought in the lawyer friend and said: "We are going to charge you in his presence, he's a good lawyer, I've known him for a long time." I said that I don't need such a lawyer: "Call my relatives, let them hire another lawyer." "Why do you need that? It costs so much money! [A private lawyer] won't help you at all...."And he deceived me, forcing me to write a statement that I don't need the lawyer. I wrote that with my own hands. It came out as if I didn't need a lawyer at all, while that was not at all what I had meant.[123]

---

[123] Human Rights Watch interview with Dmitrii El'sakov, Arkhangel'sk, July 21, 1998.

TORTURE AND CONFESSION EVIDENCE

I wanted to save what was left of me.[124]
—Boris Botvinnik, March 14, 1997

Under that kind of torture, you're no longer contemplating the possibility of suicide, you're desperately trying to find an object to kill yourself with.[125]
—Dmitrii Koligov, March 16, 1998

At that moment under that torture I would have confessed to the murder of List'ev.[126]
—Andrei Getsko, April 5, 1998.

After the resistance of the detainee wears down, police force him or her to write a confession, sometimes by prompting or dictating what is to be written. Investigators and judges often heavily rely on these confessions in the further stages of the preliminary investigation and trial proceedings. Human Rights Watch is not aware of any Russian judge who exclude a coerced confession from the evidence of a criminal case, even if medical evidence of torture was presented. Law enforcement agencies and the judiciary have been reluctant to admit mistakes in investigations and judicial errors.

The Process of Securing Confessions

Former detainees recounted the different ways in which they composed their confessions under duress.[127] Some said they wrote the confessions themselves;

---

[124] Human Rights Watch interview with Boris Botvinnik, Moscow, March 14, 1997.

[125] Dmitrii Koligov testifying at a court hearing at the Nikulinskii District Court of Moscow, March 16, 1998.

[126] Human Rights Watch interview with Andrei Getsko, Bratsk, Irkutsk province, April 5, 1998. The murder of Vladislav List'ev, a famous Russian television journalist and producer, caused a major shock in Russian society in 1995.

[127] Russian criminal procedure distinguishes between confessions obtained in the course of the criminal investigation through a formal record of a police interrogation with a suspect or defendant (*chistoserdechnoe priznanie*), and statements that the perpetrator of the crime prepares independently, and with which he reports himself to the police (*iavka s povinnoi*). A *iavki s povinnoi* can serve as a reason for beginning criminal proceedings while a *chistoserdechnoe priznanie* can be obtained only in the context of an already begun criminal case in the course of an interrogation. Police do not appear to have a clear preference for one or the other type of confession. However, all torture victims we interviewed who were

others, that police either prompted or dictated the confession, and sometimes coerced several confessions from the same victim. In yet other cases, once the detainee confessed, police attempted to force them to sign confessions to various other unsolved. Police forced many of the individuals interviewed by Human Rights Watch to state in their confessions that article 51 of the constitution (the right not to testify against oneself or close relatives) was explained to them, that they voluntarily refused a lawyer, and that they had no complaints about their treatment by the police.

Mikhail Iurochko told Human Rights Watch that his first confession was written with heavy prompting by the case investigator:

> Yes, they gave me an interrogation form, the investigator sat there, the detective was close by. The detective left, the investigator worked out together with me the place in the room [at the scene of the crime]: what, where, how. He prompted me. I wrote it with my own hand...like that. "Here, probably, you did this, and that you did like this."[128]

After Iurochko wrote this confession, a witness apparently testified to seeing three people on the roof of the victims' apartment building on the day of the murder. According to Iurochko's account, police subsequently forced him to write a second confession, this time implicating two of his friends.[129]

Mara Poliakova, a former instructor at the Procuracy General's Institute for Improving Qualifications of Top Personnel, analyzed numerous criminal cases and found evidence that police regularly force defendants to write new, revised confessions as their cases advance, with subsequent confessions reflecting new information the investigation had gathered. She illustrated her observation with the case of a man who was convicted for the murder and rape of a minor. The Moscow City Court overturned his conviction when police found an individual who appeared to be the real perpetrator of the crime:

> [D]uring the very first interrogation, he said: "I committed the murder and rape of this girl." He didn't give any concrete information about the crime. Then he changed his testimony. He said that he had committed the crime with his close friends...in this [confession], he listed the friends. Then the investigation established a fool-proof alibi for these people.... Then it turned out that certain [other] friends were, as we say,

---

initially arrested on administrative charges wrote *iavka s povinnoi*.
[128] Human Rights Watch interview with Mikhail Iurochko, Arkhangel'sk, July 21, 1998.
[129] Ibid.

fond of women, they brought some sort of pictures to their friends, of a pornographic character or simply with a sexual motif. That is, they [the investigators] established a kind of preoccupation and a new confession appeared, in which he referred to his ostensible co-offender. Then, a fool-proof alibi was established [of the man's friends]. Whenever an alibi was established, a new version appeared.[130]

Some former detainees told Human Rights Watch that police tried to force them to sign blank interrogation forms or refused to allow them to read the interrogation reports they were supposed to sign. For example, Andrei Tuzikov told Human Rights Watch, "Then one of them put a plastic bag over my head, gave [me] a piece of paper and a pen and said: 'Sign.' I had no choice and I signed.... I didn't know what he [the police officer] wanted. They later wrote in their own, they had given me a blank piece of paper."[131] Zhanna Setchikova and Tatiana Popkova described similar experiences (see below).

Several former detainees told Human Rights Watch that police tried to force them to confess to so-called *"visiaki,"* crimes that police are unable to solve for long periods. Igor Koliapin, of the Nizhnii Novgorod Society for Human Rights, told Human Rights Watch about one of his clients:

[T]hey detained a young man (seventeen to nineteen years old) for the theft of a car, almost red-handedly and started to beat him up at the precinct and demanded that he confess to some other unsolved crimes, which were "hanging" in the precinct.... They told him: "Things won't look worse, what's the difference? You're going to be doing plenty of time. We'll make sure you get vodka or whatever else. And we won't pester you anymore. Confess, you've committed a crime anyway. And you avoid unpleasantness for someone else: you'll do time not only for yourself but also for the other guy."[132]

He said that when the young man refused to confess to the other crimes, police officer beat him severely.

Several others gave Human Rights Watch similar accounts of their own ill-treatment. Police, according to his account, tried to coerce Oleg Fetisov into confessing not only to stealing a jacket but also to several apartment and garage

---

[130] Human Rights Watch interview with Mara Poliakova, Moscow, February 3, 1999.
[131] Human Rights Watch interview with Andrei Tuzikov, Bratsk, Irkutsk province, April 5, 1998.
[132] Human Rights Watch interview with Igor Kaliapin, Nizhny Novgorod, October 17, 1997.

burglaries. Altogether, they tried to make him confess to seven different crimes. The effort failed with his leap from the police station window to escape torture. Andrei Tuzikov said that after he had been tortured and confessed to one crime, police left him alone for some time:

> Five days I spent in the KPZ [temporary holding cell], nobody called me in or touched me. Then after five days he [the investigator] said: "We have some [burgled] apartments." He dictated. I signed. I didn't start to argue with him.... He said, "We have an apartment 'hanging,' you must take it [upon yourself]."[133]

Altogether Tuzikov confessed to seven different crimes, most of which were apparently not prosecuted.

Reliance on Confession Evidence

In various cases Human Rights Watch examined, investigators and judges relied heavily on coerced confessions signed by defendants. Once torture produced a confession, the emphasis of the further investigation appeared to be to corroborate and reinforce the confession; sometimes investigators disregarded other evidence or evidence exonerating the defendant.

In the case of Mikhail Iurochko, Dmitrii El'sakov, and Evgenii Mednikov, who were accused of murdering two young sisters, police coerced confessions from all three men that by and large corroborated each other. The case investigators subsequently refused to take into consideration what appeared to be legitimate evidence of the innocence of one of the men: Dmitrii El'sakov maintained that at the time of the murder he was at work at an Arkhangel'sk fire department, and various colleagues, including the head of his shift, confirmed this. The colleagues told investigators and later the court that El'sakov could never have left the fire department for a long time without his absence being noticed. Furthermore, nobody had seen him leave the building. Several colleagues said they remembered seeing El'sakov at different times during the day and one colleague said he had lunch with El'sakov at 1:00 p.m.

Like the investigators, the Arkhangel'sk Province Court refused to believe Dmitrii El'sakov's colleagues. The judge even went so far as to institute criminal proceedings against one of the firefighters for lying under oath. El'sakov's lawyer, Valentina Lutsyshina told Human Rights Watch:

---

[133] Human Rights Watch interview with Andrei Tuzikov, Bratsk, Irkutsk province, April 5, 1998.

> This man, who was on the shift...gave testimony of the following nature; he answered the court impertinently: "You can leave your court room as well but to do that unnoticed for a longer time is impossible.... You can go to the bathroom for five or ten minutes but in a small group even that soon gets noticed."[134]

Had the investigator, or court, accepted the alibi, the entire criminal case would have collapsed as it would have become clear the confessions Iurochko, El'sakov, and Mednikov gave implicating one another had been obtained through unlawful means. In May 1999, the Supreme Court overturned their convictions and sent the case back for further investigation.

Mara Poliakova, a former instructor of the Procuracy General's Institute for Improving Qualifications of Top Personnel, confirmed to Human Rights Watch that once confessions have been obtained, procuracy officials heavily rely on them and are highly reluctant to dismiss them, even if circumstances indicate that the confessions may have been obtained under coercion. The instructor trained procurators by having them reenact criminal investigations throughout the course of several years. One of the cases used during this training was that of a young man who had been wrongly sentenced to death for raping and murdering a minor on the basis of his confessions and some circumstantial evidence. He periodically withdrew his confessions, claiming that they had been coerced under torture and were dictated to him by co-detainees or police officers. After his conviction by the Moscow City Court, police found the real perpetrator of the crime and the Supreme Court overturned the young man's conviction. Poliakova told Human Rights Watch:

> All our procurators worked on this case in a traditional way.... And each time they went the same [wrong] way.... [E]ach procurator works in the following way: there is the prosecution's version and his task is to push that version through court. And everything that contradicts that version (and this is at a level of thinking or even the subconscious) is thrown off internally.
>
> In this case, there was a lot of circumstantial evidence but there were also some small contradictions. It was necessary to identify these and to clarify the reasons for these contradictions.... His [the defendant's] testimonies, in which he confessed his guilt in committing the offense, differed. Also, when you read them [the confessions], even a layman's

---

[134] Human Rights Watch interview with Valentina Lutsyshina, Arkhangel'sk, July 20, 1998.

eye can see that we're talking about different language styles, different levels of command of the language.

The procurator should have approached his testimony critically. First of all, it was necessary to...establish why [he gave] such different testimony. In this case, a psycho-linguistic expert assessment should have been carried out.... We later carried out an expert assessment and the experts, seven people, [were] specialists in different areas: psychologists, linguists.... Everyone gave a separate conclusion and when they were put together, it turned out that all results were the same. And all seven experts concluded that he [the defendant] was the author only of the retractions.... They even established that the texts [of the confessions] had been dictated by three or four [different] people.[135]

In the case of Boris Botvinnik, Dmitrii Koligov, and Mikhail Shikalenko, investigators also heavily relied on the three men's "confessions" as well as on a videotaped "investigative reenactment" at the site of the crime. Botvinnik told Human Rights Watch that after he signed a "confession," police took him to the place of the crime to reenact it. Botvinnik was supposed to show police *where* he had done *what* at the time of the crime. Botvinnik claims that police prompted him during the entire reenactment and at one point even led him down the wrong staircase, where they got stuck and had to turn back. Both Koligov and Shikalenko described in court how police had beaten them into confessing.

In court, Judge Valentina Komarova of the Nikulin District Court initially tried to avoid hearing the case on the merits; she returned the case to the procuracy for further investigation on two occasions, stating it was insufficiently investigated. On both occasions, the case eventually returned to the judge, who issued a guilty verdict in March 1999, two years after first receiving the case. During that period, Koligov and Shikalenko remained in the Butyrka pretrial detention center. In 1998, Shikalenko was diagnosed with an open form of tuberculosis.

The "confessions" and the "reenactment" provided as the basis for the conviction. As a Human Rights Watch researcher monitoring the trial observed, she inexplicably refused take into consideration several other irregularities that had occurred during the criminal investigation. The gun with which the victims were shot, a bag, and various other pieces of material evidence that had been previously confiscated by police mysteriously disappeared. Prosecutors did not respond to the defense's queries as to the fate of this material evidence, and the judge failed to

---

[135] Human Rights Watch interview with Mara Poliakova, Moscow, February 3, 1999.

require the prosecution to do so. Police also failed to question the only witness to the armed robbery and murder of which Botvinnik and his codefendants were accused. The witness, a Mongolian woman who worked at the Mongolian embassy in Moscow, had been wounded during the robbery and was taken to the hospital. She did not leave Russia for at least three weeks following the crime.

The case of death-row prisoner Sergei Mikhailov, whose innocence appears to have been irrefutably proven but who still languishes in jail, reveals the overwhelming importance given to confessions in Russia. It appears that once a confession-based conviction is obtained, the resistance to reopening or reviewing the case becomes extraordinarily high, even in the face of dramatic new evidence.

Following the murder and rape of a ten-year-old girl in the provincial town of Vel'sk in Arkhangel'sk province in October 1994, police detained twenty-one-year-old Sergei Mikhailov for ten days in December 1994 for petty hooliganism. Denied access to a lawyer, Mikhailov claimed that police beat him over the course of these ten days and threatened to throw him into a so-called "pressing room," where cell mates who are police trustees would beat and rape him. While still in incommunicado detention, Mikhailov confessed to the murder. After Mikhailov was granted access to a lawyer, he withdrew his confession. In April 1995, the Arkhangel'sk Province Court tried the case and sentenced Mikhailov to death, based largely on his confession. The Supreme Court confirmed the sentence on appeal.

In November 1996, a murder almost identical to the one for which Mikhailov had been convicted occurred in Vel'sk. In the course of the investigation, police arrested Alexander Kozlov, who reportedly confessed not only to the second but also to the first murder.

Instead of immediately starting proceedings to correct a miscarriage of justice against Mikhailov, the Arkhangel'sk procuracy tried to obscure its mistake.[136] Although the procuracy's special investigator concluded in July 1997 that Mikhailov had been wrongly convicted and recommended that the sentence be overturned, the head of the procuracy in Arkhangel'sk, Alexander Apanasenko, refused to send this conclusion to the Procuracy General in Moscow. By then, an Arkhangel'sk-based journalist had written several critical articles about the case, and her newspaper, *Pravda severa*, also hired a lawyer for Mikhailov. In November, Apanasenko appointed a second special investigator, who reached the same conclusions as his colleague. Once again, Apanasenko refused to send the

---

[136] Under Russian law, Mikhailov and his lawyer cannot themselves file a request with the Supreme Court to overturn the conviction. The regional procurator's office must file the request with the Procuracy General, which in turn must request the Supreme Court to overturn the sentence.

conclusions to Moscow. During this time, Mikhailov's lawyer had written five complaints to the Procuracy General, which finally demanded to receive the case materials.

Subsequently, the Procuracy General appointed its own special investigator, Dmitrii Buianov, to the case, this time from neighboring Vologda province. In August 1998, this investigator told a representative of Human Rights Watch that he was absolutely convinced of Mikhailov's innocence. Shortly thereafter, he presented his conclusions to the head of the Vologda procuracy, who sent them to the Procuracy General in Moscow. Inexplicably, the Procuracy General considered Buianov's conclusions insufficient to request the Supreme Court to overturn Mikhailov's conviction. It sent the case back to Vologda in October 1998, claiming that "not all witnesses had been questioned." In January 1999, Buianov submitted his next conclusion to the Procuracy General, which apparently found it insufficient and returned it to him once more in April 1999. As of this writing, Buianov had sent the results of his latest investigation into the case, but the Procuracy General had not taken a decision yet.

Meanwhile, Mikhailov continues to be held on death row at the Arkhangel'sk pretrial detention center,[137] where he has been for almost four and a half years. According to his lawyer, Mikhailov has tried to commit suicide several times. Both his lawyer and the special investigator Human Rights Watch spoke to expressed deep concern about his mental stability. As a death-row prisoner, Mikhailov does not have the right to receive visitors, except for his lawyer. From April 24, 1995 to July 1, 1997, Mikhailov had no exposure to sunlight, as death-row prisoners did not have the right to recreation. Human Rights Watch representatives met with Mikhailov briefly in August 1998, thanks to the special investigator from Vologda province. However, the representatives were forced to break off the meeting because prison authorities insisted that a guard be present at all times. Mikhailov appeared extremely distraught and depressed. Due to President Boris Yeltsin's initiative to commute the sentences of all remaining death row prisoners in June, Mikhailov's sentence was changed to twenty-five years of imprisonment. He is currently awaiting transfer to a labor colony.

Judicial Refusal to Exclude Coerced Confessions

Judges rarely exclude confessions obtained under duress, although most at trial did appear to question the defendant on the issue, summoned the alleged

---

[137] In Russia, death-row prisoners were kept in pretrial detention centers in special cells until the execution of their sentences. Although their death sentences have now been commuted to life imprisonment or twenty-five years, most former death-row prisoners are still in their death cells, waiting to be transported to a labor colony.

perpetrators for questioning, and some requested medical documents. Some judges subsequently simply dismissed the torture complaints while others sent cases back for further investigation or instructed the procuracy to investigate the torture complaints.

One judge from a Moscow district court, who acknowledged that many defendants she tries allege they were ill-treated, told Human Rights Watch that when defendants make allegations of torture, it is extremely difficult for her to exclude the confessions or testimony concerned, even if she is convinced that the allegations are legitimate:

> When a defendant alleges he was tortured, I am obliged to appoint a procuracy inquiry into the allegations before I exclude the evidence. However, these inquiries never confirm the allegations. The procuracy just writes formal replies. That makes it almost impossible for me to exclude the evidence: If I do, the procuracy will appeal and a higher court will overturn my verdict pointing to the outcome of the procuracy inquiry.[138]

In the case of Boris Botvinnik and his codefendants, Judge Komarova questioned the defendants about torture during several court hearings. She questioned the detectives and investigators who had worked on the case, who claimed that they had fully observed the law. She was provided with conclusions regarding the nature of Botvinnik's injuries from a leading eye institute in Russia and a hospital in Volgograd. However, Judge Komarova denied several requests for a forensic medical examination, and in her final verdict on the case, did not exclude the confessions or the results of the highly suspicious "investigative reenactment," which were both obtained under torture and the threat of torture, and failed to refer to the medical evidence of torture altogether. Judge Komarova gave all three men comparatively lenient sentences on March 1, 1999: Botvinnik received a suspended sentence of five years' imprisonment; Koligov, a three-year prison term (he had already spent two and a half years in pretrial detention); and Shikolenko, a four-year prison term.

During their trial in August 1997 in a Nizhnii Novgorod court, Kirill Komlev and Anton Shamberov both told the court that they were tortured and mentioned the name of police detective Popov. The judge called Popov to the stand. Anton Shamberov told Human Rights Watch:

---

[138] Human Rights Watch interview with Galina Vorontsova, Moscow, September 20, 1999. "Galina Vorontsova" is not the person's real name. See below, "Accountability," for an explanation of the deficiencies of informal procuracy inquiries into torture claims.

> When during the court hearing they [the judges] asked Popov if they had beaten Komlev and Shamberov, he said: "No, we didn't beat them, we just had a friendly talk." For almost an entire ten days they talked friendly talks. And Komlev said: "If beating up is called a friendly talk, then we had a friendly talk." Popov said further that now the defendants will say whatever in order to get themselves off and the court accepted that.[139]

As was the case during the procuracy's review of the torture allegations, the court did not question three people who allegedly saw Komlev at the police station after he was beaten: his wife, mother, and lawyer. The court ruled that the torture allegations had not been confirmed by facts.

In the case of Andrei Getsko, the judge summoned several doctors who Getsko claimed had seen how police officers beat him in an elevator at the Central Hospital-1 in Bratsk. When the doctors confirmed that they had witnessed the incident on March 20, 1998, the initially skeptical judge had no choice but to recognize that the beatings had taken place and instituted criminal proceedings. She did not exclude the confession signed by Getsko as a result of the beatings, but rather referred the criminal case against Getsko, which had lasted already four years, back to the procuracy for further investigation.

In one extreme case, a judge acknowledged in his verdict that testimony had been received under physical coercion but went on to base the guilty verdict on that testimony. Judge S.V. Romanovskii of the Klin City Court, in his verdict in the case against Aleksei Korkhov (charged with battery and murder) stated that witness Seliverstov repeatedly testified to police in favor of Korkhov.[140] However, the written verdict declares that "after physical coercion," he changed his testimony, incriminating Korkhov. Yet the judge went on to argue that he believed that the testimony obtained under coercion was the truth. Even if that testimony were truthful, the judge should have excluded it from the court proceedings under article 69 of the criminal procedure code.

---

[139]Human Rights Watch interview with Anton Shamberov, Nizhnii Novgorod, October 18, 1997.
[140]Ruling of the Klin City Court, case no. 1-731\96, November 29, 1996.

THE VICTIMS

The victims of police brutality are ordinary people who fell afoul of the law. Most of the victims are suspected or real petty or serious offenders. The victims may be charged with a whole spectrum of crimes and offenses ranging from petty theft to rape and child murder and torturers torture irrespective of the detainees race or background. Most victims Human Rights Watch spoke to were ethnic Russians; most were adult males, predominantly in their twenties and thirties, but we also found evidence, though albeit for a smaller sample of interviewees, that male minors were also subject to torture and ill-treatment with disturbing frequency. Few interviewees who alleged they were tortured were women.

Minors

Police violence against minors appears to be widespread, in particular against young men and boys accused of having committed small-scale theft or other petty crimes. According to the Committee for Civil Rights, which works with 300 minors in labor colonies, the frequency of police violence against minors increased significantly between 1994 and 1998. The group estimates that about one-third of all minors facing criminal proceedings are subjected to violence during the detention and investigation process, and that every fourth minor has been subjected to police violence on the street, unrelated to the criminal investigation process, before the age of fifteen.[141]

Russian criminal procedure grants some protection to minors who are criminal suspects, but it fails to obligate police to contact parents or a guardian before questioning them. Moreover, the protections guaranteed in law are routinely ignored. Article 49 of the criminal procedure code makes the participation of a lawyer obligatory in the inquiry and preliminary investigation phases of cases involving minors, from the moment the minor has been presented with the detention report.

This special obligation for lawyers to be present during interrogations of minors is routinely ignored. Minors in four cities in Russia told Human Rights Watch that police interrogated (and tortured) them in the absence of a lawyer.

Under article 397 of the criminal procedure code, police may, but are not obliged to, allow the parents or a teacher to be present when questioning minors,

---

[141] Human Rights Watch interview with Andrei Babushkin, chair of the Committee for Civil Rights, Moscow, February 15, 1999.

which appears to be a deviation from international standards on the protection of minors.[142]

Oleg Fetisov, Ekaterinburg

On November 21, 1996, police officers came to Fetisov's school during lunch break and told him to come to the police station. According to his account, the then fifteen-year-old Fetisov was taken to the Verkh Isetskii police station, where three police officers questioned him. When he refused to confess to stealing a jacket from another schoolboy, torture ensued. According to his account, police first beat him, kicked him, and dragged him around on the floor. Then they handcuffed him, tied him to a chair and put a gas mask over his head. They cut the oxygen supply several times for about a minute. Fetisov said he twice almost lost consciousness.

At approximately 3:00 p.m., three and a half hours after he arrived at the police station, Fetisov told his tormentors that he would write a confession. Police uncuffed his hands and gave him a pen and paper. When the officers' attention for Fetisov relented for a few moments, he got up and ran to the window. One of the police officers pulled his gun and threatened to shoot, but Fetisov jumped out.

Fetisov was taken to the hospital with a fractured skull, pelvic bone, and arm, a small cerebral hemorrhage, a damaged knee, and a concussion. Police failed to inform Fetisov's parents that they had detained the boy. In hospital Fetisov was in shock, but constantly repeated what had happened to him at the police station. Someone at the hospital obtained his parents' phone number and called them. Fetisov spent twenty-one days in the hospital and several more months at home recovering. He did not go back to jail.

Police continued to pursue the criminal case against Fetisov and his codefendants, who had both spent almost a year in detention (they were suspected of several more accounts of theft) by the time Human Rights Watch spoke to

---

[142] Rule 7.1 of the United Nations Standard Minimum Rules for the Administration of Juvenile Justice (hereinafter, the Beijing Rules) provides
"Basic procedural safeguards such as...the right to the presence of a parent or guardian...shall be guaranteed at all stages of proceedings." Furthermore, as mentioned above, Russian law does not oblige police to immediately inform the parents or a legal guardian of the arrest of a minor. Article 40(2)(b)(ii) of the Convention on the Rights of the Child treats the child's right to be informed "promptly and directly" of charges "through his or her parents and legal guardians"; article 10.1 of the U.N. Standard Minimum Rules for the Administration of Juvenile Justice provides that "[u]pon the apprehension of a juvenile, his or her parents or guardian shall be immediately notified of such apprehension, and, where such immediate notification is not possible, the parents or guardian shall be notified within the shortest possible time thereafter."

Fetisov. Hearings began in March 1998 and Fetisov and his codefendants were found guilty of robbery. Fetisov received a two-year suspended sentence.

Following Fetisov's jump, the procuracy investigated the incident and instituted criminal proceedings against Fetisov's torturers. At one point, the investigator reportedly told Fetisov's mother that he considered the police officers to be guilty of torture but said that the criminal case was now in the hands of his supervisors.[143] The case against the police officers was subsequently delayed several times and then handed over to the procuracy of the Chkalovsk district of Ekaterinburg, ostensibly to ensure greater objectivity. That procuracy closed the criminal investigation after Fetisov refused to undergo a psychiatric assessment as his lawyer considered such an assessment to be irrelevant to the investigation against the police officers.

Igor Afon'kin, Baikal'sk, Irkutsk province

Igor Afon'kin's first brush with police happened when he was thirteen years old, when he was detained for illegal entry. Since then, police have detained him on a regular basis, often beating him and forcing him to confess to a variety of crimes. In June 1997, when he was fourteen, Afon'kin was detained at a square during an outdoor dance on Youth Day:

> We walked on the square, there was the discotheque, and they took us. Brought us to the police station in a police jeep. They took us out of the car there where they have a little concrete platform by the entrance into the station. They took us out and beat us up, first sprayed tear gas into out eyes, then took us inside.

Afon'kin said he could not remember why the police detained him that time. The police released him the following day. His mother told Human Rights Watch:

> It was a nightmare when they took him out. First of all, he had a such a bruise on his head, they beat him on the head with something, a nightstick or something else.... Then I looked, he didn't tell me right away, and it turned out that they had worked on him with tear gas! Right in his eyes. Red eyes.... He was all hysterical! He had to throw up.

---

[143] Human Rights Watch interview with Oleg Fetisov and Nadezhda Fetisova, Ekaterinburg, August 11, 1997.

On his back, there were red spots, the next day bruises appeared and we photographed them on Polaroid.... There were also bruises on Igor's legs. Mostly on the hips, not round ones but stretched ones, as if they were beating with sticks.

On November 19, 1997, Afon'kin was detained again. He and some friends were standing by his house when police drove up: "They, the police came running up, beat us up, and then took us to the police jeep, threw us in and took us there [to the police station], there they beat us and beat us, they beat the codefendants as well, and then took us to the KPZ." Police did not advise Afon'kin's mother that they were taking him to the police station, although they visited her and confirmed she was unaware of the arrest:

They came by, asked where my son was and didn't tell me why [they were asking]. I asked them if anything had happened. They [told] me: "No, nothing happened. Where is your Igor?" I told him that he's outside. They left. And I had such an intuition, I immediately went outside and asked the boys: "Where's Igor?" They got scared, didn't say anything.... And then Andriushka came up, his friend: "Auntie Tania, they took Igor to the police station."

At the police station, Afon'kin said he was taken to an office and told to write "a confession": "He put a pen on the table and a piece of paper. And said: 'Write!' Well, and if you don't know what to write, he took a nightstick, beat you up and said: 'Write!.'... They beat, mostly, on the back. On the kidneys with their nightsticks."[144] Afon'kin did not have access to a lawyer from the moment of his detention. He was kept in detention for four months and released on the personal guarantee of a local human rights organization. The case was sent back for further investigation at least twice and the trial had not started as of late March 1999.

Aleksei Alekseev, Ekaterinburg

In March 1997, fourteen-year old Aleksei Alekseev and a friend were throwing snowballs from the balcony of his parents' apartment in Ekaterinburg when they hit a car in the courtyard. The owner of the car, who had been in a shop, phoned the police claiming that the snowball had dented the car. Alekseev and his friend, who had apparently gone outside to take a look at the car, were taken to the

---

[144] Human Rights Watch interview with Igor Afon'kin and his mother Tatiana Afon'kina, Baikal'sk, Irkutsk province, April 7, 1998.

local police station. Alekseev did not have access to a lawyer. Alekseev's mother told Human Rights Watch:

> They were at the police station for four hours. I didn't know where they were, despite the fact that we have a phone at home and my son gave it [to the police] immediately. They [the police] didn't phone me until they had received a confession from him.
>
> They got the confession [from him] by making him crazy, they asked the same questions over and over again, then they forced him to stand to attention so that he felt bad, then she [the female police officer] started to beat him over the head, pulled his hair so that he'd feel pain and confessed quickly. She promised to take him to the detective downstairs who would not be so nice to him. With intimidation she received a confession from him.... He just signed what she had written down for him.[145]

As a result of the beatings, Alekseev had sleeping problems and complained of a lack of energy. When his mother took him to the doctor, he was diagnosed with a possible concussion and bruises on his head. Police did not institute criminal proceedings against Alekseev because of his age.

Women
Torture of women was not a primary focus of Human Rights Watch's investigations, and we received few allegations in this regard. Women constitute about 10 percent of the Russian prison population.[146] The female victims of torture and ill-treatment Human Rights Watch interviewed were released fairly soon after their detention and, ultimately, were called as witnesses rather than suspects.

In April 1994, police in Usol'e-Sibirskoe, Irkutsk province, detained Igor Akhrimenko and Yury Morozov for their alleged participation in a murder. In the years after the detention, police allegedly tried to force the wives of both Akhrimenko and Morozov, as well as a former girlfriend of Akhrimenko, to sign statements against them. Zhanna Setchekiva, Akhrimenko's wife, told Human Rights Watch:

---

[145] Human Rights Watch interview with Aleksei Alekseev's mother, Ekaterinburg, August 8, 1997. "Aleksei Alekseev" is not the adolescent's real name.
[146] According to statistics published by the Russian government in *Prestupnost' i pravonarusheniia 1991-1995,* the number of women in prison grew between 1991 and 1995 from 84,000 to 122,000, or from 9.1 percent to 11.7 percent of the prison population.

> one fine day I went home from work, after a night shift, I went out to the bus stop and a police car drove up to me and they said: "We need to question you urgently." I sat down in the car and went, they took me to the police station. They didn't show any [ID], just said that they needed to question me because they knew I was Akhrimenko's wife.
>
> We arrived at the police station and they said: "You must sign these papers." [I replied:] "Before signing, I must read them." [They said:] "No." A police officer, I don't know his name, slapped me in the face and said: "If you won't sign and won't tell us anything, we will simply 'do you' beyond recognition." They poured me a full glass of vodka and he said: "Drink." "No, I won't." They started to scream at me, first one came close, then another and he threw me from the chair on the ground, I mean, a blow landed me on the floor...and they started to beat me, they beat me in the chest.

Setchikova said that when the police officers finally released her at 5:00 p.m., she was kicked in the back as she went out the door. She remembers being covered in blood and making her way to her mother-in-law's house, where she phoned an ambulance. Setchikova's chest, back, and legs were covered with bruises. These injuries were documented in writing at an emergency room.

Tatiana Popkova, Igor Akhrimenko's former girlfriend, also said she was forcibly taken to a police station in the fall of 1996 and also told to sign an interrogation report, which police refused to allow her to read.[147] She told Human Rights Watch:

> I asked her to [allow me to] read [it] but she categorically refused, covered the text with her hands and said: "Sign." "How can I sign, without reading? Maybe I'm signing someone's death sentence?"... A man came in...an elderly one. I understood that he had a fairly high position. He pulled my hat off me, took me by the hair and smashed my face into the wall. I got very scared, first of all, I didn't expect that that would happen because I had never come across such violence. He smashed me into the wall several times. I started feeling bad and started falling off the chair.

---

[147] In 1994, police also tried to force Oksana Bykova to sign a statement without allowing her to read it.

She said police officers also threatened to throw her into a "pressing room." Another police officer later intervened and released her.[148]

---

[148] Human Rights Watch interview with Tatyana Popkova, Usol'e-Sibirskoe, Irkutsk province, April 9, 1998.

THE LEGAL FRAMEWORK

Russia has made some progress toward bringing domestic law into conformity with international law in the areas of prohibiting and criminalizing torture and providing redress to victims. However, significant gaps remain.

Russia is a party to most major human rights conventions. It ratified the International Covenant on Civil and Political Rights (ICCPR) and the 1984 U.N. Convention against Torture and Other Cruel, Inhuman or Degrading Treatment or Punishment (hereinafter the Convention against Torture) in 1976 and 1987 respectively. Following its accession to the Council of Europe, Russia ratified the European Convention on Human Rights (ECHR) and the European Convention for the Prevention of Torture and Inhuman or Degrading Treatment or Punishment (CPT) in May 1998.

In accordance with article 15(4) of the Russian constitution, international law has priority over domestic law and is directly applicable.[149] This means that Russian officials, including police officers, prosecutors, and judges are supposed to apply international law directly, even if provisions of international law are not explicitly incorporated in domestic legislation. It is extremely improbable, however, that a defendant would be able to make practical use of article 15(4) in a court of law. In practice, knowledge of international law is extremely limited among legal professionals, and officials and defense attorneys hardly ever make use of it. In court, references to international law (and even to Russia's constitution) often elicit smirks or irritation.

Prohibition and Criminalization of Torture and Ill-Treatment

Few elements of international human rights law are as unequivocal as the ban on torture. Russian law criminalizes certain acts of torture, though not all.

A large body of international legal authority has evolved over the last fifty years that forbids the use of torture and other cruel, inhuman, or degrading treatment or punishment. The prohibition is embodied in the United Nations Universal Declaration of Human Rights, which states in article 5: "No one shall be subjected to torture or to cruel, inhuman or degrading treatment or punishment." That right is reaffirmed verbatim in article 7 of the ICCPR, and in article 21(1) of

---

[149] The provision states: "Generally recognized principles and norms of international law and the international agreements of the Russian Federation are a constituent part of its legal system. If an international agreement of the Russian Federation establishes rules other than those stipulated by a law, the rules of the international agreement shall apply."

the Russian constitution.[150] Apart from these treaties, the prohibition against torture is widely considered a *jus cogens* norm, that is, a binding and peremptory norm of customary international law from which no derogation is permitted. The Russian criminal procedure code also bans the coercion of "a defendant or other participant in a case to give testimony by means of violence, threats and other unlawful means,"[151] and since March 1999 the law on police also forbids the use of torture and ill-treatment.[152]

The Convention against Torture, article 1, defines torture as:

> any act by which severe pain or suffering, whether physical or mental, is intentionally inflicted on a person for such purposes as obtaining from him or a third person information or a confession, punishing him for an act he or a third person has committed or is suspected of having committed, or intimidating or coercing him or a third person, or for any reason based on discrimination of any kind, when such pain or suffering is inflicted by or at the instigation of or with the consent or acquiescence of a public official or other person acting in an official capacity. It does not include pain or suffering arising only from, inherent in or incidental to lawful sanctions.

Under this definition, torture is an act that causes severe pain or suffering, which can be either physical or mental, and must be inflicted intentionally.

Russia's criminal code makes torture punishable, although the relevant articles do not cover the full scope of acts that constitute torture under the definition set out in the Convention against Torture. Article 111 sets penalties of from two to fifteen years of imprisonment for premeditated, serious bodily injury, but does not specifically address perpetrators who are acting in an official capacity. Article 117 addresses ill-treatment, but also does not specifically address perpetrators who are acting in an official capacity. It states:

> Infliction of physical or psychological suffering by administering systematic beatings or other violent means, if this did not have the

---

[150] Article 21(2) of the constitution states: "No one may be subjected to torture, violence or other treatment or punishment that is cruel or degrading to the human dignity. No one may be subjected to medical, scientific or other experiments without their voluntary consent."
[151] Article 20(3).
[152] Article 5 of the Law of the RSFSR on Police, as amended on March 31, 1999, published in *Rossiiskaia gazeta*, April 8, 1999, p. 5. It states: "Police may not use torture, violence or other forms of cruel or degrading treatment."

consequences indicated in article 111 [severe damage to health] and 112 [damage to health of average seriousness] of this law is punishable by deprivation of freedom for up to three years.[153]

Torture is invoked as an aggravating circumstance in article 117(2d), which states that the above-mentioned crime "with application of torture is punishable by deprivation of freedom for a period of three to seven years." The term "torture" is not defined in the article.[154] Under Russian law, law enforcement officers do not enjoy immunity from prosecution under this article.

Article 117 is deficient because it fails to criminalize causing physical or psychological suffering by non-violent means. Thus, the use of threats against the person himself or third persons is not punishable under this article.

Russian legislators have chosen not to include torture as an aggravating circumstance in the infliction of physical or psychological suffering that caused death, severe injury, or injury of average seriousness. As a result, a police officer can be tried for "infliction of physical or psychological suffering...with application of torture" for ill-treating someone without leaving any lasting damage, but if he tortures his victim to death, he may be tried simply for murder.

Torture committed by an official is considered an aggravated circumstance of coercion to give testimony (article 302 of the criminal code). Article 302 states:

> 1. Coercion of a suspect, defendant, victim [of crime] or witness into giving testimony or coercion of an expert into giving a conclusion by means of threats, blackmail or other unlawful means by an investigator or person carrying out the inquiry is punishable by deprivation of freedom for a period of up to three years.
>
> 2. The same action, together with the application of violence, degrading treatment or torture is punishable by deprivation of freedom for a period of two to eight years.

---

[153] Article 117 of the criminal code.

[154] Although the term "torture" is not defined in Russian law, the Russian constitution at article 15 (4) provides for the direct application of international law in the Russian legal system. The provision states: "Generally recognized principles and norms of international law and the international agreements of the Russian Federation are a constituent part of its legal system. If an international agreement of the Russian Federation establishes rules other than those stipulated by a law, the rules of the international agreement apply." Thus, it may be possible to interpret the term in light of the definition provided in the Convention against Torture, to which Russia is a party.

This article makes coercion by public officials of suspects to confess punishable. However, article 302 fails to apply to third parties who inflict pain and suffering at the behest of, or in complicity with, a public official, which is common in Russia through the phenomenon of the "pressing room."

Treaties and declarations developed during the last two decades prohibit *both* torture *and* cruel, inhuman, or degrading treatment. The Declaration on the Protection of All Persons from Being Subjected to Torture and Other Cruel, Inhuman or Degrading Treatment or Punishment, adopted by the U.N. on December 9, 1975 (hereinafter the Declaration on Torture), states in article 2 that "[T]orture constitutes an *aggravated and deliberate* form of cruel, inhuman or degrading treatment or punishment" (emphasis added), while stressing in article 3 that no state may permit or tolerate it under any circumstances. The European Court of Human Rights ruled that the distinction between torture and inhuman or degrading treatment "would appear to have been embodied in the Convention to allow the special stigma of "torture" to attach only to deliberate inhuman treatment causing very serious and cruel suffering."[155]

The European Court of Human Rights further established a strict threshold for physical force against detainees. In the case of *Ribitsch* v. *Austria*, the court ruled that:

> In respect of a person deprived of his liberty, any recourse to physical force which has not been made strictly necessary by his own conduct diminishes human dignity and is in principle an infringement of the right set forth in Article 3.[156]

Forced Confessions in Court/The Right not to Testify against Oneself

Russian and international law both unequivocally forbid forced confessions. Article 15 of the Convention against Torture orders states parties to ensure that statements obtained through torture not be used as evidence in, except against the person accused of torture.[157] This provision is closely related to article 14(3g) of the ICCPR, which states that anyone charged with a criminal offense shall not "be

---

[155] *Ireland* v. *the United Kingdom* judgment, January 18, 1978, para. 167.
[156] *Ribbitsch* v. *Austria* judgment, December 4, 1995, para. 38.
[157] Article 15 states:
Each State Party shall ensure that any statement which is established to have been made as a result of torture shall not be invoked as evidence in any proceedings, except against a person accused of torture as evidence that the statement was made.

compelled to testify against himself or to confess guilt."[158] Similarly, article 51(1) of the Russian constitution states that no one is obliged to testify against himself, his spouse or close relatives.[159] Article 69 of the criminal procedure code precludes the use in court of testimony taken in violation of the law cannot be used in court.[160]

Investigation of Torture Allegations

Article 12 of the Convention against Torture obliges states parties to initiate a prompt and impartial investigation of torture complaints whenever circumstances give "reasonable ground to believe that an act of torture has been committed." Article 13 of the ECHR requires states to establish "an effective remedy before a national authority" for anyone whose rights and freedoms as set out in the convention have been violated. In addition, the European Court of Human Rights has ruled that article 1 of the ECHR, in conjunction with article 3, requires an effective investigation of torture complaints whenever the applicant has an "arguable claim."[161] For example, in the case of *Assenov and others* v. *Bulgaria* it stated:

> The Court considers that, in these circumstances, where an individual raises an arguable claim that he has been seriously ill-treated by the police or other agents of the State unlawfully and in breach of Article 3, that provision, read in conjunction with the State's general duty under Article 1 of the Convention to "secure to everyone within their jurisdiction the rights and freedoms in [the] Convention," requires by implication that there should be an effective official investigation [of alleged violations of the rights set forth in the Convention.] This

---

[158] Article 14(3g) states:
[I]n the determination of any criminal charge against him, everyone shall be entitled:] [N]ot to be compelled to testify against himself or to confess guilt.

[159] Article 51(1) of the Russian constitution states:
No one is obliged to testify against himself, his spouse and close relatives, the range of which being defined by a federal law.

[160] Article 69(3) of Russia's criminal procedure code states:
Evidence obtained in violation of the law shall be recognized not to have legal force, and can neither be used as a basis for the indictment nor to prove the circumstances enumerated in article 68 of this code.

[161] Article 1 states: "The High Contracting Parties shall secure to everyone within their jurisdiction the rights and freedoms defined in Section I of this Convention." Article 3 states: "No one shall be subjected to torture or to inhuman or degrading treatment or punishment."

obligation...should be capable of leading to the identification and punishment of those responsible.[162]

The court elaborated upon the need for a sufficiently thorough and effective investigation in various decisions, as in the case of *Assenov and Others* v. *Bulgaria*, in which the court held that Bulgaria had denied the applicant an effective remedy. In this case, prosecutors had failed to immediately question a series of witnesses to a police beating of a Roma adolescent in public. In addition, prosecutors at various levels had concluded, without a proper investigation, that "even if the blows were administered on the body of the juvenile, they occurred as a result of disobedience of police orders" and that the boy's father had caused the injuries.[163]

In another decision (*Aksoy* v. *Turkey*), the European Court of Human Rights ruled that if an applicant was in good health when detained and injured at the time of release, the burden of proof lies with the government:

> [W]here an individual is taken into police custody in good health but is found to be injured at the time of release, it is incumbent on the State to provide a plausible explanation as to the causing of injury, failing which a clear issue rises under Article 3.[164]

Article 13 of the Convention against Torture also obliges states to ensure individuals the right to complain and to be protected against repercussions for filing a complaint.[165]

The U.N. Principles on the Effective Prevention and Investigation of Extra-legal, Arbitrary and Summary Executions encourage states to investigate all suspected cases of extra-legal, arbitrary, and summary executions. These authoritative standards explicitly include deaths in custody if there are "complaints by relatives or other reliable reports" which suggest that an unnatural death occurred. The investigation, which must be thorough, prompt, and impartial, should

---

[162] *Assenov and Others* v. *Bulgaria* judgment, October 28, 1998, para. 102.
[163] Ibid., para. 106.
[164] *Aksoy* v. *Turkey* judgment, December 12, 1996, para. 61.
[165] Article 13 states:
> Each State Party shall ensure that any individual who alleges he has been subjected to torture in any territory under its jurisdiction has the right to complain to, and to have his case promptly and impartially examined by, its competent authorities. Steps shall be taken to ensure that the complainant and witnesses are protected against all ill-treatment or intimidation as a consequence of his complaint or any evidence given.

The Legal Framework

"determine the cause, manner and time of death, the person responsible, and any pattern or practice which may have brought about that death" and should result in a publicly available written report.[166]

In Russia, the procuracy is the primary body responsible for ensuring observance of human rights, including the procedural and other rights of criminal suspects, defendants, and other detainees. However, the procuracy also plays the principal role in prosecuting crimes, as it is in charge of investigating certain categories of criminal cases and prosecutes defendants in court. Human Rights Watch's research has shown that procuracy review of a torture complaint is in most cases a mere formality, and that an effective remedy for torture victims does not exist. In some death in custody cases, however, those alleged responsible for the detainees death were brought to trial.[167]

Redress and Compensation

Under article 14 of the Convention against Torture, states parties are obliged to provide for an enforceable right to adequate and fair redress and compensation

---

[166] Provision 9 of the Principles states:
> There shall be thorough, prompt and impartial investigation of all suspected cases of extra-legal, arbitrary and summary executions, including cases where complaints by relatives or other reliable reports suggest unnatural death in the above circumstances. Governments shall maintain investigative offices and procedures to undertake such inquiries. The purpose of the investigation shall be to determine the cause, manner and time of death, the person responsible, and any pattern or practice which may have brought about that death. It shall include an adequate autopsy, collection and analysis of all physical and documentary evidence and statements from witnesses. The investigation shall distinguish between natural death, accidental death, suicide and homicide.

Provision 17 of the Principles states:
> A written report shall be made within a reasonable period of time on the methods and findings of such investigations. The report shall be made public immediately and shall include the scope of the inquiry, procedures and methods used to evaluate evidence as well as conclusions and recommendations based on findings of fact and on applicable law. The report shall also describe in detail specific events that were found to have occurred and the evidence upon which such findings were based, and list the names of witnesses who testified, with the exception of those whose identities have been withheld for their own protection. The Government shall, within a reasonable period of time, either reply to the report of the investigation, or indicate the steps to be taken in response to it.

[167] See below, "Accountability," for a detailed discussion of the procurator's office's practice regarding torture complaints. Torture victims can also complain to the Russian Ombudsman. It is, however, thus far unclear how effective this remedy is.

for the victims of torture.[168] The European Court of Human Rights considers the requirement of an "effective remedy" under the ECHR to include a right to compensation.[169]

Russian law provides the right to compensation for both material and moral damages suffered by torture victims. However, with several exceptions, this right is essentially unenforceable. The general provision of article 53 of the Russian constitution, in combination with articles 1069, 1070, and 151(1) of the civil code, provide a sufficient legal basis for compensation for both moral and material damages for torture victims.[170] According to these articles, damages (including moral damages) caused by the unlawful actions committed by the agencies of the

---

[168] Article 14 (1) states:
> Each State Party shall ensure in its legal system that the victim of an act of torture obtains redress and has an enforceable right to fair and adequate compensation, including the means for as full rehabilitation as possible. In the event of the death of the victim as a result of an act of torture, his dependents shall be entitled to compensation.

[169] See for example, *Aksoy* v. *Turkey* judgment, para. 98.

[170] Article 53 of the Russian constitution states: "Everyone has the right to compensation from the state for damage caused by unlawful actions (or inactions) of organs of state power or their officials."

Article 1070(2) of the civil code states:
> Damage caused to a citizen or legal person as a result of an unlawful action of an agency of the investigation, the criminal prosecution, or the procuracy, which has not led to the consequences mentioned in paragraph 1 of this article [unlawful application of a measure of restraint, unlawful criminal prosecution, unlawful conviction], is indemnified on the basis and in the manner established by article 1069 of this law....

Article 1069 states:
> Damage caused to a citizen or legal person as a result of illegal actions (non-actions) of state organs, organs of local self-government or officials of these organs, including as a result of issuing an act of a state organ or organ of self-government not complying with a law or other legal act, is subject to indemnification. The damage is indemnified out of the applicable treasury of the Russian Federation, the subject of the Russian Federation, or the municipal formation.

Article 151(1) of the civil code states:
> In case moral damage (physical or moral suffering) has been caused to a citizen by actions which violate his personal immaterial rights or infringe on other immaterial goods that belong to him, as well as in other cases provided for by the law, a court can oblige the violating side to provide material compensation of the indicated damage.

investigation, criminal prosecution, or by the procuracy are subject to compensation.

In the absence of a sufficient body of case law, it further remains unclear whether Russian law provides for "fair and adequate" compensation of damages suffered by torture victims. According to articles 151(2) and 1101(2 and 3) of the civil code, courts determine the size of such a compensation. In determining this, courts must take into consideration, among other things, the character and level of physical and moral suffering of the victim, and the level of guilt of the person who caused the damage.[171] Under article 1064 of the civil code, material damages must be compensated in full.[172]

Human Rights Watch knows of only one case in which a court granted compensation for damages to torture victims and their relatives. In 1998, the Supreme Court of the Republic of Mordovia awarded 200,000 rubles (at the time approximately U.S.$33,333) in compensation for damages to the mother of Oleg Igonin, a young man who died as a result of torture. It granted several other torture victims compensation damages ranging from 30,000 to 50,000 rubles (approximately, U.S.$5,000 to U.S.$8,333).

---

[171] Article 151(2) of the civil code states:
> In determining the size of material compensation of moral damage, the court takes into consideration the level of guilt of the violating party and other circumstances that deserve attention. The court must also take account of the level of physical and moral suffering, related to the individual features of the person, to whom the damage was caused.

Article 1101 (2 and 3) of the civil code states:
> The size of compensation of moral damage is determined by courts, depending on the character of the physical or moral suffering caused to the victim, and also on the level of guilt of the party that caused the damage in case their guilt is the ground for compensating the damage. In determining the size of compensation of the damage, the requirements of rationality and fairness must be taken into account.
>
> The character of physical and moral suffering is determined by the court, taking into account the factual circumstances under which the moral damage was caused, as well as the individual particularities of the victim.

[172] Article 1064 (1) of the civil code states: "Damage caused to the person or property of a citizen, as well as damage caused to the property of a legal entity, must be compensated in full by the person who caused the damage."

HOLDING RUSSIA TO ITS INTERNATIONAL OBLIGATIONS

Russia's compliance with its obligations under the Convention against Torture and other international agreements for the prevention of torture has been under the scrutiny of a range of intergovernmental bodies and mechanisms in the 1990s, notably by European and United Nations bodies. This oversight, as well as Russia's bilateral relations with a number of states, has led to significant reporting and advocacy regarding the prevention of torture, unfortunately to little avail.

In this chapter we primarily discuss the international community's response to allegations and well-established cases of torture aimed at eliciting confessions from suspects and detainees. In the summary of U.N. Special Rapporteur Nigel Rodley's findings, however, we also discuss conditions in pretrial detention as essential to an understanding of the atrocious conditions in which many torture victims are held, often for years on end, before their eventual transfer to a prison colony or release.

United Nations
Committee against Torture

The Soviet Union ratified the Convention against Torture in 1987. Russia, as the Soviet Union's successor state, submitted its second periodic report on implementation of the convention in 1996, which the Committee against Torture considered in November 1996. In its conclusions, the Committee found that Russia had made considerable progress in legislation toward protecting its citizens against torture, and it commended in particular the human rights provisions of Russia's 1993 constitution.

However, the committee expressed concern about "widespread allegations of torture and ill-treatment of persons in custody with a view to securing confessions, general allegations of ill-treatment of detainees and the absence of effective machinery to address such complaints promptly." It further decried Russia's failure to create a specific crime of torture in domestic law as well as the slow rate at which domestic legislation is being harmonized with constitutional and international norms of human rights.

The Committee recommended that Russia introduce the crime of torture, using the definition of the Convention against Torture, as a separate crime, with sufficiently severe punishment to reflect the gravity of the offense. It further called for the establishment of an "effective machinery to monitor the conditions under which investigations of crimes are conducted" and "an appropriate process for the prompt investigation of complaints of suspects, detainees and prisoners and the prosecution of offenders."[173]

Special Rapporteur on Torture

At the invitation of the Russian government, U.N. Special Rapporteur on Torture Nigel Rodley visited Russia from July 17 to 28, 1994 to investigate questions relevant to torture in Russia, and specifically conditions in pretrial detention centers. During the visit the special rapporteur visited various police detention centers, pretrial detention centers, prison colonies, and a hospital for detainees in Moscow, St. Petersburg, and their immediate vicinity. He also spoke to numerous officials and human rights activists. On November 16, 1994, the special rapporteur issued a detailed report with his findings.[174]

Ill-treatment and Coercion to Confess

The special rapporteur reported receiving numerous allegations of police brutality at the time a suspect is taken into custody, and of investigators and representatives of the procuracy pressuring suspects to confess. He noted:

> [T]here is an initial period where a person may be held, formally for no more than three hours, for screening, identification checks and verification of any earlier police record. During this period the suspect is not logged in. The logging in only occurs after the investigator has produced a form confirming the details the screening is designed to elicit. During this period, there is no record of the detainee's presence... Accordingly, the period of temporary detention could provide an opportunity for abuse to occur.[175]

He noted in his report that he was unable to investigate allegations of police brutality and torture by proxy in detail, as he was not able to speak to detainees in private, because an official of the Ministry of Internal Affairs was present during all meetings with detainees.[176] In the context of these limitations, the special rapporteur stated that although beatings and other forms of ill-treatment appear to be frequent, he did not conclude that they are routine.[177] The special rapporteur

---

[173] For the full text of the Committee's report, see Appendix A.
[174] Report by the Special Rapporteur on Torture, Sir Nigel Rodley, November 16, 1994, E/CN.4/1995/34/Add.1
[175] Ibid., para. 66.
[176] Ibid., para. 20 and 57.
[177] Ibid., para. 20.

further reported "persistent reports from reliable sources" that violent inmates are intentionally placed in cells to brutalize other inmates and break their will with a view to securing a confession.[178] The special rapporteur stated that most police appeared to believe they could act with impunity and were not deterred by the criminalization of torture and ill-treatment in Russia's criminal code.[179]

Detention Policies, Court Review, and Length of Detention

The special rapporteur severely criticized Russia's detention policies. He stated in his report:

> Article 9 (3) of the International Covenant on Civil and Political Rights guarantees that persons awaiting trial shall not generally be kept in detention. Detention before trial should be used only where it is lawful, reasonable and necessary. The Human Rights Committee has interpreted the "necessity" requirement narrowly. The Committee has found that detention may be necessary "to prevent flight, interference with evidence or the recurrence of crime"...or "where the person concerned constitutes a clear and serious threat to society which cannot be contained in any other manner."... The seriousness of the crime or the need for continued investigation, considered alone, do not justify prolonged pre-trial detention.... Under this interpretation of article 9 (3) it would be difficult to justify the all-too-common practice within the Russian Federation of detaining non-violent first-time suspected offenders.[180]

In fact, the special rapporteur found that investigators and procurators rarely choose any other measure of restraint than custody: "Indeed, the entire investigative and judicial procedures to determine the guilt or innocence of a suspect places pressures on the investigator, prosecutor and judge to remand even non-violent first-time offenders."[181] The special rapporteur further noted that the judicial review process of the lawfulness of detention is of limited use as "courts almost always confirm the lawfulness of the detention."[182]

He further criticized the long periods of time many detainee spend in pretrial detention centers:

---

[178] Ibid., para. 57.
[179] Ibid., para. 21.
[180] Ibid., para. 38.
[181] Ibid., para. 37.
[182] Ibid.

> Article 9 (3) of the International Covenant on Civil and Political Rights also guarantees the right to trial within a reasonable time or to release. Although the Human Rights Committee has not provided specific guidelines on what constitutes a reasonable time, it is clear that the 18-month limit on pre-trial detention in the Russian Federation is incompatible with article 9 (3) of the Covenant, particularly in the light of the fact that the length of detention may be extended by years due to unreasonable delays during the course of a trial.[183]

Since the special rapporteur's visit, the Russian legislature has extended the maximum term for pretrial detention to two years.

Conditions in Detention

The special rapporteur's criticism of conditions in pretrial detention centers (SIZOs) was vivid and harsh:

> The Special Rapporteur would need the poetic skills of a Dante or the artistic skills of a Bosch adequately to describe the infernal conditions he found in these cells. The senses of smell, touch, taste and sight are repulsively assailed. The conditions are cruel, inhuman and degrading; they are torturous. To the extent that suspects are confined there to facilitate the investigation by breaking their wills with a view to eliciting confessions and information, they can properly be described as being subjected to torture.[184]

Describing a cell at Butyrka pretrial detention center, the special rapporteur wrote:

> When the door to such a general cell is opened, one is hit by a blast of hot, dark, stinking (sweat, urine, faeces) gas that passes for air. These general cells may have one filthy sink and a tap, from which water does not always emerge, near a ground-level toilet around which the inmates may drape some cloth for a minimum of privacy and to conceal the squalor of the installation. There is virtually no daylight from covered or barred windows, through which only a small amount of fresh air can penetrate. Artificial lighting is weak and not always functioning.

---

[183] Ibid., para. 39.
[184] Ibid., para. 71.

Due to the overcrowding in the general cells visited at both Butyrskaya and Matrosskaya Tishina No. 1, there is insufficient room for everyone to lie down, sit down or even stand up at the same time. At Matrosskaya Tishina No. 1 the Special Rapporteur saw some detainees lying on the floor underneath the lowest bunk (about 50 cm above the floor). All the detainees in these cells suffer from swollen feet and legs due to the fact that they must stand for extensive periods of time. The inmates tend to be half-clothed and are even stripped to their undershorts (at least in the summer, when the Special Rapporteur visited). Their bodies are perspiring and nothing can dry due to the humidity. Despite the existence of some medical and even hospital facilities (often without sufficient medicines), the general cells are the obverse of a hospital regime: they are disease incubators. Festering sores and boils abound; most if not all inmates suffer from skin diseases that cause pervasive itching.[185]

Recommendations

The special rapporteur recommended to the Russian government to remove from SIZOs all detainees in excess of the officially proclaimed capacity of existing institutions. He proposed that all nonviolent first-time offenders be released and that the remaining overcrowding could be eliminated by transferring the excess population on a temporary basis to indoor stadiums or other comparable public places.[186] This recommendation was not carried out. Instead, the SIZO population increased from 238,000 in 1994 to about 300,000 in 1999.

He further recommended a much greater use of noncustodial measures of restraint, such as bail and release on one's own recognizance and stated that laws restricting the use of such measures of restraint should be amended and that all deprivations of freedom should require judicial sanctioning.[187] Furthermore, he encouraged the Russian government to build additional pretrial detention centers to the extent that other measures of restraint would not eliminate the overcrowding, and to refurbish existing institutions.[188]

Council of Europe
Parliamentary Assembly Monitoring Procedure

On January 25, 1996, the Parliamentary Assembly of the Council of Europe adopted Opinion No. 193, granting Russia's accession for request to the Council of

---

[185] Ibid., para. 43 and 44.
[186] Ibid., para. 77.
[187] Ibid., para. 79, 80, and 81.
[188] Ibid., para. 82.

Europe. The opinion contains a number of accession obligations. Among others, these conditions include an obligation to adopt a new criminal procedure code that conforms to Council of Europe standards, to reform the procuracy, and to establish a professional bar association.

In a report released on June 2, 1998, the Council of Europe co-rapporteurs for the Monitoring Committee, Rudolf Bindig and Ernst Muhlemann, presented their findings on Russia's honoring of Council of Europe obligations. The report noted that "allegations of ill-treatment or even torture during police custody and pretrial detention, mainly to obtain coerced confessions, are still being made." It recommended that "the Russian authorities should intensify their efforts to protect detainees from such abuses by law-enforcement agents, and should ensure that offending guards and policemen are promptly brought to justice."[189] Human Rights Watch believes that the rapporteurs failed to note the real extent of torture and used far too weak wording to characterize and condemn the practice of torture in Russia.

The rapporteurs noted that Russia had apparently made no progress toward reforming the procuracy. The report stated:

> [I]n practice, this means that, in court, the equality of arms between the prosecution and the defense is not always guaranteed. Outside of court, it means that the prosecutor's office has powers which in most Council of Europe states have been transferred to other bodies, such as administrative courts, ombudsman institutions or judges.[190]

> [I]n principle, the function of supervising the administration should clearly belong to administrative courts, and the function of defending human rights equally clearly belong to an institution independent from the prosecutor's office, such as the Human Rights Commissioner, and ombudsman or another similar institution. An institution whose primary function is to accuse persons (e.g. of a criminal offense), and thus fights, a priori, for the interests of the state, cannot at the same time ensure that the rights of the arrested person are not violated.

The rapporteurs added that since institution-building in Russia is still in progress, "[i]t might be acceptable for the current practice to continue until a more

---

[189] Rudolf Bindig and Ernst Muhlemann, *Report on the Honouring of obligations and commitments by the Russian Federation* (Strasbourg: The Council of Europe, June 2, 1998), para. 47.
[190] Ibid., para. 28.

appropriate institution can take these functions over without hindering the effectiveness of the service."[191]

The rapporteurs did not themselves analyze the draft criminal procedure code that the Russian State Duma adopted in its first reading in June 1997. The report merely reflects the critical opinions of independent experts and nongovernmental organizations on the draft. At the request of Russia's presidential administration, the Council of Europe's Directorate for Human Rights carried out an expert assessment of the draft and presented the results to the presidential administration in September 1999.[192]

The report furthermore underscored the importance of achieving a change in mentality toward suspects and defendants. It stated that "the presumption of innocence does not seem to be automatically applied in the Russian Federation. Many policemen and prison officials consider a person guilty as charged as soon as he or she is remanded in custody, and the high conviction rates in Russian courts (especially when the defendant has made a confession) point to some judges and jurors sharing this view."[193]

Committee for the Prevention of Torture

Russia ratified the European Convention for the Prevention of Torture and Inhuman or Degrading Treatment or Punishment in May 1998. Under the convention, the Committee for the Prevention of Torture can carry out surprise visits to member states and has full access to police stations, pretrial detention centers and prison colonies.

A Committee delegation carried out its first visit to Russia from November 16 to 30, 1998. The delegation visited Moscow, Nizhnii Novgorod, and Saratov. In September 1999, the Committee carried out its second visit to Russia, and traveled to Vologda, Cheliabinsk, and St. Petersburg. During both visits, Committee members and experts inspected police stations, SIZOs, colonies and other places of detention. On both occasions, the delegation met with both the relevant officials and representatives of NGOs. The information gathered by the Committee remains confidential unless the Russian government sanctions publication of the report.

As of this writing, the Committee for the Prevention of Torture had not yet announced whether it plans to visit Russia again in 2000.

---

[191] Ibid., para 28 and 29.
[192] Ibid., para. 21.
[193] Ibid., para. 50.

Directorates for Human Rights and Legal Affairs

The Council of Europe's directorates for human rights and legal affairs provide assistance to, and training for law enforcement agencies, the judiciary, and lawyers through a trilateral program also involving the European Commission and the Russian government. So far, these joint programs have focused primarily on the judiciary and lawyers. Cooperation with the procuracy and the Ministry of Internal Affairs is still in the early stages of development.

Organization for Security and Cooperation in Europe

The Organization for Security and Cooperation in Europe (OSCE) stated in its Copenhagen Document of the Conference on the Human Dimension of the Conference for Security and Cooperation in Europe (CSCE) that "no exceptional circumstances whatsoever, whether a state of war or a threat of war, internal political instability or any other public emergency, may be invoked as a justification of torture."[194] The 1993 CSCE Implementation Meeting on the Human Dimension called for all member states to make the prevention of torture a priority area of implementation.[195]

Despite these words of commitment and numerous reports on torture in Russia by Russian and international NGOs and in the Russian media, Human Rights Watch is not aware of any work by the OSCE on torture in Russia. The OSCE does not have an office in Russia, but maintains a small field mission in Chechnya.

European Union and Member States

Human Rights Watch is not aware of any specific initiatives of the European Union to address the issue of torture in Russia, apart from its member state, Sweden, having raised the case of Sergei Mikhailov (see above) with former Procurator General Yuri Skuratov.

The European Union announced a decision in December 1998 to begin issuing yearly human rights reports on non-European Union countries. One of the European Union's main issues of concern, apart from the abolition of the death penalty, is torture and ratification of the United Nations torture convention.

The European Union as such does not provide any direct assistance to Russia's law enforcement agencies, the judiciary or the legal profession. Most European Union assistance is channeled through the trilateral joint programs run by the Council of Europe.

---

[194] Copenhagen Document of the Conference on the Human Dimension of the CSCE. (1990) para 16.3.
[195] Report of SWB.1. para. 7, adopted at the Human Dimension implementation meeting of the CSCE in 1993.

United States of America

The U.S. Department of State's *Country Report on Human Rights Practices for 1998* stated that in Russia "there are credible reports that law enforcement personnel regularly use torture to coerce confessions from suspects and that the Government does not hold most of them accountable for these actions." The report discussed a number of torture methods used by Russian police, as well as a number of concrete incidents that were widely discussed in the Russian press. This recognition has borne no discernable impact on U.S. policy on security assistance to Russia. The U.S. government provided an estimated $10 million in training and technical assistance to Russian law enforcement in 1998. It appeared that the U.S. government had not yet made any significant progress toward implementing the Leahy amendment, a legislative provision that calls for assurances that no U.S. assistance benefits units of security forces responsible for gross violations of human rights, unless those responsible have been brought to justice. According to State Department officials, the implementation of this amendment is apparently complicated by the fact that the Russian procuracy does not keep centralized records on abuse by security forces. In a departure from practice with respect to some other countries, the U.S. government has not made assistance to law-enforcement agencies in Russia conditional on the Russian government's monitoring of abuses by security forces and providing the U.S. with the appropriate information. It also appeared that U.S. authorities gave insufficient priority to the implementation of the Leahy amendment, failing to provide to U.S. embassy employees in charge of such matters the extra resources they would need to perform such a task, given Russia's chaotic law-enforcement environment. The Moscow embassy's efforts to track abusive security officials was clearly too passive, as it appeared to merely accept the failure by Russian authorities to gather and maintain centralized, meaningful statistics on abusive officials. U.S. authorities did not, apparently, exhort their interlocutors to keep such statistics, or even make such practices a condition for future assistance.

In its technical assistance programs to law enforcement agencies, the U.S. government did not appear to make sufficient linkages to respect for human rights, and in particular to prevention of torture. The goals of these training programs do not even make a direct reference to improving respect for human rights but merely refer to the rule of law. The assistance programs have a component called "human dignity," but the U.S. government does not appear to monitor implementation of such training.

CRISIS IN THE CRIMINAL JUSTICE SYSTEM

Police torture in Russian takes place against the backdrop of a chaotic criminal justice system. The political crisis that arose in the course of dismantling the Soviet Union's authoritarian political system has stalled desperately needed reforms of the Soviet-era criminal justice system, leaving it in great disarray. In addition, unrelenting economic crises have meant drastic reductions in public expenditure across the board, which left the criminal justice system with inadequate funding. The police, procuracy, and judiciary all face high turnover rates, underfunding, increased workloads, and corruption; further, they all suffer from an acute lack of public trust. The legal profession, which was severely underdeveloped in Soviet times, has grown but is still far from effective and professional. Corruption and unethical practices are widespread.

The Police Force

Opinion polls conducted in recent years have shown that Russia's police force is in a deep crisis of legitimacy: Russian citizens do not trust their own police. One poll found that in 1998 more than 50 percent of respondents assessed police performance as bad or very bad. Thirty percent believed police are primarily concerned with protecting their own interests instead of those of citizens, and 15 percent believed police mainly protect the interests of the mafia.[196] According to data from the Scientific Research Institute of the Ministry of Internal Affairs, around 60 percent of crime victims do not want to report crimes to the police as they see them not as a protector but as a source of increased danger.[197] A television opinion poll carried out by the daily program *Segodniachko* on NTV (Russia's independent television channel) on December 10, 1998, found that the vast majority of Russians believe the police beat detainees. The question, "Do you believe that police sometimes beat detainees?" generated a record number of calls that were not, as is usually the case, evenly divided between "yes" and "no." Of the 22,871 people who phoned the studio during the half-hour program, 21,910 answered in the affirmative, 758 believed police do not beat detainees and 203 people answered that they did not know. In June 1998, the daily newspaper *Segodnia* [Today] reported that an opinion poll in Moscow found that 43 percent of Muscovites would not

---

[196] Oleg Arifjanov, "Rossiiskia militsiia rabotaet gorazdo khuzhe sovetskogo" (Russian militia performs significantly worse than the Soviet one), *Izvestiia* [The News](Moscow) April 17, 1998, p. 1.

[197] Vladimir Indiriakov, "Uchastkovyi po prozvishu 'liutyi'" (Precinct inspector nicknamed "the cruel one"), *Trud* [Labor] (Moscow) May 14, 1998.

contact the police under any circumstances, including opening the door to their apartment to police officers, and 37 percent feared police as much as criminals.[198]

Personnel, Recruitment, and Turnover

Since the early 1990s, the police force has experienced a serious turnover problem. Attracted by much higher salaries, large numbers of police officers, detectives, and investigators have left the police force to join private security firms or become lawyers or businessmen. According to Vladimir Vorozhtsov, an aid to then-Minister of Internal Affairs Sergei Stepashin, some 1.2 million employees of the Ministry of Internal Affairs, or 80 percent of its entire staff, have left their jobs for employment outside the ministry since the early 1990s.[199] The police chief of Arkhangel'sk province, Boris Uemlianin, told Human Rights Watch that around 50 percent of police detectives work in the force for only three years. Detectives with working experience as detectives of more than ten years constitute only about 5 percent. Uemlianin added:

> If we look at criminal investigation— it's three and a half years since I worked as head of the criminal investigation department.... Only a few are left with whom I worked, from over forty people, around 15 percent.[200]

Uemlianin further said that in order to become an effective detective, one needs to have at least three years of experience. Vitalii Bartoshevich, deputy chief of police in Irkutsk province, told Human Rights Watch that more than 50 percent of police detectives leave the force within five years.[201]

These high turnover rates obviously also result in the loss of institutional memory. In his book about the police, a journalist with the Moscow-based newspaper *Obshchaia gazeta,* Maksim Glikin,[202] quotes two police detectives as saying:

---

[198] Svetlana Sukhova, "Kaznit' deshevle, chem pomilovat'" (Executing is cheaper than granting clemency), *Segodnia* (Moscow) June 4, 1998.

[199] Human Rights Watch interview with Vladimir Alferov, deputy head of the investigative department of the MVD, and Vladimir Vorozhtsov, assistant to the minister of interior, Moscow, March 30, 1999.

[200] Human Rights Watch interview with Boris Uemlianin, Arkhangel'sk, July 22, 1998.

[201] Human Rights Watch interview with Vitalii Bartoshevich, Irkutsk, April 9, 1998.

[202] Maskim Glikin has covered the criminal justice system for *Obshchaia gazeta* [Everyone's Newspaper] for the last five years. He is also the author of two books on crime and criminal justice in Russia.

The continuity has stopped, the normal transfer of experience. Before, in criminal investigation, there were gray-haired men with twenty years of experience and in the first two or three years you weren't even allowed to come close to something serious.... Now, a detective who has worked for three years is considered senior.[203]

Yet, simultaneously with this outflow of experienced officers, the number of employees of the Russian Ministry of Internal Affairs has grown since the collapse of the Soviet Union. According to Stepashin, the size of the Russian Ministry of Internal Affairs now exceeds the number of Ministry of Internal Affairs employees the Soviet Union had and is relatively one of the highest in the world.[204] According to the daily newspaper *Novye izvestiia,* there is currently a police officer for every ninety-three inhabitants of Russia.[205]

Recruitment standards have also been lowered. The percentage of investigators with a legal education is no more than 50 percent.[206] A police chief in Irkutsk even said that at most 34 percent of police investigators had a legal education.[207] One procurator reflected with a bit of amusement and exaggeration that "if they don't have a criminal record, they are accepted automatically."[208] Former police officer Oleg Egorov told Human Rights Watch that when he started working for the police in 1992, recruitment procedures were fairly strict and included background checks and a psychological test. However, once accepted into the force, proceedings were less strict:

---

[203] Maksim Glikin, *Militsiia i bespredel* (Police and lawlessness), (Moscow: Tsentrpoligraf, 1998), p. 338.
[204] *Izvestiia,* January 21, 1999, p. 1.
[205] *Novye izvestiia,* [The New Izvestiia], (Moscow) May 20, 1999, p. 1.
[206] The Russian term *"sledovatel'"* means investigator. The "sledovatel'" leads and coordinates criminal investigations, and following the investigation is responsible for drafting the indictment before sending the case to the procurator, for approval, and to court. In Russia, police, procuracy, Federal Security Service, and other law enforcement agencies each have their own investigative departments and "sledovateli," who are responsible for investigating crimes that fall under the jurisdiction of that law enforcement agency. The "sledovatel" is supposed to have a legal education, which he can receive by attending a law faculty, or by attending a four-year program at a police school with a specialization to become investigator, or a special school for investigators.
[207] Human Rights Watch interview with Vitalii Bartoshevich, deputy head of police for the Irkutsk province, Irkutsk, April 9, 1998.
[208] Human Rights Watch interview with Vladimir Byzenkov, Ekaterinburg, August 12, 1997.

I initially applied for a job with the Ministry of Internal Affairs, didn't know where I would go [to work], and for myself thought that I could count on precinct inspector at the most. But when they had received all the documents, ran all the [background] checks, they called me in and said: "Write a statement, you're going to the crime police." That shocked me. They took me downstairs to the department for criminal investigation, introduced me to the chief, with the deputy, and said: "You'll start today." They explained to me what I had to do.[209]

Despite this grim picture, Boris Uemlianin expressed hope that recruitment and professional preparation of police officers would improve over the next few years in Arkhangel'sk province and elsewhere. Vladimir Alferov of the Ministry of Internal Affairs told Human Rights Watch that most police investigators without a law degree are taking courses in the evenings.[210]

Material Difficulties and Workload

Policemen receive low salaries[211] and face massive workloads and extremely poor working conditions. Maksim Glikin has also described how the lack of equipment affects police work: police precincts often have only one computer for ten to fifteen people; and xerox machines are a rarity. As a result, he claims detectives spend nearly half their time copying documents by hand.[212] Mikhail Pashkin of a Moscow police union said that he knows of police departments that have one telephone for seven detectives.[213] According to Glikin, a country-wide police database has recently been developed, but many police officers do not yet know how to use it and it is poorly maintained. Also, much information is still kept in non-computerized card form. By his account, the number of fingerprints alone on such cards is around thirty million. Glikin also decries the absence of special telephone lines for fast and reliable police communications.[214] At the same time, all

---

[209] Human Rights Watch interview with Oleg Egorov, April 21, 1999. "Oleg Egorov" is not the man's real name.

[210] Human Rights Watch interview with Vladimir Alferov and Vladimir Vorozhtsov of the Ministry of Interior, Moscow, March 30, 1999.

[211] According to Mikhail Pashkin of a Moscow police union, police detectives and investigators receive between 1,500 and 2,000 rubles, or U.S.$60 and $80, per month, respectively. Traffic police receive between 700 and 1,200 rubles, or U.S.$28 and $48, per month, respectively.

[212] Glikin, *Militsia i bespredel*, pp. 266, 283.

[213] Human Rights Watch interview with Mikhail Pashkin, Moscow, March 4, 1999.

[214] Glikin, *Militsiia i bespredel*, pp. 274 - 292.

of the police officers and chiefs Human Rights Watch spoke to complained that workloads have increased drastically over the last few years.

Police Extortion and Violence[215]

The scale on which police extort money from ordinary citizens is dramatic. In a 1998 study on corruption in Russia, President Boris Yeltsin's former political advisor, Georgii Satarov, stated that grassroots corruption in Russia is "deeply entrenched in the everyday life of society" and "penetrates into all spheres where a citizen has to interact with the state or, vice versa, the state summons a citizen." The study concluded that law enforcement agencies (and especially the police) are the second most corrupt state agencies, trailing only the housing system.[216]

The *propiska* (obligatory residence permit) system, for example, commonly serves as a pretext for police extortion, especially against nonethnic Russians.[217] The conduct of the Moscow police is particularly predatory: it is not uncommon for a person from the Caucasus or Central Asia to choose not to leave the house rather than confront the likely prospect of having to pay a police bribe or worse. Police extract what amounts to a monthly "tax" from UNHCR-recognized refugees residing in Moscow who, due to that city's restrictive rules, cannot obtain residence permits; the alternative to paying the "tax" is certain eviction, incarceration, or the threat of deportation.

---

[215] In addition to extortion and violence, police involvement in organized crime has become a daily recurring theme in the Russian media. See, See for example, Glikin, *Militsiia i bespredel*, pp. 30, 31, 39, 40; Sergei Il'in, "Proshchai oruzhie" (Goodbye to Arms), *Novye izvestiia*, (Moscow) December 16, 1998, p. 8; Pavel Morozov, "Militsioner ugodil za reshetku" (A Policeman Ended up Behind Bars), *Segodnia*, Moscow, June 1, 1998, p. 7; Al'bert Sanitarov, "Militsionery pomogali narkodel'tsam sbyvat' opium" (Police Helped Drug Dealers Sell Opium), *Segodnia*, (Moscow) December 11, 1998, p. 7; Konstantin Demin, "Praporshchik za god stal leitenantom-milionerom" (Within a Year, a Warrent Officer Became a Millionaire Lieutenant), *Segodnia*, (Moscow) June 11, 1998, 7; Vadim Nesvizhkii, "Nachatoe grabiteliami dovershili militsionery" (Police Finished What Robbers Started), *Segodnia*, Moscow) October 8, 1998, p. 1; Nikolai Grittsin, "Ne pishite "operu"" (Don't Write the Detective), *Izvestiia*, (Moscow) February 13, 1998. In, 1996, the MVD established an internal security service to fight police corruption. Human Rights Watch is not aware of any reports issued by this agency regarding its effectiveness.

[216] INDEM Foundation, *Russia vs. Corruption: Who Wins? Analytic report,* Moscow 1998, p.26.

[217] See, Human Rights Watch, "Moscow: Open Season, Closed City," *A Human Rights Watch Report*, Vol. 9, No. 10 (D) September 1997; Amnesty International, "Failure to Protect Asylum Seekers" (EUR 46/03/97), April 1997.

Traffic police are possibly the most notorious of all police divisions for their corrupt practices. It would be difficult to find a driver in Russia who has never paid an on-the-spot "fine" to a traffic police officer for any violation of traffic rules, real or imagined. Asking for a receipt more often than not prompts threats and worse. Failure to pay results in having one's licence revoked. Police are further reported by the media as being closely linked to the prostitution business or even controlling it.[218] Human Rights Watch researchers have even seen policemen forcing elderly women who were begging passers-by for money to pay bribes to be allowed to beg at a specific location.

This kind of extortion is frequently accompanied by senseless violence.[219] In the course of researching torture practices, Human Rights Watch also found numerous cases of violence by traffic police and in drunk tanks. The media, furthermore, regularly report about violent crimes committed by police officers that are unrelated to their duties. In some cases, officers have tried to justify gratuitous violence by fabricating criminal proceedings against their victims.[220]

There are also widespread allegations of police corruption involving large sums of money. A procuracy official in St. Petersburg, for example, recounted to Human Rights Watch how an official in the economic crime unit of the local police was allegedly involved in a car import scheme that evaded taxes on a large scale.[221] Maksim Glikin discusses similar alleged scams, including bribery in the registration of weapons, and the establishment of special charitable organizations as a cover for shady business deals.[222]

The Procuracy

The procuracy appears to be facing personnel problems similar to those in the police force, although in an interview with Human Rights Watch the Procuracy General's office would not confirm this. Lower-level procuracy staff interviewed for this report, however, said that numerous qualified and experienced officials have left for better paying jobs in the private sector and have been replaced with young and inexperienced staff. For several years, the Procuracy General has allowed procurators, as an apparent consequence, to hire fourth- and fifth-year law students

---

[218] Irina Bogoran and Grigorii Sanin, "Devochki s Tverskoi—v obiatiiakh zakona" (Girls from Tverskaia Street—In the Arms of the Law) *Segodnia* (Moscow), February 4, 1998, p. 7.
[219] See, Human Rights Watch, "Moscow: Open Season, Closed City," and Amnesty International, "Failure to Protect Asylum Seekers" (EUR 46/03/97), April 1997.
[220] For a good example, see Glikin, *Militsiia i bespredel*, p. 74.
[221] Human Rights Watch interview with Elena Topil'skaia, St. Petersburg, July 15, 1998.
[222] Glikin, *Militsiia i bespredel*, pp. 127, 133 and 147.

Crisis in the Criminal Justice System 109

as procurators' assistants. In addition, workloads appear to have increased significantly, while a new criminal code brings several new categories of crimes under the jurisdiction of the procuracy.[223] As a result, according to some law enforcement specialists, the quality of investigations has suffered. Mara Poliakova, who worked as an instructor at the Procuracy General's Institute for Improving Qualifications of Top Personnel from 1979 to 1997, said she saw the professional qualifications of procuracy personnel decline throughout her years of training:

> In the course of many years I saw that professionalism is the problem of problems. During the last years, I noticed that [the level of professionalism] started to fall dramatically, even that low level [of professionalism that existed previously] disappeared.... If you judge even by those who came previously and who come now to us at the Institute for Improving Qualifications of Top Personnel.... For the first time we started teaching law school students. Our institute is the Institute for Improving Qualifications of Top Personnel. An institute for improving qualifications, *improving*, and people started coming to us...to improve qualifications which they didn't have. They didn't even have a degree, what qualification can there be then?[224]

Elena Topil'skaia of the Leningrad province procuracy commented:

> When I started working, in order for an investigator to be put on a case of premeditated murder under aggravating circumstances, you needed to be a senior investigator with five years of experience. Now, children, practically, start to work and are immediately put on several contract killings, and they investigate [those] as they see fit.

> Today, cases are much more complicated, voluminous, and the skills of investigators have become much lower, because people capable of working try to find better paying work, and here students work, today's and yesterday's, or people who are about to leave on pension.[225]

---

[223] Under Russian criminal procedure, a variety of different law enforcement agencies (the MVD, procuracy, tax police, Federal Security Service, military commanders) are charged with conducting the preliminary investigation into various categories of crimes. Several new crimes, such as environmental and computer crimes, have been added to the jurisdiction of the procuracy (article 126 of the criminal procedure code).
[224] Human Rights Watch interview with Mara Poliakova, Moscow, February 3, 1999.
[225] Human Rights Watch interview with Elena Topil'skaia, St. Petersburg, July 15, 1998.

However, Anatolii Korotkov, first deputy head of the investigation department of the procuracy general's, claimed that there are no specific material or personnel problems in the procuracy:

> Mostly, in the procuracy there is a stable situation with employees. Vacancies are between 3 and 5 percent. The outflow has ended, although there used to be an outflow at one time, but now everything is stable, even more so, there are many people who want to come and work in the procuracy because it is the most stable agency, which makes for the smallest number of mistakes.[226]

The Judiciary

Judicial vacancies and a rise in the number of court cases have clogged Russia's dockets. Russia has around 15,000 judges for a population of approximately 147 million people; proportionally about half the number of judges in the Netherlands. According to Viacheslav Lebedev, chair of Russia's Supreme Court, the number of vacancies hovers at around 1,000.[227] The newspaper *Novye izvestiia* reported 1,169 vacancies in November 1998.[228] At the same time, the number of court cases has grown significantly over the last few years, resulting in an increased workload for judges.

Courts suffer from severe underfunding, especially since the August 1998 economic crisis. In an April 1998 interview, Lebedev said that salaries are paid on time but there is no money for operating the courts. After the August crisis, salary arrears appeared and the material situation at courts has deteriorated even further. The telephones and heating of many courts have been turned off, and signs asking citizens to bring in their own stationary are the rule rather than exception. Some courts are located in rented buildings that the Ministry of Justice can no longer afford. Courts have large debts to security firms.[229] According to Lebedev, district

---

[226] Human Rights Watch interview with Anatolii Korotkov, Liudmila Kurovskaia, Viktor Kamyshanskii, and Elena Duganova of the Procuracy general, Moscow, March 1, 1999.
[227] "Ne sudite, da ne sudimy budete" (Don't judge and you will not be judged), *Obshchaia gazeta*, April 23 - 29, 1998, p. 13.
[228] *Novye izvetsiia*, November 11, 1998, p. 1.
[229] See, Oleg Odnokolenko, "Esli Femida pravitel'stvu ne po karmanu.... Kriminal'nyi mir okhotno voz'met sudej na soderzhanie" (If the Government Can't Pay for Femida... the Criminal World Will Happily Support Judges), *Segodnia*, June 24, 1998, p. 2; Viacheslav V'iunov, "Rossiiskii sud v tesnote I v obide" (Russian Courts in a Tight Spot), *Nezavisimaya gazeta regiony*, No. 2, 1998, p. 2; Vagif Kochetkov, "Nishchii sud ishchet sostoiatel'nogo sponsora" (Poor Court Looks for Wealthy Supporter), *Novye izvestiia*,

courts can sometimes not even send decisions to province courts for appeal hearings because the postal system will not accept mail from courts until they have paid off their debts.[230] In the winter of 1998, many courts were apparently threatened with closure due to heat and electricity cuts. *Izvestiia* reported in December 1998 that all twenty-three courts in Tomsk province had ceased functioning and that courts in various other regions were on the verge of following this example.[231] The workload of criminal law judges has also reportedly increased significantly in recent years.

The Legal Profession

The Russian constitution grants everyone the right to qualified legal assistance and guarantees free legal aid to the poor.[232] Unfortunately, this provision has not yet led to any significant improvements in the position of detainees and defendants.

In Soviet times, there was a deficit of lawyers. That problem is quickly being resolved, in part by numerous former police and procuracy investigators becoming lawyers, attracted by the higher salaries. However, many lawyers—especially if appointed by an investigator or judge—do not sufficiently represent the interests of their clients, if they do not outright cooperate with the prosecution.

November 17, 1998, p. 2; "Sudam otkliuchaiut otoplenie, I oni zakryvaiutsia" (Heating of Court Cut, the Courts Close), *Novye izvestiia*, November 20, 1998, p. 1.

[230] "Ne sudite, da ne sudimy budete," *Obshchaia gazeta*, April 23 - 29, 1998, page 13.

[231] Konstantin Katanian, "V Rossii Femida - golaia. Na radost' prestupnikam ee razdelo gosudarstvo" (The Russian Femida is Naked, to the Joy of Criminals, the State Undressed Her). *Izvestiia*, December 1, 1998, p.7.

[232] Article 48.

STALLED REFORM

Under the Soviet criminal justice system, criminal suspects and defendants were practically stripped of the rights granted to them in international law and standards. Fair trial standards were systematically violated as an independent judiciary did not exist and suspects and defendants were generally considered guilty before trial. Crime policy was based on a state plan, requiring police and procuracy to solve specific numbers of crimes. The system did not allow for any form of public oversight over prisons or other detention centers.

The year 1990 saw the first serious attempts to reform this system. New laws were adopted that established a theoretically independent judiciary and provided due process rights, and crime policies were temporarily changed. However, the reforms came to a premature end several years later as they met great resistance from both the criminal justice institutions and the political establishment. As a result, Russia's criminal justice system remains a hybrid of half-reformed and purely Soviet institutions and laws. The procuracy remains unreformed. The judiciary is legally independent but in practice is still very dependent on local governments. Crime policies are once again based on a seemingly rigid a government plan, attitudes toward suspects and defendants have seen little change, and the entire system still lacks transparency.

Institutional Reform

In October 1991, the Supreme Soviet of the R.S.F.S.R. (the parliament) adopted a Concept for Judicial Reform, drafted by a group of independent experts, which was to serve as a guideline for future draft laws.[233] In 1992, the Department for Judicial Reform and Court Proceedings was formed under the presidential administration with a mandate to draft a proposal on judicial reform. This proposal, the Concept for Judicial Reform, called for the transformation not only of courts but of almost all law enforcement agencies with respect to the preliminary investigation, trial, and implementation of court decisions. The Concept envisaged the creation of an independent judicial corporation that would enjoy the trust of the people. One of the most important guarantees of independence was seen to be life-long tenure for all professional judges. The concept further called for the transformation of the procuracy into an agency that would have only policing and prosecutorial functions and would cede certain functions to the judiciary, the reintroduction of jury trials, the introduction of justices of the peace, a constitutional court, and judicial control over the validity of arrests.

---

[233] The independent group was appointed in 1990 by the Supreme Soviet.

Some of these ideas were implemented. The Supreme Soviet adopted laws on the constitutional court, on arbitration courts, and on the status of judges; introduced judicial control over arrests (*habeas corpus*); and amended the criminal procedure code to allow for the gradual introduction of jury trials. However, as prospects for Russia's timely transition to democracy, rule of law, and a market economy dimmed, the initial optimism about reforming Russia's criminal justice system faded. It became clear that the changes needed to transform the system would have to go much deeper than any of the authors of the reforms had apparently foreseen. The reforms sparked institutional rivalries, and many of those who worked in the system, being used to the old proceedings and afraid of losing their jobs, came to oppose the reforms. At the same time, the government's political will to carry out real reforms, not only of the criminal justice system but across the board, disappeared and in some areas the government returned to Soviet-style policies. For example, politicians reverted to their previous formulaic positions on crime in reaction to increased crime rates.

A new criminal procedure code that would introduce real adversarial proceedings (as called for in the Russian constitution) has not been adopted,[234] and the procuracy was never reformed. Justices of the peace (an institution which could greatly have relieved the overburdened court system) were introduced, but after delays. The gradual reintroduction of jury trials came to a stop. In 1995, the Department for Judicial Reform was dissolved and judicial reform appears to have largely ceased. The reform effort has thus come to a stop before it really started, leaving the criminal justice system in great disarray.

Problems Reforming the Procuracy

The reform of the procuracy proposed in the Concept for Judicial Reform was aimed at removing the conflict of interest that currently arises in the procuracy's dual functions of both investigating and prosecuting crimes, and guaranteeing due process and human rights. Reform did not progress, and the procuracy has aggressively defended its current structure.

Procuracy officials do not see their functions as contradictory. Anatolii Korotkov, first deputy head of the investigative department of the Procuracy General, maintained that combining law enforcement and rights protection carries

---

[234] Article 123(3). The State Duma adopted a draft criminal procedure code in June 1997. Moscow Center for Prison Reform, *Proekt Ugolovno-protsessual'nogo kodeksa RF - otzyvy iuristov, ekspertov, pravozashchitnikov* (Moscow 1997).

no conflict of interest, and that the procuracy's prosecutorial work should be seen as a form of protecting the rights of crime victims.[235]

In practice, however, the procuracy does not adequately protect the rights of defendants it is investigating and prosecuting for crimes. The prosecutorial function is clearly given priority over defense of the rights of criminal suspects and defendants and numerous (and often gross) violations of their rights are silently tolerated.

Reforms of the Judiciary

A 1992 law on the status of judges establishes, and is intended to safeguard, the independence of the judiciary. This flagship of judicial reform, however, is in many respects undermined by the practical dependence of the judiciary upon local authorities and law enforcement agencies. The judiciary, moreover, has yet to show that it is prepared to become a truly independent arbiter.

Although Russia's constitution requires that courts be financed from the federal budget alone, and that sufficient funds be allocated to the judiciary to allow it to fully and independently perform its tasks, federal financing of courts is not sufficient for basic upkeep of the court system.[236] As a result, court presidents are forced to beg for help from local authorities—who are under no obligation to financially or otherwise support the courts—to add resources to their budgets and to ensure the delivery of electricity, postal, and telephone services. In an interview with *Obshchaia gazeta* in 1998, the chair of the Supreme Court, Viacheslav Lebedev actually encouraged such practices. He said:

> I would not judge a president of a court who goes to the leader of his province and asks him for money for the work of the court. I am grateful to those governors who gave money to the courts for operating expenses, who have helped restore buildings.[237]

---

[235] Human Rights Watch interview with Anatolii Korotkov, Liudmila Kurovskaia, Viktor Kamyshanskii and Elena Duganova of the Procuracy General, Moscow, March 1, 1999.
[236] Article 124 of the constitution states:
> The financing of courts is effected solely from the federal budget and must ensure the possibility of the complete and independent exercise of justice in accordance with a federal law.

[237] *Obshchaia gazeta*, "Ne sudite, da ne sudimy budete" (Don't judge and you will not be judged), April 23 - 29, 1998, p. 13.

A study by the University of Toronto in Canada found that more than half of the 300 district court judges questioned received money from regional governments.²³⁸ Sergei Pashin, a judge on the Moscow City Court, gave an example of how this assistance works in practice. He told Human Rights Watch that Moscow Mayor Yuri Luzhkov has been paying bonuses to all judges (apparently between 1,500 and 2,000 rubles for district level judges) in Moscow several times a year. Pashin also said that the Moscow city police had donated a luxurious jeep to the Moscow City Court. As a result, court presidents have clear incentives to respond to "requests" local authorities might have in judicial matters. Vladimir Mironov, formerly a judge on the Moscow City Court, told Human Rights Watch:

> [T]he court is that agency that doesn't have anything of its own...and therefore always walks with a stretched-out hand. If they give little, of course, there is going to be dissatisfaction and nothing in the pocket, therefore the court is like that beggar who goes with his stretched-out hand. And what can [the court system] bargain with? Only political decisions.
>
> What is the policy of the [Moscow] city court? For example, Yuri Mikhailovich Luzhkov said: There is the fight against crime. If there is fight against crime, the functions of the court are as follows: to pass maximum sentences on those criminals and not to hinder other law enforcement agencies by verifying...evidence, resolving...doubts [applying], the presumption of innocence, or even acquitting someone.... The court is the agency which must precisely carry out a set task in the city of Moscow.²³⁹

Several judges told Human Rights Watch that court presidents, who administer the assignment of cases, encourage judges to consult with them before issuing decisions, even though this is illegal under Russian law.²⁴⁰ For example, Nadezhda Kovaleva, a former judge with Meshchanskii District Court in Moscow, said at a seminar on the judiciary in September 1998:

---

²³⁸ Peter J. Solomon and Todd S. Foglesong, "Courts and Transition in Russia: The Challenge of Judicial Reform," (University of Toronto, 1998) unpublished manuscript cited with permission of the authors.
²³⁹ Human Rights Watch interview with Vladimir Mironov, Moscow, April 13, 1999.
²⁴⁰ Article 16 of the criminal procedure code states that judges are independent and subordinate only to the law.

> About what kind of independence, about what kind of individual authority can there be when the president of the court, so to speak, expresses surprise because Kovaleva goes into the judge's chamber to make a ruling, doesn't call [the court president], doesn't deliberate with [the court president], doesn't ask which decision should be issued?[241]

Court presidents pressure judges to rule on cases as quickly as possible and to pass severe sentences. Sergei Pashin told Human Rights Watch that a favorite theme at court planning meetings is for judges to review cases faster. He said:

> [A large backlog of cases] hinders his [the court's president] career. A good administrator is someone who doesn't have any specific problems, under whom work is done quickly. Qualitatively or not, that doesn't matter.[242]

Court presidents have ample means of exerting pressure on judges. For example, court presidents play a decisive role in deciding which judges are eligible for apartments or improved living conditions. Under the law on the status of judges, local authorities are obliged to provide apartment to judges who need them within six months after the judge's appointment or within six months of the moment the need for a better apartment arose. However, this rule is often not observed. Vladimir Mironov told Human Rights Watch:

> If I work for an apartment, I need to fit into the system. If only I made a step to the right or to the left, that's an attempt to depart from my main goal and therefore I can no longer count on getting an apartment.[243]

Furthermore, court presidents can make the lives of judges miserable in various other ways. For example, the court leadership can assign the judge to very large cases and criticize him or her for considering too few cases per year.

In addition, in practice judges are not fully independent of the procuracy and police. Judge Sergei Pashin told Human Rights Watch the following:

> For instance, if these agencies don't like a judge, defendants won't be brought to him [by police for court sessions]. Witnesses won't come,

---

[241] Transcript of the round table "Crisis in the Judiciary and the Judicial System in Russia," organized by the Glasnost' Foundation for Human Rights, September 29, 1998.
[242] Human Rights Watch interview with Sergei Pashin, Moscow, January 28, 1999.
[243] Human Rights Watch interview with Vladimir Mironov, Moscow, April 13, 1999.

nobody will bring them in and deliver them. The next step is to accuse the judge of "red-taping," even though he isn't guilty of anything, and fire him from the judicial system.[244]

Several judges also said that procurators can make the life of a judge very unpleasant by writing protests against every decision the judge issues as a form of revenge for issuing an undesired decision. In such cases, the judge loses a lot of time defending his decisions and may face criticism from the court president for being the object of too many protests.

Some judges who have pressed for reform of the system to eliminate some of the pressures on judges have themselves been forced out of the judiciary or compelled to fight against dismissal. Sergei Pashin is the most prominent judge who was stripped of his status on seemingly political grounds; he was later reinstated after a major international and domestic campaign on his behalf. The Moscow Judicial Qualification Commission and later the High Qualification Commission found him guilty of discrediting the honor of judges by violating certain legal norms regarding decision-making on criminal cases. However, it is widely believed that Pashin was stripped of his status in fact for refusing to submit to the demands of Moscow City Court president Zoia Korneva, especially regarding verdicts, and in particular acquittals he had issued. The Supreme Court's civil chamber reinstated Pashin saying that, although Pashin had violated criminal procedure, it did not consider this violation to be intentional or discrediting the honor of the judiciary.

Proceedings to strip Vladimir Mironov, a judge on the Moscow City Court, of his status began the very day he testified in court in favor of Sergei Pashin during the hearings on the latter's case. The Moscow Qualification Commission stripped Mironov of his status less than a month later, claiming his health no longer allowed him to work as a judge. Although Mironov indeed has some health problems, he believes he is capable of working as a judge and is convinced that he was stripped

---

[244] Human Rights Watch interview with Sergei Pashin, Moscow, January 28, 1999. In 1993, the Plenum of the Supreme Court issued a decision in which it recommended qualification commissions (bodies made up of judges that have the power to recommend the appointment of judges and strip judges of their status) to view "red-taping" criminal cases as "an act discrediting the honor and dignity of the judge" and to strip such judges of their status (Decision 7 of the Plenum of the Supreme Court "On the terms of review of criminal and civil cases by the courts of the Russian Federation" of August 24, 1993). Judges often allow for, or cause, unjustifiably long delays in reviewing criminal cases by constantly postponing hearings, often for months at a time, and in some cases reached a verdict only several years after the case was transferred to court. In Russian, this practice is referred to as *"volokita,"* or "red-taping."

of his status in retaliation for his support of Sergei Pashin. The High Qualification Commission and the Supreme Court upheld the decision of the Moscow Qualification Commission on his case.

Elena Raskevich, formerly a judge on the Noginsk City Court, was stripped of her status in 1998 for a series of alleged violations that she considers to have been fabricated. Raskevich believes that she was in fact fired for her refusal to follow the court president's instructions. She told Human Rights Watch that her problems started when she acquitted Vadim Gesse, a conscientious objector, who had been imprisoned for refusing to perform military service. The court president later criticized her for being soft, she said, when she issued suspended prison sentences to two pensioners who had attempted to steal potatoes that belonged to the government.[245]

Pressure to Convict

> *[Public concern is] aroused by the court practice of passing unwarrantably soft sentences and even acquittals with regard to persons having committed grave crimes.... The already difficult work of the law-enforcement agencies, which is associated with enormous risks for life and health of their employees, is rendered pointless by this.*

—President Boris Yeltsin in his speech to the State Duma in 1995[246]

Acquittals are rare in Russia. Only about one half of one percent of all criminal cases end in acquittal in court, although most judges and former judges interviewed by Human Rights Watch maintained that a large percentage of cases that are sent to court are badly investigated.[247] It appears unlikely that the extraordinary number of convictions was the result of careful prosecution policies aimed at bringing only the best-supported cases to trial. Rather, members of the judiciary described to Human Rights Watch extraordinary pressure from law enforcement agencies, local, and federal authorities, and the media upon the judiciary to convict. Furthermore, procedural requirements are in place that discourage acquittals, including routine procuracy appeals to higher courts. Hence, they maintained, it was easier procedurally and less risky for judges to issue a guilty verdict.

---

[245] Human Rights Watch interview with Elena Raskevich, Moscow, July 9, 1998.
[246] *Rossiiskaia gazeta* February 17, 1995, p. 7.
[247] "Rabota sudov Rossiiskoi Federatsii v 1997 godu" (The work of courts of the Russian Federation in 1997), in: *Rossiiskaia iustitsiia* [Russian justice], no. 6, 1998, p. 56.

Among other things, judges told Human Rights Watch that an acquittal demands much more work than a conviction. As a legal journalist for *Novye izvestiia* put it:

> Every judge knows it. To write a guilty verdict is not difficult — you can base it on the indictment. That's what the majority of judges do.... The oversight institutions usually relate to guilty verdicts leniently: agree with it without looking. A not-guilty verdict is a different issue. The "[oversight] institutions" will review every word under a microscope.[248]

While the prevention of corrupt practices provides an important rationale for monitoring acquittals, this does not appear to be the primary objective of such monitoring. Judge Vasilii Martyshkin of the Supreme Court of the Republic of Mordovia told Human Rights Watch:

> I consider that in order to issue an acquittal you have to have great courage as a judge...everything must be justified.... You practically have to argue every piece of evidence in the indictment...and every nuance is a separate theme for discussion. Everything should be argued in such a way that there is not the slightest reason [for overturning the verdict].[249]

The procuracy, which prosecutes criminal cases in court, meticulously studies acquittals; if there is the slightest lack of clarity in the verdict, it launches protests requesting a higher court to overturn the decision.[250] Possibly as a result of this, the Supreme Court overturned 33.1 percent of not-guilty verdicts in 1997 (29.4 percent in 1996) while it overturned only 2.5 percent of guilty verdicts (2.2 percent in 1996). The Supreme Court's practice thus strengthens what might be termed a no-acquittals doctrine.[251] Unfortunately, Human Rights Watch was unable to discuss the Supreme Court's position on this issue as the chairman of the criminal chamber of the court refused to meet with Human Rights Watch representatives.

---

[248] Georgii Tsel'ms, "Opravdatel'nyi prigovor, eto vsegda chudo — iz sta podsudimykh opravdyvaetsia tol'ko odin" (An acquittal is always a miracle — out of one hundred defendants only one is acquitted), *Novye izvestiia*, September 18, 1998, p. 7.

[249] Human Rights Watch interview with Vasilii Martyshkin, Moscow, March 28, 1999.

[250] Judgments in trials of first instance are not final. Therefore, appeals in higher courts cannot be considered to be double jeopardy.

[251] "Rabota sudov Rossiiskoi Federatsii v 1997 godu" (The work of the courts of the Russian Federation in 1997), in: *Rossiiskaia iustitsiia*, No. 6, 1998, p. 57.

Apart from intense scrutiny from the procuracy, judges who acquit face often hysterical reactions from the police, media, and the court president. Several judges told Human Rights Watch that these critics react to the very news of an acquittal and do not even read the verdict. Acquittals are often followed by charges that the judge accepts bribes. Judge Martyshkin told Human Rights Watch about a case in which he acquitted several men of murder charges:

> I read that verdict and ruling various times and thought: Did I really write all that? It was so detailed, it was watertight. They [the procuracy] wrote protests for half a year...the detective agencies, the press.... When you issue a death sentence, they say: "Oh, Martyshkin is such a great guy...," [but when you issue an acquittal,] they create such a fuss, this and that, possibly there is something unclean going on. That is what sometimes happens. And then, after half a year they say: "Ok, it's all correct."

Martyshkin told Human Rights Watch that by the time the procuracy abandons its attempts to have the verdict overturned, the judge's reputation has been irreparably compromised.

Until recently, judges frequently avoided issuing acquittals by sending criminal cases back to the procuracy for further investigation. Elena Topil'skaia, an employee of the procuracy of Leningrad province told Human Rights Watch that many judges send cases back for further investigation in the hope that the procuracy will close them:

> The court is just afraid of taking a decision on the case, even though a qualified judge could take a decision, could investigate the evidence in the appropriate manner. Further investigation is a compromise. In more than 50 percent of the cases of further investigation, the judges don't have the courage to issue an acquittal, in other words, he doesn't want to be the final instance in the case, and sends [it] for further investigation so that it is the procuracy that closes the case.[252]

In 1997, 9.7 percent (9.4 percent in 1996) of all criminal cases were sent back for further investigation. Some cases were even sent back multiple times. For example,

---

[252] Human Rights Watch interview with Elena Topil'skaia, St. Petersburg, July 15, 1998.

lawyer Genri Reznik told a press conference in February 1999 that he knew of a case that was sent back for further investigation thirteen times.[253]

In April 1999, a landmark Constitutional Court decision found provisions allowing judges to send cases back for further investigation to violate the presumption of innocence and several other constitutional guarantees. Under the provisions of the criminal procedure code declared unconstitutional, judges were obliged to conduct their own court investigation into the circumstances of the case and gather sufficient evidence to issue a verdict on the case. If the inquiry or preliminary investigation conducted before the court hearing was incomplete and the gaps in the investigation could not be filled during the court hearing, judges were, under the provisions challenged, supposed to send the case back to the procuracy for further investigation.[254] This implied that, in case of doubt about the grounds of the accusation, judges had to return the case for further investigation, rather than issue an acquittal. The Constitutional Court held that this practice served only the interests of the prosecution:

> [T]his allows for the correction of deficiencies of exactly the prosecutorial activity, when neither the procurator, nor the victim [of the crime] have removed doubts about the grounds of the accusation (including in court). For the sake of the defense return of the case for further investigation is not necessary because the defense can rightfully count on the court issuing a not-guilty verdict if the case has not been proven...or doubts exist about the accusation.
>
> [I]f the criminal prosecution agencies could not prove the guilt of the defendant fully...this must lead—in the system of current criminal procedural norms in constitutional interpretation—to the issuing with respect to the defendant of a not-guilty verdict, or a guilty verdict which establishes the guilt of the defendant of less serious criminal activity.[255]

---

[253] Genri Reznik speaking at a press conference about the case of Alexander Nikitin, February 3, 1999, National Press Institute, Moscow.

[254] Article 232(1) of the criminal procedure code states that:
  A judge sends a case for further investigation in the following cases:
  1) Insufficiency of the conducted inquiry or preliminary investigation, which cannot be corrected during the court hearing.

[255] For the full Constitutional Court decision, see *Rossiiskaia gazeta,* April 27, 1999, p. 4.

Hence, judges can no longer send criminal cases back for further investigation in case of insufficient evidence.[256]

The Constitutional Court decision is no doubt a major step in the right direction. However, under current circumstances it is likely to make convictions without sufficient evidence even more frequent. Before the Constitutional Court decision, many judges compromised by sentencing defendants whose guilt had not been proven, including those who claimed confessions were made under torture, to the term they had already spent in pretrial detention. Elena Raskevich, a former judge with the Noginsk City Court, approximately fifty kilometers east of Moscow, told Human Rights Watch that judges frequently adopt this practice because "this is acceptable for everyone."[257] The procurator is satisfied because he has achieved another conviction, the defendant walks free out of the court room, and the judge successfully avoided issuing an acquittal or sending the case for further investigation. According to official information cited in a Council of Europe report, 65 percent of pretrial detainees are not sent to prison after trial because the sanction imposed is either noncustodial or the length of the sentence is shorter than the pretrial period already served.[258]

Crime Policy Reform

In the late 1980s and early 1990s, the MVD departed briefly from the Soviet-era practice of basing crime policy on a formulaic plan for solving crimes. During the Soviet era, the state closely regulated the correlation between the number of crimes registered and the number of crimes solved, and every police officer had a

---

[256] Russia's Constitutional Court can rule only on provisions that are specifically mentioned in complaints it receives. In the current case, the court was asked to decide on the constitutionality of provisions one and three of article 232 of the criminal procedure code, both of which it found to violate the constitution. It did not rule on provisions two, four and five, which allow judges to send cases back for further investigation if norms of criminal procedure law have been seriously violated during the inquiry or preliminary investigation, or if there are grounds to prosecute other persons on the case if they cannot be prosecuted separately, or if the case has incorrectly been joined with or separated from another case (other cases). The court may rule on the constitutionality of these provisions if it receives a complaint dealing specifically with them, provided all other formal requirements have been met.
[257] Human Rights Watch interview with Elena Raskevich, Moscow, July 9, 1998.
[258] Rudolf Bindig and Ernst Muhlemann, *Report on the Honouring of Obligations and Commitments by the Russian Federation* (Strasbourg: The Council of Europe, June 2, 1998), paragraph 47.

quota for the number of crimes they were to solve per day.[259] It appears that the Russian government returned to a similar crime policy around 1994, and with "the fight against crime" high on almost every politician's agenda, there is once again significant political pressure on law enforcement agencies to produce unrealistic crime-solving statistics. At the same time, strict mechanisms for quality control of police work apparently not exist. This appears to be a factor encouraging the use by police of such methods as torture, falsification of evidence, and the concealment of the crime.

Crime-solving statistics serve as the main indicator for the evaluation of law enforcement work.[260] This system of appraisal applies at all levels of the police and apparently the procuracy. Local police chiefs pressure their officers, regional police chiefs pressure local police chiefs, and the federal government pressures regional police chiefs to turn in statistics showing a high level of cases solved. Pressure to produce good statistics is a factor that rewards police for seeking confessions, whether or not confessions are extracted through physical abuse. Oleg Egorov, a former police officer from Moscow province, told Human Rights Watch:

> [I]f you came to work, you have to produce. [If] you deliver no results, you, as a specialist, did not succeed. But by what means you give the result, doesn't interest anyone. You have your crime solving rates, you don't have "hangers" [crimes that remain unsolved for a long time]—that suits everyone. It's desirable, of course, that there aren't too many complaints against you.[261]

President Boris Yeltsin's controversial decree 1226 on organized crime of June 1994, which gave police sweeping powers to detain suspects without presenting a warrant or charge, may have launched the most recent campaign for

---

[259] In the eyes of the police, a crime is considered to be solved, and appears in the statistics of the Ministry of Internal Affairs as such, as soon as the criminal investigation has been finalized, an indictment been written, and the case has been submitted to the procurator for approval and transfer to court.

[260] Maksim Glikin observes in his book that the regions with the most authoritarian leaders produce the best statistics: Kursk province, with governor Alexander Rutskoi— 84.4 percent and the Republic of Ingushetiia of President Ruslan Aushev—90.4 percent. Maksim Glikin, *Militisiia I bespredel*, p. 258.

[261] Human Rights Watch interview with Oleg Egorov, April 21, 1999. "Oleg Egorov" is not the man's real name.

good statistics.²⁶² Since 1994, crime-solving statistics have soared every year.²⁶³ In April 1998, after a cabinet reshuffle, then-Acting Prime Minister Sergei Kirienko and then-Minister of Internal Affairs Sergei Stepashin announced plans to change the system of appraisal, stressing that the crime picture presented by the police should be more objective.²⁶⁴ These intentions, however, have been of no consequence. According to official figures, in 1998 and the first quarter of 1999, police solved respectively 74.4 and 73.8 percent of all registered crimes, up from 45.1 percent in 1993.²⁶⁵

The Ministry of Internal Affairs appears to issue an annual plan in some form in order to continuously improve crime-solving statistics. This "plan" reportedly contains instructions as to the number of criminal cases that must be solved per year and the number of people a police officer must detain per year. In its book, *In Search of a Solution: Crime, Criminal Policy and Prison Facilities in the Former Soviet Union*, the Moscow Center for Prison Reform refers to a copy of an internal letter from the deputy head of the Department of Internal Affairs of the Moscow Eastern Administrative District, written in December 1995, which states that every district militia officer must solve no fewer than two serious crimes per year and no fewer than sixteen crimes under certain articles of the criminal code, record 800 administrative violations, and keep an eye on no fewer than two released prisoners.

Mikhail Pashkin of a Moscow police union has described what he maintains is constant pressure at every level to meet crime-control quotas:

> Formally, that list does not oblige anyone to anything but orally, the police chiefs will say at every meeting...how many people every...officer should detain, how many administrative protocols should be filled out, how many criminal cases should be instituted; and that is per month. So

---

²⁶²Presidential decree 1226 of June 14, 1994, On Urgent Measures to Defend the Population from Banditry and Other Manifestations of Organized Crime. This decree, which was issued on June 14, 1994, allowed police to detain an individual suspected of links to organized crime for up to thirty days without an arrest warrant or formal charge. President Yeltsin rescinded the decree in the summer of 1998.

²⁶³ Official statistics on crime-solving rates (the ratio: of registered crimes vs. crimes on which the criminal investigation has ended in an indictment) showed a crime-solving rate of 84.3 percent in 1986 at the beginning of perestroika, when rigid plans for solving crimes existed. The late 1980s showed a continuous drop in crime-solving rates; in 1993, official statistics showed that 45.1 percent of registered crimes was solved. Since then, the rates have gone up again; In 1998, the Ministry of Internal Affairs claimed that 74.4 percent of registered crimes was solved.

²⁶⁴ NTV *Segodnia* news program, Moscow, cited in WNC, April 14, 1998.

²⁶⁵ See the MVD's website: http://www.mvdinform.ru/gic/home.htm

this whole faulty scheme leads to the officer [trying to fulfill the plan] when he goes to work.[266]

According to Pashkin, because local police chiefs may sometimes be fired for failing to meet crime-solving targets, they consequently establish a "reign of terror"—by pressuring officers through their pocket books— at their precincts. They assign police officers the number of crimes they must solve and if they fail, police chiefs have sufficient means to make the lives of these police officers extremely difficult, including by threats to their income or indeed their livelihood.

Police officers resort to physical abuse to coerce confessions in the context of pressure to meet the demand for "solved" crimes. A former police officer from Irkutsk, who asked to remain anonymous, linked torture with the intense pressure to solve crimes in an interview with Human Rights Watch. Noting that his supervisors never discussed the inadmissability of physical abuse, he commented:

> [T]hat would just have been funny. If they jail you, they jail you, but to discuss that "it is forbidden to work in such a way" is funny because you'll be forced to work like that anyway: you have to deliver your crime-solving statistics. What's the point of discussing it? Just that everyone sits down and laughs? And suddenly someone will say [to the police chief]: remember, you told me this and that [that torture is forbidden]? What is the chief going to say then? It's a stupid and funny theme. If they catch you—you go to jail. That's a lesson for you: Don't get caught."[267]

Another consequence of rigid crime policies is concealment of crimes that police believe they will not be able to solve: if such crimes do not figure in official statistics they will not affect the crime-solving rate. It has been widely acknowledged by police and political authorities that duty officers frequently fail to record reported crimes; Human Rights Watch found during an investigation into

---

[266] Human Rights Watch interview with Mikhail Pashkin, Moscow, February 25, 1999.
[267] Human Rights Watch interview with former police officer Sasha Sidorov, April 9, 1998, Irkutsk. "Sasha Sidorov" is not the man's real name. Maksim Glikin estimates that if all crimes that are currently concealed by police would be registered, crime-solving statistics would fall to around 14 percent, and asserts that rates would fall further if all confessions that were received under torture were excluded.

Russia's state response to domestic violence and rape, for example, that police routinely refuse to register such reports.[268]

Absence of Public Monitoring over Places of Detention

In 1998, a group of well-known Russian legal experts prepared a draft law on public monitoring of places of detention at the request of State Duma deputies Valerii Borshchev and Saak Karapetian. This draft would enable certain members of the public to have unlimited access to all place of detention to investigate conditions of detention and treatment of detainees by officials. In particular, the draft provided for the appointment of so-called public inspectors who would have the right to visit police stations, IVSs, SIZOs, colonies, and other places of detention without prior warning, at any time. Their remit would be to ensure that the rights of all persons deprived of their freedom are fully observed, and to provide humanitarian aid. The draft law also called for the establishment of so-called trusted specialists (physicians, lawyers, psychologists) who would assist public inspectors in their work.

In September 1998, the State Duma Committee for Public and Religious Organizations sent the draft to the Russian government for comments. In late October, first deputy prime minister Yuri Masliukov rejected the concept of public monitoring altogether, calling it "unacceptable interference with the activities of state agencies and their officials." According to Masliukov, his position was shared by the Procuracy General and the Supreme Court.[269]

In a reply to Masliukov, Borshchev pointed out that the lack of transparency in the prison system and among police institutions is one of the main reasons for widespread torture and other violations of due process. He furthermore underscored that both the law on the police and prisons law allow for such public monitoring. Borshchev also criticized the government for lobbying for a draft law prepared by the Research and Investigative Institute of the Ministry of Interior that allows for "public control" following prior agreement with the administration of each place of detention, saying that such control "by special permission" cannot be called control.[270]

In May 1999, however, the State Duma adopted in first reading a slightly different draft law on public monitoring. Under the draft law, Russia's ombudsman

---

[268] Human Rights Watch, "Russia: Too Little, Too Late: State Response to Violence Against Women," *A Human Rights Watch Report,* vol. 9, no.13 (D), December 1997. See also, Glikin, *Militsiia i bespredel,* pp. 265, 266.

[269] Letter from Yuri Masliukov to Gennadii Seleznev dated October 27, 1998, No. 5132 p. P4.

[270] Letter from Valerii Borshchev to Yuri Masliukov dated November 5, 1998, No. 1791/98.

Stalled Reform 127

would appoint up to fifty public inspectors, who would have the right to visit police stations, IVSs, SIZOs, colonies and other places of detention, without prior warning, at any time. Their remit would be to ensure that the rights of all persons deprived of their freedom are fully observed, and to provide humanitarian aid. In order for this draft to become law, the draft has to be approved by the State Duma in second and third reading, approved by the Council of the Federation, and signed by the Russian president.

A Predisposition to Brutal Methods

Closely linked to the failure to carry out sufficient institutional reform, the attitude of law-enforcement officials toward the rule of law, suspects, and defendants remains unreconstructed, a hold-over from the Soviet era. To many who work in the criminal justice system, the law is often merely an abstract guide that has only limited relevance to daily life, and that can be twisted and disregarded if circumstances demand so. At the highest level, President Boris Yeltsin disregarded Russia's constitution when he issued decree 1226, which allowed police to detain criminal suspects for thirty days without charge. Similarly, at an official meeting, Sergei Stepashin, then the head of the Federal Counter-Intelligence Service (the successor to the KGB, and later renamed the Federal Security Service, FSB), commented on that decree saying that he was "for the violation of the rights of a person if that person is a criminal."[271] Human Rights Watch found these views even among law-enforcement officials with otherwise progressive ideas about law-enforcement. For example, procuracy employee Ekaterina Zamiatina told Human Rights Watch:

> officials of the procuracy sometimes are in a bind, they are forced, this is very unpleasant to admit, to deny that violence was used against defendants using any possible more or less plausible excuse in order for the case on the main charges to go on successfully to court. If it is established that violence was used during the investigation, even if there is other evidence, judges, of course, look at that very negatively and the results of the investigation are put in doubt, [judges] may even acquit the person.[272]

---

[271] V. Osin, "Neotlozhka protiv banditov" (Urgent action against bandits), *Rossiiskaia gazeta,* June 24, 1994.
[272] Human Rights Watch interview with Ekaterina Zamiatina, July 15, 1998. "Ekaterina Zamiatina" is not the woman's real name.

She also gave a concrete example, from a murder case in 1995, in which police beat the defendants:

> They beat their heads into the safe, threatened them, got a gun, promised to use it. The physical injuries were documented by a medical institution: upon reception at the SIZO, they were examined, of course.... And they said that the unlawful methods were used on them from the very beginning of the investigation up until trial. But the procuracy was forced to take a position saying that there was insufficient evidence that the police officers used force, because otherwise they wouldn't have convicted them for murder.[273]

A former judge told Human Rights Watch about a 1996 case against several racketeers in which she issued a guilty verdict, despite the fact that all evidence had been gathered through serious violations of the law, including through ill-treatment. She told Human Rights Watch that she issued a guilty verdict because she was convinced that the men were guilty, but gave them suspended sentences.[274]

According to Mara Poliakova, at the Procuracy General's Institute for Improving Qualifications of Top Personnel, the procurators she trained knew very well that they must exclude evidence received in violation of the law, but that they themselves presumed they were not expected not to apply these standards. Poliakova gave an example that she said she had used when training procurators; a procurator had made a significant mistake and the law demanded that the defendant would walk free. She said she asked the trainees what should be done: "[T]hey all simultaneously raised their hands and said that the case should be closed. I said: 'And if in reality in your practice you get such a case, what would you do?'...They said that 'of course, we would leave it as it is.'"[275] Illustrating this in practice, the deputy procurator of Nizhnii Novgorod province told Human Rights Watch that if he would strictly apply the criminal procedure code when deciding whether to send a criminal case to court, not a single case would be transferred.[276]

Among police, the attitude toward the law is still considerably worse: Many police officers do not know the law or do not care about it. For example, according to Moscow deputy procurator Yuri Sinel'shchikov, out of 311 detentions that were

---

[273] Ibid.

[274] Human Rights Watch interview with Natalia Ivanova, July 9, 1998. "Natalia Ivanova" is not the woman's real name.

[275] Human Rights Watch interview with Mara Poliakova, February 3, 1999, Moscow.

[276] Human Rights Watch interview with Vladimir Nikolaev, October 23, 1997, Nizhnii Novgorod.

carried out by Moscow's organized crime unit in 1997, 238 were carried out in violation of the law.[277] Former police officer Oleg Egorov told Human Rights Watch:

> [Police officers] generally don't talk about the law. I can say that the criminal procedure code, as well as the criminal code, is not, as it should be, a Bible for the detective, including myself. We knew that there was such a book.
>
> I knew that detention reports are written in accordance with article 122 [of the criminal procedure code] but didn't know it by heart, as I do now as a lawyer. Then, it was something far off. I knew that article 144 [of the criminal code] concerned theft, and 102 murder. I think most [police detectives know the law] at that level, there is no deep knowledge, not even the minimal necessary knowledge.[278]

A police detective from Irkutsk reflected a practical distinction between the ideal and the real world in a letter to the editor of the weekly newspaper *Obshchaia gazeta*:

> Any authority, even the most democratic, is unthinkable without violence. Especially unthinkable is work in detective units without the use of tough, cruel, and brutal methods.... I read the newspapers and know all those beautiful words about humanism, presumption of innocence, and inviolability of the individual. But chattering is one thing, working a completely different one.[279]

The attitude among police officers, procuracy employees, and even judges toward criminal suspects and defendants is usually highly negative if not outright hostile. Hostility toward suspects weakens the presumption of innocence at high levels of the judicial system. Judge Sergei Pashin of the Moscow City Court described this:

> At the qualification commission, when they stripped me of my status as a judge, an absolutely "monstrous fact" was discovered. [I had] taken a

---

[277] Yuri Sinel'shchikov, "Nezakonnoe zaderzhanie," *Zakonnost'*, no. 2, 1999, p. 9.
[278] Human Rights Watch interview with Oleg Egorov, April 21, 1999. "Oleg Egorov" is not the man's real name.
[279] Letter published in *Obshchaia gazeta,* April 9-15, 1998, p. 4.

decision to release a person from [pretrial] custody, the case was on a Friday. I was on a holiday but came [to court] anyway to decide the matter.... And he was in the SIZO, he was in quarantine [hospital]. I phoned the administration [of the SIZO] to say that a decision had been taken [to release him], that he should urgently be taken to the SIZO so that he could be released that day. The first deputy president [of the Moscow City Court] told me: "I don't have a car...[to take the necessary documents to the SIZO]." I hired a taxi with my own money, gave the money to my secretary, she went to the SIZO. And on Friday he was free.

This fact was discovered at the qualification commission. And president Andreeva [said], "And why is it that a judge cares about a criminal?!" That is what she said.... Can you imagine, during his holiday he came and gave money so that they could release him.[280]

---

[280] Human Rights Watch interview with Sergei Pashin, January 28, 1999, Moscow.

ACCOUNTABILITY

The authorities are hypocrites, they know that if you fully observe of the law, you, the hardworking detective, are physically not able to keep crime at an acceptable level. The authorities understand perfectly well that you can frequently only expose a criminal and bring the case to a conviction with the help of torture. Therefore, the authorities silently permit you to torture those citizens who end up in the friendly embrace of Femida.

—Letter to the editor of *Obshchaia gazeta* from police detective Vladimir K.[281]

Due to conflicts of interest inherent in the procuracy, strong corporate solidarity in the police force, pressures on prosecutors, and intimidation of the victims themselves, the overwhelming majority of the abusive police officers who torture criminal suspects are not held accountable. Procuracy inquiries into torture complaints rarely lead to a criminal investigation against abusive police officers, and complaints filed during the defendant's trial are usually dismissed without serious consideration. Criminal investigations of police abuse have yielded a mixed record, and very few torture victims have received compensation for the injuries they suffered. Victims can also seek accountability through the Russian ombudsman, which started to work on torture when it was established in 1998. However, it remains difficult to assess the effectiveness of this complaint procedure as it came into effect only fairly recently. While international remedies, like appeals to the European Court of Human Rights, are theoretically open for torture victims, it appears that international bodies have not yet heard any torture cases from Russia.

The Procuracy Inquiry

The procuracy is responsible for ensuring that criminal justice system officials—detectives, investigators, judges, and the like—fully observe the rights and freedoms of suspects and defendants, and is therefore responsible for investigating complaints of ill-treatment and torture.[282] At the same time, the

---

[281] Published in *Obshchaia gazeta*, April 9-15, 1998, p. 4.

[282] According to the 1995 Law on the Procuracy of the Russian Federation, the procuracy is in charge of exercising supervision over implementation of the law (article 21-25), over respect for rights and freedoms (article 26-28), over search and investigation activities, inquiries and preliminary criminal investigations (article 29-31) and over places of detention (articles 32-34). In accordance with article 27(1), officials of the procuracy "review and

procuracy brings criminal cases to court and conducts criminal investigations on certain categories of cases. This combination of tasks produces a conflict in which officials of one and the same body are charged with both investigating and prosecuting a defendant in a criminal case and reviewing the defendant's torture complaint.

The procuracy investigates torture or ill-treatment complaints by first conducting an informal inquiry;[283] if this produces credible evidence that criminal abuses occurred, the procuracy then institutes a criminal investigation within three days.[284] The informal inquiry is, however, frequently superficial and plagued with delays, and few inquiries end in criminal proceedings. Indeed, procuracies appear generally to treat these inquiries as a mere formality.

Superficiality

Under a 1992 instruction issued by the procurator general, all complaints of abuse must be fully and objectively investigated and the complainant must be informed of the decision taken on the complaint.[285] In practice, our research and that

---

check reports, complaints and other statements on" and "take measures to prevent and intervene with" such violations. It further institutes criminal proceedings "if there is reason to believe that the violation of rights and freedoms of man and citizen constitutes a crime" (article 27(2)). Under article 109 of the criminal procedure code, procurators are obliged to accept reports on any crime and decide within three, or in exceptional cases, ten days whether to institute criminal proceedings.

[283]Human Rights Watch did not receive any reports that detainees had problems submitting their complaints from pretrial detention centers or IVSs.

[284] A criminal case is instituted if it is established that "there are sufficient facts which point at signs of a crime" (article 108 of the criminal procedure code). According to a commentary on the criminal procedure code, sufficient facts exist when their "sum total and quality allow one to make a well-founded assumption that a crime was committed or was being prepared" (V.M. Lebedev, *Nauchno-prakticheskii kommentarii k ugolovnomu-protsessual'nomu kodeksu RSFSR*, Moscow 1998, p. 211).

[285]There is confusion as to the term within which the procurator's office must review torture complaints. Most procurator's office officials we spoke to mentioned a one-month term for reviewing complaints (this coincides with a general one-month term set for government officials for responding to complaints in article 4 of the 1993 law on complaints). However, the criminal procedure code requires that the procurator's office must take a decision on any report on the commission of a crime within three days or, in exceptional cases, ten days. The 1992 law on the procuracy established a general rule that procurators should review complaints within one month but with respect to a violation of a constitutional right (like torture) this term was five days. This article was dropped altogether from the new law on the procuracy (adopted in 1995). However, an instruction of the procurator general from 1992 (No. 33 of July 30, 1992, "On the manner of review of letters, complaints, statements and

of numerous human rights groups in Russia's regions shows that this informal inquiry is exceedingly superficial. It is conducted primarily by young and inexperienced procurator's assistants, who often merely forward complaints to the chiefs of police precincts for a response, take these responses at face value, and neither interview the complainant or seek other evidence of abuse. The procedure frequently ends with a letter informing the complainant in a few stark sentences that because his complaint "was not confirmed by the facts," no criminal proceedings will take place, without further explanation.[286] Most torture complaint procedures end after this decision, since many complainants are not aware of their right to study the records of the procurator's inquiry and to challenge it.[287]

The informal inquiry is also limited procedurally in the same manner as initial inquiries into reports on any other crimes. It has an informal nature, meaning that the official conducting the investigation has less power than an investigator in a criminal investigation. For example, the official may not subpoena the alleged perpetrators or witnesses, who are thus not obliged to appear and are not under oath, and does no formally record interviews he or she conducts. The official also cannot order a forensic examination of the complainant.[288]

The criminal procedure code sets no standards for the informal inquiry, beyond the requirement in the 1992 instruction that it be "full and objective." This lack of specific standards facilitates sabotage of the inquiry by procuracy officials who do not work in good faith, allowing them to dismiss complaints without conducting a thorough and objective investigation.

A provision in the 1992 instruction encourages procurators to "decide the question of the expediency of involving the complainant and specialists in conducting [the inquiry]"; in practice, however, the procurator's assistant often does not question the complainant during the review. Andrei Babushkin of the Committee for Civil Rights told Human Rights Watch that he recently studied

---

reception of citizens in the organs of the procuracy of the Russian Federation") still sets the norm contained in the 1992 law, and, as far as Human Rights Watch is aware, this instruction has not been rescinded.

[286] In article 113 (3)of the criminal procedure code requires such replies to supply explanations for decisions.

[287] Article 8 of Instruction No. 33 of July 30, 1992, "On the manner of review of letters, complaints, statements and reception of citizens in the procuracy agencies of the Russian Federation" states that after a decision is issued, the complainant must be given the opportunity to study the materials of the procurator's review "to the extent that that does not violate the rights of other citizens...."

[288] Article 109 of the criminal procedure code merely gives the procuracy the right to "demand the necessary material" and to "receive explanations" in order to investigate reports on crimes.

seventeen informal inquiries conducted by the Butyrskaia district procuracy in Moscow, all of which ended in a refusal to launch a criminal investigation. In none of the cases had the procuracy assistant even questioned the complainant: "In seventeen out of seventeen cases, they had limited themselves to questioning the people who were the subject of the complaints."[289]

It seems standard practice for many procuracies to limit the inquiry to raising the allegations with the superiors of the alleged torturers; the denial of any wrongdoing generally suffices for the procuracy not to pursue criminal proceedings. A former police officer told Human Rights Watch that generally the procuracy does not question the alleged torturers themselves but sends the complaint on to the chief of the appropriate police precinct with instructions to look into it and reply in writing. He said that the procuracy questions the police officers only if the complainant himself submits medical or other convincing evidence of ill-treatment or torture.[290] However, in five of the cases Human Rights Watch investigated criminal proceedings were not begun even when medical evidence was available.

Tatiana Popkova's case was apparently typical. She was forcibly taken to the police station in Usol'e-Sibirskoe, Irkutsk province, and reportedly beaten in relation to the case of Igor Akhrimenko. She told Human Rights Watch the following about the response to her complaint to the procuracy: "They called me into the police station, the same investigator who conducted the case against Igor Akhrimenko.... She asked me to recount what happened—that was it. I told her and she didn't believe me, she smiled maliciously and said that 'that can't be' and that I 'was making it all up.'"

Procurator's assistants often ignore evidence of torture that is provided by the complainant and, according to Babushkin, they sometimes deliberately lose documents that confirm the torture.[291] Medical and other documentation that is necessary for an objective inquiry of the complaint is almost never requested. In various cases, torture victims and their relatives told Human Rights Watch that the procuracies refused to question witnesses who saw the victim after the torture with clear signs of abuse.

The father of Andrei Semenov told Human Rights Watch that in 1995, the procuracy of Ekaterinburg's Kirov district refused to investigate his son's torture complaint and wrote its formal reply without even questioning several witnesses who reportedly saw Semenov with clear signs of violence after police ill-treated him for hours.

---

[289] Human Rights Watch interview with Andrei Babushkin, Moscow, February 15, 1999.
[290] Human Rights Watch interview with Vladimir Federov, Moscow, June 8, 1999.
[291] Human Rights Watch interview with Andrei Babushkin, Moscow, February 15, 1999.

> They took him to the place where the burglary took place at around 3:00 p.m. of that same day.... The witnesses, the neighbors saw it all...saw that he was all beaten up.
>
> Whoever we turn to, we wrote to the province procurator twice, the city procurator, we receive formal replies. We live in the Kirov district ourselves, they send the case to the procurator of the Kirov district, who arrested him, do you understand?...We write, they delay for a month or two, then...the answer: "No violations." How can you investigate a case when neither witnesses nor anyone else is called, and my boy is already in jail for the third year.[292]

When complainants send their complaints to higher-level procuracies, the claims often bounce back to the local level. For example, Andrei Potanin's father told Human Rights Watch a similar story, in which the handling of the complaint was ultimately handed on to a subordinate of the officer—Kolosovskii—who he said had tortured his son:

> [W]hen I found out that after that [violent arrest] they continued to treat him badly and threatened to rape him, I wrote a complaint demanding that [the policeman] be brought to justice. I sent it to the Kirov [district procuracy], sent it to the city...province, and further [procuracies]. They sent everything back and the investigation was carried out by a subordinate of Kolosovskii, a young man, who is only interested in protecting his boss.[293]

In several cases we researched, the procuracy carried out a more extensive inquiry, but failed to question witnesses who could have confirmed the torture, and assessed testimony of other witnesses and evidence with a clear bias in favor of police officers. For example, on October 14, 1997, the Nizhnii Novgorod province procuracy replied to a complaint lodged by the mother of Anton Shamberov and Kirill Komlev, who were, respectively, acquitted and sentenced to twelve years' imprisonment in August 1997. In its reply, the procuracy cited the following reasons to explain why it would not launch a criminal investigation into the alleged abusive treatment:

---

[292] Human Rights Watch interview with Vladimir Semenov, Ekaterinburg, August 7, 1997.
[293] Human Rights Watch interview with Andrei Potanin's father, Ekaterinburg, August 8, 1997.

Explanations from police officers, who detained the defendants, stating that Komlev and Shamberov were not subjected to physical and psychological coercion during investigative activities; documents received from the IVS and SIZO, from which it is clear that neither Komlev nor Shamberov asked for medical assistance during the course of the investigation and which state that at the time of entry [into the detention center] after carrying out investigative activities, medical check-ups did not discover any physical injuries.[294]

The procuracy failed, without explanation, to interview three people who say they saw Kirill Komlev in the days following the detention with clear signs of injuries. Komlev's mother, Liubov' Shamberov, told Human Rights Watch that she saw her son on September 7, two days after his arrest, at the police station:

> I walked into the office and before me [I saw] the following picture: Investigator Bubnov, two detectives...and my son turned toward me. You know, he was all beaten up, his face was crimson...all swollen, and tears ran from his eyes.
>
> When I clasped him to me, he said: "Mom, they're killing me, threatening to kill me during an escape attempt." That's what he whispered, when I embraced him.[295]

In addition, Komlev's lawyer and his wife said they saw him on September 5 with signs of beatings.

In the Shamberov and Komlev case, the procuracy and the court blithely accepted at face value the interrogation report's claim that the investigation used no coercion, explained to the defendants their rights, and granted them access to an attorney. The procuracy's October 14 reply cited the court's verdict:

> The verdict states that "the conclusions of the defendants that their testimonies were fabricated, recorded incorrectly, given under psychological and physical coercion cannot be taken into consideration by the court because they are refuted by the factual circumstances of the case. In the course of the investigation, article 51 of the Constitution of

---

[294] Letter from the procuracy of Nizhnii Novgorod province, number 15/1-104941097 of October 14, 1997 to Shamberova, L.V.
[295] Human Rights Watch interview with Liubov' Shamberova, October 17, Nizhnii Novgorod.

the Russian Federation was explained to the defendants, the testimony was given with participation of lawyers. The correctness of the testimony of each of the defendants has been certified with an indication in the interrogation report regarding the absence of any form of pressure on them."

The court and the procuracy ignored the fact that Komlev and Shamberov were granted access to a lawyer only eight days after their detention on September 5, 1996. Shamberov told Human Rights Watch that he saw a lawyer only on September 13; Komlev was briefly given access to a duty lawyer on September 5, after he had been tortured. However, investigative activities were subsequently carried out without this lawyer and continued until September 13.

The procuracy (as well as judges, see below) also tend to ignore the length of time between the actual time of detention and the time the suspect is registered at the police station (the "procedural" time of detention). In the case of Alexander Volod'ko, the procuracy of Aleksin failed to explore what happened during the four-and-a-half hour interval between the time police detained him at his home at 12:00 midnight and the time he was registered at the local police station at 4:30 a.m. Procurators and judges also frequently fail to examine whether the defendants were lawfully detained. This is significant, for an indicator that foul play may have occurred is when a defendant confesses to a criminal offense after he has been detained for an administrative offense. However, in most cases procurators and judges refuse to acknowledge any relevance of these circumstances to allegations of ill-treatment or coerced confessions.

Delays

If victims of police abuse or their advocates remain unsatisfied by the superficiality of the informal inquiry and are undeterred by intimidation and the lack of cooperation of the procuracy, they may challenge the review's outcome with the procuracy at a higher level. However, they then face lengthy delays as the complaint wends its way through many levels of the hierarchy of procuracies—district, city, province, and federal.[296] As the process drags on, evidence of torture disappears and the likelihood of a criminal investigation of the torture claim diminishes.

In many cases, the higher-level procuracy merely forwards the complaints to the local procuracy that has already "answered" the complaint, and the complainant receives a short notice that the complaint has been passed on to the local procuracy.

---

[296] In theory, complainants can also challenge the review outcome in court. However, Human Rights Watch is unaware of any such attempts, and long delays in the judicial process would be unavoidable.

For example, in 1994 Oksana Bykova wrote numerous complaints to the local procurator about the torture of her husband. The local procurator rejected her complaints, claiming that "the case is being conducted correctly." After that, she wrote to the procuracy of Irkutsk province and to the Procuracy General in Moscow. She told Human Rights Watch:

> I knew that there would be formal replies from Moscow to Irkutsk, and from Irkutsk to Chudov [the local procurator]. That's exactly what happened: on the Moscow letter [complaint to the Procuracy General] Chudov answered that "the case is being conducted correctly." It's a vicious circle, you can't achieve anything.[297]

Very few people have the endurance to battle the unwilling procuracy for long, especially because most do not believe the procuracy will ever conduct a criminal investigation. But even if a criminal case is finally instituted and investigators are willing to investigate police abuses scrupulously, they face considerable problems. Elena Topil'skaia of the Leningrad province procuracy told Human Rights Watch:

> It usually goes like this: the complaints are received, the complaints are handed over to the procurator's assistant, he carries out a review. That all takes time. According to the [1992] instruction, they answer in the course of a month. They conduct the inquiry for a month, issue a decision refusing to institute a criminal case. The person who was subjected to the unlawful methods appeals this again. That takes more time once again and, finally, we [the investigators] end up receiving cases for investigation that are a half a year or eight months old. That obviously makes the task much more difficult.
>
> In some cases, it is even expedient to immediately institute criminal proceedings on such facts...when people haven't forgotten yet, when it's still possible to determine the exact time, down to the hour, because [if] a case that has gone back and forth ends up with an investigator after half a year, it will be very difficult for him to ask a question about confirmation of an alibi, for example, and receive a response. About the events of, say, yesterday I can talk with the precision of an hour, in a half a year I can't remember that anymore.... [298]

---

[297] Human Rights Watch interview with Oksana Bykova, Usol'e-Sibirskoe, Irkutsk province, April 9, 1998.
[298] Human Rights Watch interview with Elena Topil'skaia, St. Petersburg, July 15, 1998.

Paradoxically, a poorly coordinated and insufficient informal inquiry may serve to warn abusive police officers, allowing them to eliminate evidence of torture and conspire with their co-abusers. Igor Kaliapin of the Nizhnii Novgorod Society for Human Rights worked closely on a case that involved this practice. In September 1996, police wrongly detained and severely beat Timofei Petrov (not his real name). The man refused to confess, and had no relation to the crime under investigation. When the procuracy refused to sanction the man's arrest, police released him with clear signs of beatings. After his release, he filed a complaint with the procuracy. According to Kaliapin:

> The procuracy begins some sort of review. Two weeks later, he [the torture victim] receives a standard notification that there was nothing of the kind [torture], everything was fine and correct. Then, when we started working with the case fairly meticulously, it turned out that all the participants in the beating, having found out that there is a complaint [against them] with the procuracy and that the [complainant] might not be satisfied with a standard notification that institution of a criminal case has been refused, that he may pursue his complaint further, they were immediately on their guard and immediately agreed among themselves, clarified all the details.
>
> As it turned out, [the victim] had at first not been registered in the registry [at the police station]. When someone is detained for drunkenness, they [police] should enter him into the detention registry in the duty room: That, yes, he was brought in by so-and-so, a report. There was nothing of the kind [at first]. It was all put in only when the procuracy started its review. In this case, all those ends that can be used to pull [the case together] and prove [torture], had been redone retroactively, [missing] documents suddenly appeared.[299]

Kaliapin, however, still succeeded in gathering sufficient evidence of the abuse to have criminal proceedings instituted against the police officers for knowingly unlawful detention and violent coercion to testify.

Criminal Investigation and Court Action

In the minority of cases in which criminal proceedings are begun, abusive police may threaten and intimidate the complainants or case investigators, or the

---

[299] Human Rights Watch interview with Igor Kaliapin, Nizhnii Novgorod, October 17, 1997.

procuracy itself can undermine the investigation. The court record on such cases is mixed, ranging from acquittals to lenient to appropriate sentences.

The Case of Vitalii Sokolov (Nizhnii Novgorod province)

Vitalii Sokolov was beaten by a police officer in 1997 and then released; the local procuracy resisted investigating the case, and the abusive officer persistently harassed Sokolov. In April 1997, Sokolov was on his way home from work when an intoxicated police officer pulled him from a bus, accused him of illegal drug possession, and started beating him. The next morning, Sokolov was released after signing a statement that he had drunk alcohol in the bus, sworn, and thrown nut shells on the ground. After visiting a travmapunkt, where all his injuries were recorded, Sokolov filed a complaint to the procuracy in Bor. Sokolov told Human Rights Watch:

> Kolbovskaia, who they gave the case to, she didn't question me about anything and on the basis of the report of the person who carried out the internal investigation, she issued a refusal to institute criminal proceedings. I didn't agree with that, wrote a complaint about that. After that, she organized a meeting for me with the procurator of the city of Bor, who listened sarcastically to what I told him....After that, he did open a criminal case.[300]

At the time of Human Rights Watch's visit to Nizhnii Novgorod in October 1997, the criminal case had been under way for four months.

> So far, there is no movement. The only thing is that after the criminal case was instituted, I started getting phone calls from out of town [from people connected to the police officer].[301] They called me at home, talked to my mother and called me by a different name. My mother answered that they should stop phoning, bothering.... After they failed to get in touch with me, [the police officer who allegedly beat Sokolov] himself came to my house.... After he received a refusal [to see Sokolov] and was told to leave us alone, he pronounced the following phrase: "Well, if I pulled him off the bus, that doesn't mean that I beat him."

---

[300] Human Rights Watch interview with Vitalii Sokolov, Nizhnii Novgorod, October 19, 1997.
[301] In Russia, long distance phone calls are distinguishable from local calls from the length of the ring.

[A]fter that, he came to my work...and tried to talk to me there, but in the presence of my boss and several other people. I told him: "I have nothing to talk to you about." I just couldn't imagine how I could talk to this person after he had beaten me up.

The procuracy in Bor dropped proceedings against the police officers and closed the criminal case in July 1998 for a lack of merits.

The Case of Timofei Petrov[302]

On September 10, 1996, police requested Timofei Petrov and two colleagues to come to the police station in Nizhnii Novgorod for a "friendly chat"; they were severely beaten in an attempt to coerce confessions on theft charges, and released the following day. Under pressure from Petrov and the Nizhnii Novgorod Society for Human Rights, the procuracy instituted criminal proceedings in October 1996. After three months of intense harassment by the precinct police, Petrov dropped his complaint and the procuracy closed the criminal case. According to the Nizhnii Novgorod Society for Human Rights, Petrov's colleagues did not file torture complaints with the procuracy for fear of reprisals. Igor Kaliapin, who represented Petrov, told Human Rights Watch:

> I insisted that they be taken into custody because they had [begun to] actively put pressure on [Petrov]: they came to his home, to his work, talked to his boss, saying that they were, after all, the district police. They, of course, talked to the management of [Petrov's workplace], which in some situations depends on [the police]. We got testimony from a large number of people, a whole file of those things, forced [the procuracy] to add this to the criminal case.
>
> It ended with the police officers definitively getting to [Petrov]. He just took money from them: they bought him. Not a lot, by the way [1.5 million rubles, around U.S.$ 250 at the 1996 exchange rate]. They told him they'd leave him alone, that he wouldn't have any more problems. He quieted down at that and withdrew all complaints against them. On the day [the procuracy] was supposed to issue the indictment against [the police officers], [Petrov] went with [the police] to the procuracy and said: "You know, they...accidentally pushed me, I thought it was on

---

[302] "Timofei Petrov" is not the man's real name.

purpose but it turns out to have been accidental. There were no beatings with a stool, I just said all that out of anger."

We tried to talk to him, appealed to his conscience, but he said: "I'm afraid, I'm tired of all this, I don't want anything anymore, please leave me alone."[303]

The Case of Oleg Fetisov

The Verkh-Isetsk district procuracy of Ekaterinburg opened a criminal investigation against the police officers who reportedly tortured Oleg Fetisov (see above, "A Persistent Patter of Torture and Ill-Treatment" and "Victims") on December 5, 1996, and appointed senior investigator Popov to the case. Popov investigated the case, drafted an indictment, and submitted the case to his superiors for approval and transfer to the court. His superiors, however, stalled and then closed the case, grounding its action on Fetisov's refusal to submit to a psychiatric exam. Fetisov's mother told Human Rights Watch:

> He [Popov] told us: "I've done my job. I believe that they are guilty. Now the leadership must take a decision." The leadership decided to put the brakes on the case. They started to put the brakes on the case, to extend the terms.... We now see that all of this was done to drag it out, to red-tape it, and eventually it ended with the case being closed.
>
> They found the following way: they ordered a psychological-psychiatric expert assessment for Oleg. We then sought advice from the lawyer. There were no reasons for carrying out such an expert assessment.... We requested that the decision to carry out an assessment be canceled.... The assessment was scheduled for May 15, we didn't show up.... That was enough to close the case explicitly for that reason. The investigator told me: "If you don't need it, who does? You didn't show up for the assessment—that's it."[304]

Fetisov's lawyer, Sergei Kotov, told Human Rights Watch that he had objected to the examination because the investigators hinted that Fetisov's jump from a police precinct window may have been a consequence of mental illness, and not motivated by police torture, and because a psychiatrist had already examined Fetisov in the

---

[303] Human Rights Watch interview with Igor Kaliapin, Nizhnii Novgorod, October 17, 1997.
[304] Human Rights Watch interview with Nadezhda Fetisova, Ekaterinburg, August 11, 1997.

hospital immediately after his jump. The procuracy used Fetisov's failure to cooperate as grounds to close the case. After Fetisov received a suspended sentence for robbery, his parents abandoned their efforts to bring the abusive police officers to justice.

The Case of Sergei Kolosovskii

In 1997, the procuracy of Ekaterinburg's Verkh-Isetsk district began a criminal investigation of Sergei Kolosovskii, deputy head of criminal investigation of the Kirov district police precinct, and two of his subordinates. Procurator Evgenii Ergashev told Human Rights Watch that Kolosovskii had beaten a young man by the name of Paivin for hours at the police station, and had asphyxiated him by forcing a gas mask over his head and spraying alcohol or an ammonia mix into the trunk. Several witnesses, including Paivin's mother, heard him scream. In addition, his mother saw him with a swollen head after the beatings. The three officers were charged under article 171(2) of the criminal code (exceeding one's authority through the use of force). Kolosovskii was also charged in relation to another incident of torture.

Ergashev told Human Rights Watch that he had initially not taken Kolosovskii into custody, although he was suspended from active duty pending conclusion of the investigation. However, he arrested Kolosovskii when the latter threatened the procurator's investigation. Ergashev told Human Rights Watch:

> I called him into my office and told him that if he would continue to threaten investigators, I would have to arrest him. Kolosovskii said that he was a high-ranking police officer and would do what he wanted. At that point, I arrested Kolosovskii. During the arrest, we discovered that Kolosovskii was carrying a loaded gun, even though he did not have the right to carry weapons any more.[305]

Ergashev said that since the arrest of Kolosovskii, he had received seven more complaints of torture against the police officer. Indeed, Ergashev believed that because other detainees had recognized Kolosovskii as their torturer and attacked him, Kolosovskii had to be transferred from the Ekaterinburg SIZO to the Nizhnii Tagil SIZO.[306]

Police in Ekaterinburg launched a campaign on behalf of their colleague, with the support of several newspapers. Ergashev told Human Rights Watch that large

---

[305] Human Rights Watch interview with Evgenii Ergashev, Ekaterinburg, August 12, 1997.
[306] Ibid.

numbers of armed police had sat demonstratively outside his office in the corridor as well as in the court to intimidate employees of the procuracy and court. Kolosovskii was eventually released from pretrial custody and ran (unsuccessfully) for a seat in the Russian State Duma.

The Sverdlovsk Province Court heard the case against Kolosovskii in the fall of 1998. The court acquitted Kolosovskii on one charge and returned the charge that he had ill-treated Paivin to the procuracy for further investigation. Local human rights activists told Human Rights Watch that Paivin did not appear at the court hearing on Kolosovskii's case because he feared for his life.[307]

In her interview with Human Rights Watch, Elena Topil'skaia of the Leningrad province procuracy also asserted that police show a strong corporate solidarity: "the agencies that investigate such cases encounter active resistance, simply with a wall from the side of the corporate brotherhood of police officers, who do not want to give their brothers over to the justice system to be torn to pieces, irrespective of whether or not they are guilty."[308]

The Case of Mikhail Sobolev

On March 28, 1995, police officers violently detained Mikhail Sobolev, of Ekaterinburg, in his house and beat him so severely that he required a month of hospitalization and a month of bed rest to recover. The day after the abuse, he sent a complaint to the procuracy. After his recovery, Sobolev went to the city procurator to ask why he had received no response to the complaint.

> He [city procurator Kornilov] laughed in my face: "What, are you going to teach me what to do?" I asked: "Why haven't you opened a criminal case? According to the criminal procedure code that must be done within three, maximum ten days." Only after three months...the lawyer talked to the deputy city procurator and a criminal case was begun retroactively. From that moment on I have been trying to achieve the punishment of the guilty....
>
> They changed investigators on the case five or six times in three years and they closed the case for alleged absence of corpus delicti.... Despite the fact that we identified the defendants right in the face, they recognized them as defendants only after nine months. And they didn't recognize us [Sobolev's wife witnessed the detention of her husband but

---

[307] Human Rights Watch telephone interview with Petr D'iakonov of Memorial-Ekaterinburg, April 19, 1999.
[308] Human Rights Watch interview with Elena Topil'skaia, St. Petersburg, July 15, 1998.

was not beaten herself] as victims immediately but only after six months of investigation. One investigator closes the case, a second investigator closes the case. We've already gone through all our [local] law-enforcement agencies, [and] began to write to Moscow. I wrote to the government in Moscow, to Yeltsin, to the Commission on Human Rights, to the State Duma,...to the Procuracy General. All these papers from there...are sent back to those people about whose actions we complain.... I went to see both the city procurator and the province procurator Tulkov. They openly told me: "You'd better, man, take the money and leave it. We have to put a stop to this case and forget everything."

The first year especially there were a lot of threats, from the defendants...and from my boss [the head of a private security firm that is made up primarily of former police officers]. He came to me and said: "Come on, forgive them." He [the boss] offered money and threatened...saying that I would regret it. Still, we succeeded in bringing the case to court in three years.[309]

On January 1, 1997, the procuracy transferred the case to the Kirov District Court. Judge Ryndia scheduled the first hearing for July 14. The day of the hearing, Sobolev was surprised to learn that a different judge, who had apparently not studied the case materials, would preside. The prosecutor failed to appear at the hearing, and the judge banned the press from the courtroom. According to Sobolev, the judge clearly sympathized with the police officers and frequently interrupted him and his wife. After two days of hearings, the judge remanded the case for further investigation in view of "newly discovered facts."

In 1999, the case was transferred to the procuracy of neighboring Perm province, which was continuing the investigation as of this writing.

The Case of Andrei Getsko

On March 20, 1998, a judge in Bratsk began a criminal investigation against police officers who had beaten Andrei Getsko on September 30, 1994—after several doctors testified in court that they had witnessed police officers beating Getsko in an elevator at the Central Hospital-1 in Bratsk. Despite this irrefutable evidence of ill-treatment, the procuracy that had been instructed to investigate the beatings dropped criminal proceedings in early 1999. Human Rights Watch was

---

[309] Human Rights Watch interview with Mikhail Sobolev, Ekaterinburg, August 11, 1997.

unable to establish what formal grounds the procuracy gave for closing the criminal case.

Convictions

Although comprehensive statistics do not seem exist, it appears that only a small number for abusive police officers have been convicted for crimes related to torture.[310] Human Rights Watch on two separate occasions requested from the Procuracy General statistics on convictions of law-enforcement officials for the abuse of detainees, but was informed by letter merely that "the requested statistical data about the crime situation in Russia are regularly published in the media." Vladimir Byzenkov of the Sverdlovsk province procuracy, however, told Human Rights Watch that no statistics are gathered on the number of complaints or convictions for police abuse. However infrequent, convictions of police for crimes against detainees have attracted widespread attention in the Moscow and regional press. They include the following:

- In 1998, seven police officers were convicted in Mordovia for torturing Oleg Igonin to death (see below).
- In 1998, two police men from Saratov were given three-year suspended sentences for beating and using electroshock on three suspects. The judge reportedly told the *Moscow Times* that the sentences were adequate because the torture had had no long-term ill effects on the victims' health and the performance records of the policemen had been exemplary.[311]
- In 1997, the Verkh-Isetsk District Court in Ekaterinburg sentenced one policeman to three years' imprisonment and gave another a three-year suspended sentence for asphyxiating a man they suspected of having stolen a car and forcing a hockey stick up his anus.[312]
- In 1997, the Voronezh Province Court sentenced three police officers to eight, nine, and ten years' imprisonment for torturing to death a criminal suspect and burning his body. The officers tortured the detainee and his brother for several hours, beating and asphyxiating him. When they realized one of them had

---

[310] A U.S. State Department official told Human Rights Watch that the implementation of the Leahy amendment (see above "Holding Russia to its Obligations") is apparently complicated by the fact that the Russian procuracy does not keep centralized records on abuse by security forces.
[311] Simon Sarandzhian, "Saratov Policemen Convicted of Torturing Suspects," *Moscow Times,* October 31, 1998.
[312] Human Rights Watch interview with Evgenii Ergashev, Ekaterinburg, August 12, 1997.

died, they tried to dispose of the body by burning it and dumping it in a sewer.[313]
- In October 1996, a Nizhnii Novgorod court sentenced two police officers to two- and four-year suspended sentences for causing the death of detainee Chistiakov. When Chistiakov demanded that police release him from his cell, the officer took him out, beat him and, after tying him up in the "konvertik" position, threw him in a punishment cell, where he died. A forensic expert examination found forty bruises from night sticks on his body.[314]
- In 1994, the press reported that seven policemen who had tortured witnesses were sentenced to prison terms of from three to ten years.[315]
- In 1994, two policemen were sentenced to two and three years of imprisonment for two separate torture episodes in Nizhnii Novgorod. In 1993, the officers had unlawfully detained and beaten a minor, whose injuries were later recorded at an emergency room, and, later that year, had beaten another detainee in the head with a nightstick. A friend of the detainee witnessed the beating when she walked into the precinct office.[316]

The Case of Oleg Igonin

The torture death in 1995 of nineteen-year-old Oleg Igonin in Mordovia (See above, "Deaths in Custody and Permanent Injury") drew unprecedented attention from the Russian media, which followed the case, beginning with Igonin's death through to the historic conviction of several police officers for a range of related crimes three years later. On February 2, 1998, the Supreme Court of the Republic of Mordovia sentenced seven police officers, including officers Daev, Sazonov, and Guliaikin, to prison terms ranging from three to nine and a half years. The court found the policemen guilty of two episodes of torture under article 171(2) of the old criminal code.

Presiding Judge Vasilii Martyshkin issued, in addition to the verdict, a separate statement (*chastnoe opredelenie*) to the Russian Ministry of Internal Affairs accusing Mordovian police authorities of knowingly tolerating widespread torture practices in Mordovia. The statement castigated Mordovian police in particular for inaction on previous torture complaints against two of the convicted

---

[313] Gennadii Litvintsev, "Samosud v militseiskom zastenke," *Rossiiskaia gazeta,* April 8, 1997, p. 8
[314] Nizhnii Novgorod Society for Human Rights, "The Use of Torture on the Territory of the Nizhnii Novgorod Province, 1997," p. 13.
[315] "Osudzhdeny za nasilie protiv svidetelei," *Izvestiia,* June 15, 1995, p. 1.
[316] Anatolii Ershov, "Militsionery poluchili srok za izbienie liudei," *Izvestiia*, September 8, 1994.

officers (Daev and Sazonov). Together with S. Antonov, in 1994 they had called three men to the police station for "informal questioning." In the course of this questioning, the policemen asphyxiated the three men and forced them to sit in the "konvertik" position while beating them. Police had suspected the men of having stolen a tractor. Judge Martyshkin's statement reads:

> The procuracy of Saransk opened a criminal case under article 171(2) of the criminal code of the RSFSR against the criminal investigation officers [Daev and Sazonov] on June 7, 1994, about which the leadership of the MVD of Mordovia, the Bol'shebereznikvoskii and Lenin ROVD were informed. On July 25, 1995, investigator Savinov D.A. of the Saransk procuracy wrote the indictments against Daev, Sazonov, Antonov, Frolkin, and Tutaev.
>
> However, despite the results of the investigation of the criminal case against Daev, Sazonov, Tutaev and Frolkin, the leadership of the Mordovian MVD did not take the necessary measures, including relieving [them] from [their] official positions. *This carelessness and tolerance, the attempt to defend [the police officers] led to Daev and Sazonov committing an offence with even more grave results against minor Lavrent'ev A.S. and Igonin O.V.*[317]

Complaints to the Russian Ombudsman

Under the Russian law on the ombudsman,[318] the ombudsman considers complaints on human rights violations only after initial administrative or judicial review has yielded a response unsatisfactory to the victim. In practice, this means that after a procuracy review rules not to bring criminal charges, the torture victim may seek the ombudsman's involvement. The victim must file his or her complaint with the ombudsman within a year from the administrative or judicial decision. If the ombudsman decides to consider the complaint on its merits, he has a variety of tools to investigate the complaint, including unlimited access to documents and officials. After concluding the investigation, the ombudsman informs the complainant and the responsible agency of the conclusions and can take a number of measures that are provided for by law. These include:

---

[317] *Chastnoe opredelenie* by judge Vasilii Martyshkin of the Supreme Court of the Republic of Mordovia, Case 2-4/98, February 12, 1998. Emphasis added.
[318] The State Duma adopted the law on the ombudsman on December 25, 1996.

- Filing a human rights complaint with an ordinary court and participating in the hearings;
- Requesting the applicable government agencies to institute disciplinary action or administrative or criminal cases against the violating official;
- Requesting a court or procuracy to review a court decision that has entered into force;
- Presenting his conclusions to those officials who have the right to bring protests against court decisions and be present during court hearings in oversight proceedings.[319]

Although the ombudsman himself cannot overturn decisions by the procuracy or courts, his intervention could be an effective way of forcing a breakthrough when the police, procuracy, and courts refuse to take action on credible cases of torture. In addition, the ombudsman can put torture on the political agenda. For example, he has the right to draw up suggestions and recommendations to both federal and regional state agencies, to address the State Duma about gross and systemic violations of human rights, and to request the Duma to appoint a special parliamentary commission to investigate these reports and initiate parliamentary hearings on the issue. He may also participate both in the special commission and the hearings.

In May 1998, the State Duma appointed Oleg Mironov, a member of parliament from the communist party, as Russia's first ombudsman. On his initiative, a Department for Criminal Justice was created, which deals with individual torture complaints. Mironov told Human Rights Watch that about 28 percent of the complaints he receives concern violations in the criminal justice system. "The most serious violations of human rights happen at the moment of detention, when physical methods of coercion are used, when detainees are beaten up and tortured," he told Human Rights Watch.[320]

Using his right under the law to raise his concerns with government officials, Mironov sent a letter to then- Minister of Internal Affairs Sergei Stepashin in December 1998, in which he expressed concern about the widespread nature of torture and asked Stepashin to take the necessary steps to end it. In particular, Mironov stated in the letter that "during personal meetings of the ombudsman with people who are held in SIZOs and colonies, every second person said that he was subjected to beatings and humiliation by police officers from the moment of

---

[319] In Russia, the procuracy has the right to oversee court decisions. It can initiate proceedings to overturn court decisions (even after the appeal period has expired or if there is no right to appeal) even after they have attained legal force.

[320] Human Rights Watch interview with Oleg Mironov, Moscow, February 16, 1999.

detention until being sent to SIZOs."³²¹ The letter raised a number of concrete cases of the use of electroshock and asphyxiation. Mironov has the authority to request the State Duma to appoint a special commission or to hold hearings to investigate the torture problem, but has not yet done so.³²²

Compensation for Damage

At the time of writing, legal provisions for compensation for damages to crime victims largely remained a dead letter for torture victims. Human Rights Watch knows of only one case of this kind: As noted, the Supreme Court of the Republic of Mordovia ordered compensation to be paid by the Russian state for moral "damages" to victims in the case of Daev, Guliaikin, Antonov, and others, who stood trial for two episodes of torture (see above, "Legal Framework"). The court awarded 200,000 rubles (after the January 1, 1998 denomination, or approximately U.S.$33,333) to Valentina Igonina, Oleg Igonin's mother. The court also granted compensation for moral damages to three other torture victims, ranging from 30,000 to 50,000 rubles (approximately, U.S.$5,000 to U.S.$8,333).

Compensation for damages can also be awarded in civil cases. However, civil courts are unlikely to grant compensation for damages to torture victims unless a criminal court has found the perpetrators guilty of such a crime. As long as the procuracy does not actively prosecute perpetrators of torture, victims of torture will have little chance of receiving compensation for damages.

Fear as a Deterrent to Complaints

Police and procuracy officials warned some torture victims about repercussions should they lodge a complaint, a form of intimidation that violates Russian and international law.³²³ Dmitrii Ivanov's mother gave up all attempts to have the torturers of her son brought to justice after procuracy officials threatened to pursue a further criminal investigation against him. Ivanov, as noted above, had jumped out of a police precinct window after torture in a city in central Russia in

---

[321] Release of the press service of the ombudsman of the Russian Federation, December 29, 1998.

[322] Human Rights Watch interview with Oleg Mironov, Moscow, February 16, 1999.

[323] The 1995 Law of the Russian Federation on Detention of Persons Suspected or Accused of Committing Crimes states that "persecution in any form of suspects and defendants for appeals with suggestions, statements or complaints connected to violations of their right and legal interests is not allowed" (article 21(7)). The Convention against Torture states in article 13 that "Steps shall be taken to ensure that the complainant and witnesses are protected against all ill-treatment or intimidation as a consequence of his complaint or evidence given."

1997, where he was being questioned for a burglary. Following his jump, which left him paralyzed for life, police changed his procedural status to that of witness. When Ivanov's mother, with the help of a local human rights organization, tried to file a complaint about the treatment her son was subjected to, she was told that if she would pursue the torture complaint, her son's "status could easily be changed from witness to defendant."[324]

Oksana Bykova, whose husband was detained in April 1994 in the village of Usol'e-Sibirskoe (Irkutsk province), told Human Rights Watch that she was harassed and threatened by police investigator Muzyka when she complained about her conduct. When ordered to sign a protocol, written by investigator Muzyka, containing an admission that Bykova's husband was in possession of an illegal weapon:

> I refused to sign and she told me she would not give me a meeting [with my husband]. Then she called in police officers and they put me in a police cell...when the day ended, she released me.
>
> The next day, I went to the city procurator of Usol'e-Sibirskoe Chudov. I wrote a complaint against her.... I received a reply several days later. They told me: "Muzyka is conducting the case correctly."...Anyway, she [Muzyka] told me: "Don't get into this, otherwise we'll put you in jail as well."[325]

Tatiana Popkova, the ex-girlfriend of another defendant in the same case in Usol'e-Sibirskoe, told Human Rights Watch she received a similar warning:

> They told me this literally immediately after they applied force; there immediately was this "advice": "...better to forget this case and not to appeal anywhere, that's better for you and for Igor [the defendant]. [If] you don't listen to this advice, it will have very bad consequences for Igor."[326]

---

[324] Human Rights Watch telephone interview with a representative of the human rights organization, Moscow, June 3, 1999.
[325] Human Rights Watch interview with Oksana Bylova, Usol'e-Sibirskoe, Irkutsk province, April 9, 1998.
[326] Human Rights Watch interview with Tatiana Popkova, Usol'e-Siberskoe, Irkutsk province, April 9, 1998.

Similarly, Andrei Tuzikov from Irkutsk told Human Rights Watch that he had not told a procurator in Irkutsk that police had asphyxiated and beaten him, even though he had been taken to the procurator's office. He told Human Rights Watch: "They said that 'if you open your mouth, that will be it....' The detectives said that, they said that 'we'll find you in prison.'"[327]

---

[327] Human Rights Watch interview with Andrei Tuzikov, Bratsk, Irkutsk province, April 5, 1998.

RUSSIA'S OFFICIAL REACTION TO TORTURE

Russian government agencies are generally willing to discuss torture but fail either to acknowledge the nature and extent of the problem or to support institutional reforms required to end it. In April 1998, the Presidential Human Rights Chamber initiated some important public discussions of torture in which both the Ministry of Internal Affairs and the procuracy admitted that torture was a problem. However, none of the government agencies were willing to go beyond these initial discussions of the problem, and the Ministry of Internal Affairs and the procuracy even dismissed torture as an issue in subsequent discussions.

President and Presidential Structures

At the level of Russia's presidential structures, there has been a certain degree of acknowledgment that torture is a problem in Russia. In his annual speech to parliament in April 1998, President Boris Yeltsin spoke of the need to use actively the potential of human rights organizations to protect the rights of citizens and specifically mentioned the possibility of establishing a system aimed at preventing degrading and cruel treatment of defendants.

The Permanent Chamber on Human Rights of the Political Consultative Council under the president (the Presidential Human Rights Chamber), headed by State Duma deputy Valerii Borshchev, organized a special session on the problem of torture on April 7, 1998. At the meeting, officials from the Moscow police, the Procuracy General, and the Moscow city procuracy, several deputies of the State Duma, and numerous human rights organizations discussed the reasons and solutions for the torture problem, and concluded that torture was systematic in Russia.[328]

The Presidential Human Rights Chamber took a series of decisions aimed at ending torture. It endorsed a draft law on public oversight over places of detention and asked the State Duma to consider the draft as a matter of priority. The Chamber requested the Russian president, government, and the State Duma committee on legislation to initiate proceedings to amend the criminal code and other laws to introduce torture and cruel and degrading treatment as a separate offense. It established a working group under the Presidential Human Rights Chamber charged with drafting an anti-torture program, and extended invitations to representatives of the Ministry of Interior and the Procuracy General to participate in it. It further suggested that the Ministry of Interior discuss forms of public control possible

---

[328] Decision of April 7, 1998 "On gross violations of human rights in the agencies of internal affairs." See Appendix E for the full text of the decision.

under current legislation. Finally, it requested the Ministry of Internal Affairs and the Procuracy General to draft legislation on the work of duty lawyers at police stations and IVSs, and to make it mandatory to present all detainees with a printed card listing their rights. To date, these proposals have not been implemented.

Another human rights body under the Russian president, the Presidential Human Rights Commission led by Vladimir Kartashkin, did not mention the problem of torture in its report on 1996 and 1997, which was published in late 1998. In 1998, however, the presidential administration requested the Council of Europe to conduct an expert assessment on the conformity of the draft criminal procedure code with Council of Europe standards, which will of necessity address the issue of safeguards against torture, or cruel, inhuman or degrading treatment. The results of this assessment were presented to the presidential administration in September 1999, but remain confidential.

Ministry of Internal Affairs

The Ministry of Internal Affairs does not acknowledge the extent of torture in police custody in Russia. In an interview with Human Rights Watch, Vladimir Vorozhtsov, an aid to then-Minister of Interior Sergei Stepashin, dismissed the notion that torture was a problem:

> The method of referring to torture has these days been taken up as a weapon by most representatives of the criminal world, as a means of pressure to make cases collapse. Understanding that the problems of protection of human rights are fairly pressing, this has become one of the methods of countering justice. This is mostly groundless, often during the investigation and in court they start to withdraw their earlier testimony, claiming that they were subjected to torture.[329]

The Ministry of Interior officials argued that torture of detainees is practically impossible, because the procuracy and court system were expected to uncover any instance of torture and the police officers would be held criminally responsible. Vladimir Alferov, deputy head of the investigative committee of the Ministry of Internal Affairs, maintained this emphatically:

---

[329] Human Rights Watch interview with Vladimir Alferov and Vladimir Vorozhtsov of the Ministry of Interior, Moscow, March 30, 1990.

[U]nder our procedure, established today by law, there are no obstacles, absolutely no obstacles for achieving a full and official investigation of such facts in case unlawful methods were indeed applied.

In my opinion, the attempts by some policemen to beat, roughly speaking, confessions out [of suspects or defendants] do not produce the effect at which these unlawful actions are aimed because the process doesn't end with getting testimony. There, fortunately, are too many possibilities to, first of all, expose these people's unlawful methods of investigation, and secondly, to put everything right and not be convicted unlawfully....

I don't idealize the situation, there apparently are some facts, when a defendant may confess to the commission of a crime in the context of violence, such facts exist which go to court. But in court, in any case, during a public hearing, he can say that "yes, unlawful methods of investigation were used against me, and I confessed to [the crime] but I didn't commit the crime." The court immediately sends the case back for further investigation or acquits him.

If our crime-solving statistics were built only on confessions, as one must admit that courts are an absolutely independent system today, the third power, then the courts would issue acquittals much more often than they do now.... Today, the number of acquittals confirms that there is no massive coercion into confessions.[330]

According to Vorozhtsov, some 2,000 police officers per year face criminal prosecution, including for common criminal offenses. Vorozhtsov said he believes that only around twenty or thirty of these cases concern torture. Of a total of 900,000 criminal cases per year, this would mean that torture led to prosecutions in less than one hundredth of a percent of all criminal cases. When Human Rights Watch countered that its research had shown that the procuracy's inquiries are often no more than a formality, Vorozhtsov replied that even if that were the case the number of cases in which torture is used would still be insignificant.

The Ministry of Internal Affairs' representative, Vladimir Alferov, told Human Rights Watch that Russia's high crime solving rates are in fact realistic:

---

[330] Ibid.

It can be explained by the fact that the overwhelming mass of crimes are committed by people who do not try to avoid responsibility.... If 30,000 premeditated murders are committed per year here, then 28,000 murders are domestic murders on grounds of drunkenness or family fights, when everything is obvious, when the murderer, all in blood, lies next to his victim, still drunk.... Secondly, it can explained by the fact that the people who work in our law-enforcement agencies, despite, as you say, the insufficient salary and technical equipment, have kept their commitment to the work, to selfless work, to fulfilling their task as honorably as possible. Also, our crime is structured totally differently.[331]

At the Presidential Human Rights Chamber's session on torture in April 1998, several representatives of the Ministry of Internal Affairs were present but did not speak. A Ministry of Internal Affairs representative who spoke at a seminar on torture organized by the Moscow Center for Prison Reform in February 1998, in turn, had said on the one hand that there was no torture problem in Russia, while on the other that torture is a new problem for the police. Officials from the ministry's legal department are participating in the working groups on torture that were established by decision of the Presidential Human Rights Chamber.

Regional police chiefs were generally willing to meet with Human Rights Watch researchers. Most downplayed or denied outright the existence of a problem with police torture while admitting that there were occasional excesses and that common criminal offences were committed by police officers. In a departure from this tendency to minimize the problem, at the Presidential Human Rights Chamber's session on torture, Vladimir Vershkov of the Moscow city police testified that in his opinion torture had become significantly more frequent than ten to fifteen years ago.

The ministry's dismissive attitude toward torture in Russia is one of the principle causes of the lack of accountability for torture. In various cases of credible police torture, the police authorities neither fire abusive officers nor put them on desk duty. For example, in its statement to the Ministry of Interior, Judge Vasilii Martyshkinth of the Supreme Court of Mordovia stated that the failure of Mordovian police authorities to take appropriate measures against police officer Daev and several others, who were under a criminal investigation for torture in 1995, allowed them to continue torturing detainees, one of whom eventually died as a result. The St. Petersburg Times reported in July 1998 that a police officer who had been sentenced to eight years' imprisonment in 1997 for sexual and other abuses in office, but was released under a State Duma amnesty, was allowed to

---

[331] The acquittal rate in Russia is .5 percent. See above, "Stalled Reform."

resume his work at the local police precinct No. 44 following his release. The police officer was fired only after this was denounced as a scandal in the press.[332] Similarly, author Maksim Glikin reported that one of the police officers implicated in the torture of Alexander Volodko was promoted from senior lieutenant to captain.

The Ministry of Internal Affairs' dismissal of torture as a problem is made easier by the absence of express definitions of torture or ill-treatment in Russian criminal law. Acts that constitute torture are parsed out in a series of articles in the criminal code, including exceeding authority and infliction of mental or physical harm (with consequences of varying seriousness) and coercion to give testimony. As a result, it is very difficult to establish how many policemen were convicted or prosecuted for torture and ill-treatment of those in their custody, in contrast to these prosecuted for other abuses of office or crimes committed as a private person. Furthermore, as Russian legislation does not contain a definition of torture, police officers may claim that they do not know exactly what acts of violence against detainees constitute torture. For example, some police officers told Human Rights Watch that they do not consider beatings to be torture.

Procuracy General

The sometimes contradictory statements by procuracy officials suggest that the procuracy does not take police torture seriously and that no official policy to deal with the problem exists. To Human Rights Watch, officials of the Procuracy General flatly denied that torture or ill-treatment is a problem. The procuracy was said not to collect specified statistics on torture complaints or the number of police officers prosecuted for ill-treating detainees.

During a meeting with several officials from the Procuracy General in Moscow in February 1999, Anatolii Korotkov, first deputy head of the investigation department, told Human Rights Watch the following about the use of unlawful methods of investigation in Russia:

> There are no particular problems with respect for rule of law in Russia.... I believe that such a phenomenon exists but we do not misuse [the law] more than American police officers. In fact, trips of our delegation to America showed that there is even more unjustified use of violent means toward citizens there than in our police. Here, if a police officer uses his

---

[332] Evgeniia Borisova, "Police Reinstate Convicted Molester," *St. Petersburg Times*, July 17, 1998; Evgeniia Borisova, "Police Say Molester To Be Fired," *St. Petersburg Times*, July 24, 1998; Evgeniia Borisova, "Sex Crime Policeman Sacked," *St. Petersburg Times*, August 3, 1998.

nightstick, he will spend the next month or two writing explanations: how, where, why. He will deliberate: to hit or not. In America, you can very easily get [beaten] with a nightstick.[333]

At the Presidential Human Rights Chamber's session on torture, Korotkov's colleagues, Iakov Pister of the Procuracy General and Yuri Sinel'shikov of the Moscow City Procuracy, expressed very different opinions. Sinel'shikov said that according to his observations, torture has become much more widespread over the last few years:

> I think that five to ten years ago, police officers beat citizens much less frequently. These tendencies have become especially frequent since the events of 1993 [Yeltsin's armed attack on parliament].... We receive fairly few, in my opinion, complaints; a thousand complaints per year of course does not reflect the number of such incidents.[334]

Iakov Pister said:

> The Procuracy General has become especially worried about the situation of respect for the law in the organs of interior. Lately, we, the Procuracy General, devote the most intent and permanent attention to this direction.[335]

In the statistics it gathers, the procuracy does not have a special statistical category for complaints of torture or ill-treatment, which makes it impossible for the procuracy to provide an overview even of complaints. Despite assurances that complaints of torture and ill-treatment are taken seriously and considered objectively, our research indicates that the exact opposite is the case (see "Accountability"). Furthermore, during the Presidential Human Rights Chamber's session on torture, Yuri Sinel'shikov of the Moscow City Procuracy expressed support for the introduction of public control over places of detention. However, a letter from first deputy prime minister Yuri Masliukov regarding the draft law on

---

[333] Human Rights Watch interview with Anatolii Korotkov, Liudmila Kurovskaia, Viktor Kamyshanskii and Elena Duganova of the procurator general's office, Moscow, March 1, 1999.
[334] Transcript of the Human Rights Chamber's session on torture, April 7, 1998 (Human Rights Watch's translation).
[335] Ibid.

public control states that the Procuracy General is against the idea of this form of oversight.

The Procuracy General's publicly dismissive attitude toward measures to check torture and its unwillingness to take complaints seriously has been reflected in the promotion of procuracy officials who failed to investigate torture complaints thoroughly and objectively. For example, Arkhangel'sk province procurator Alexander Opanasenko was promoted to his current position after supervising the criminal investigations against Mikhail Iurochko and his codefendants (see above, "A Persistent Pattern of Torture and Ill-Treatment"), and Sergei Mikhailov (see above, "Torture and Confession Evidence"). All defendants in these cases alleged they confessed under torture. Charges against Iurochko and his codefendants have since been dropped, while several independent procuracy investigators have concluded that Mikhailov is not guilty of the crime for which he was convicted. In 1999, Opanasenko received the honorary title of Honored Jurist of Russia.

State Duma

Several members of the State Duma have been actively involved in attempts to address the problem of torture in Russia. The above-mentioned Presidential Human Rights Chamber's session on torture in April 1998 was co-chaired by deputies Valerii Borshchev and Galina Starovoitova, who was brutally murdered later that year. Valerii Borshchev was also the initiator of the draft law on public control.

However, as a whole the State Duma has done little to resolve the problem of torture. In June 1997, the State Duma adopted a draft criminal procedure code which perpetuates the current system of criminal justice, ignoring the CIS model criminal procedure code drafted primarily by Sergei Pashin, which would bring Russia's criminal justice system in line with international standards. Some 3,000 amendments have been proposed to this draft criminal procedure code. It is unclear when the second reading of the document will take place.

APPENDIX A: UNITED NATIONS COMMITTEE AGAINST TORTURE

Excerpts from the U.N. Convention against Torture and Other Cruel, Inhuman or Degrading Treatment or Punishment

Article 17

1. There shall be established a Committee against Torture (hereinafter referred to as the Committee) which shall carry out the functions hereinafter provided. The Committee shall consist of ten experts of high moral standing and recognized competence in the field of human rights, who shall serve in their personal capacity. The experts shall be elected by the States Parties, consideration being given to equitable geographical distribution and to the usefulness of the participation of some persons having legal experience.

Article 19

1. The States Parties shall submit to the Committee, through the Secretary-General of the United Nations, reports on the measures they have taken to give effect to their undertakings under this Convention, within one year after the entry into force of the Convention for the State Party concerned. Thereafter the States Parties shall submit supplementary reports every four years on any new measures taken and such other reports as the Committee may request.

2. The Secretary-General of the United Nations shall transmit the reports to all States Parties.

3. Each report shall be considered by the Committee which may make such general comments on the report as it may consider appropriate and shall forward these to the State Party concerned. That State Party may respond with any observations it chooses to the Committee.

4. The Committee may, at its discretion, decide to include any comments made by it in accordance with paragraph 3 of this article, together with the observations thereon received from the State Party concerned, in its annual report made in accordance with article 24. If so requested by the State Party concerned, the Committee may also include a copy of the report submitted under paragraph I of this article.

Appendix A: United Nations Committee Against Torture 161

Article 20

1. If the Committee receives reliable information which appears to it to contain well-founded indications that torture is being systematically practised in the territory of a State Party, the Committee shall invite that State Party to co-operate in the examination of the information and to this end to submit observations with regard to the information concerned.

2. Taking into account any observations which may have been submitted by the State Party concerned, as well as any other relevant information available to it, the Committee may, if it decides that this is warranted, designate one or more of its members to make a confidential inquiry and to report to the Committee urgently.

3. If an inquiry is made in accordance with paragraph 2 of this article, the Committee shall seek the co-operation of the State Party concerned. In agreement with that State Party, such an inquiry may include a visit to its territory.

4. After examining the findings of its member or members submitted in accordance with paragraph 2 of this article, the Commission shall transmit these findings to the State Party concerned together with any comments or suggestions which seem appropriate in view of the situation.

5. All the proceedings of the Committee referred to in paragraphs I to 4 of this article shall be confidential, and at all stages of the proceedings the co-operation of the State Party shall be sought. After such proceedings have been completed with regard to an inquiry made in accordance with paragraph 2, the Committee may, after consultations with the State Party concerned, decide to include a summary account of the results of the proceedings in its annual report made in accordance with article 24.

Concluding Observations on Russia's Second Periodic Report to the U.N. Committee against Torture

A/52/44, paras.31-43
14 November 1996

Concluding observations of the Committee against Torture : Russian Federation. 14/11/96. A/52/44, paras.31-43.

(Concluding Observations/Comments)

COMMITTEE AGAINST TORTURE
CONSIDERATION OF REPORTS SUBMITTED BY STATES PARTIES UNDER ARTICLE 19 OF THE CONVENTION

Conclusions and recommendations of the Committee against Torture

A. Russian Federation

31. The Committee considered the second periodic report of the Russian Federation (CAT/C/17/Add.15) at its 264th, 265th and 268th meetings, held on 12 and 14 November 1996 (see CAT/C/SR.264, 265 and 268), and adopted the following conclusions and recommendations.

1. Introduction

32. The second periodic report of the Russian Federation was not submitted on time, a fact that may be attributed to the transition that the country is undergoing. The report conforms, on the whole, to the guidelines adopted by the Committee for the submission of State reports.

33. The Committee expresses its appreciation to the representatives of the Russian Federation for their presentation of the report and especially for the effort made to answer almost all of the many questions raised by the Rapporteur, the Co-Rapporteur and the members of the Committee.

2. Positive aspects

34. The Constitution of the Russian Federation safeguards human rights in a comprehensive way, including the right to personal safety and bodily integrity.

35. The Constitution prohibits torture and every form of degrading treatment of the individual.

Appendix A: United Nations Committee Against Torture

36. The introduction of a new criminal code is welcomed, particularly in view of the criminalization of a series of acts the commission of which by law enforcement agents would constitute torture.

37. The setting up of the Presidential Commission on Human Rights and the establishment of an ombudsman for human rights are, without doubt, steps in the right direction. The positive aspects of the creation of those offices will be further enhanced if their powers to monitor the application of the Convention and deal with abuses are comprehensively defined.

38. The withdrawal of the reservation to article 20 and the declarations of acceptance of the procedures under articles 21 and 22 of the Convention are welcomed.

39. The allocation of additional resources for the improvement of prison conditions, as referred to by the delegation, is a step forward.

40. The will to reform State institutions, albeit with difficulty, in order to bring them into conformity with the provisions of the Constitution and fundamental human rights norms is duly noted.

3. Factors and difficulties impeding the application of the provisions of the Convention

41. The Committee acknowledges the existence of the following difficulties:

(a) The break with the past left an institutional vacuum that is proving difficult to fill. The State apparatus, as experience teaches, is resistant to change;

(b) The reorientation of State institutions and machinery is a difficult process. However, awareness of the obstacles to this process should lead those in authority to redouble the efforts to overcome them;

© The absence of properly trained personnel in sufficient numbers to make possible a swift change to the legal framework and the manner of running the State which is envisaged by the Constitution;

(d) The vastness of the country and diffusion of authority between central and regional authorities places additional difficulties in the way of establishing the new order;

(e) The lack of adequate resources to address the problems that are being encountered in the change from the old to the new legal order; the allocation of the necessary resources for the reform of legal practices should be seen as a priority.

4. Subjects of concern

42. The Committee is concerned about the following:

(a) The failure to create a specific crime of torture in the domestic law, as required by article 4 of the Convention;

(b) Presidential Decrees Nos. 1815 of 2 November 1993, 1226 of 14 June 1994 and 1025 of 10 July 1996, which allow the detention of suspects incommunicado for up to 9 days in one case and 30 days in the other cases, leave the door open to the abuse of the rights of detainees;

(c) Widespread allegations of torture and ill-treatment of suspects and persons in custody with a view to securing confessions, general allegations of ill-treatment of detainees and the absence of effective machinery to address such complaints promptly;

(d) The fact that, according to the materials presented to the Committee, young soldiers in the Russian army were brutalized by older soldiers without the authorities taking appropriate remedial measures;

(e) The failure to establish effective machinery for the prompt examination of prisoners' complaints about ill-treatment and conditions in prisons;

(f) The slow rate of harmonizing domestic legislation with the Constitution and with norms concerning human rights. The disharmony leaves a gap between the legal order respecting human rights established under the Constitution and the application of the law;

(g) Overcrowding in prisons, made all the worse by the poor and insanitary conditions prevailing in them;

Appendix A: United Nations Committee Against Torture

(h) Lack of proper training of police and prison personnel and the personnel of agencies engaged in law enforcement with regard to the rights of suspects and prisoners and their duties under the law;

(I) Lack of appropriate measures to give comprehensive effect to the provisions of article 3 of the Convention and to ensure its applicability in all relevant circumstances, including in relation to extradition;

(j) Absence of extraterritorial jurisdiction makes difficult or impossible the implementation of article 5, paragraph 1 (b), of the Convention;

(k) Reported widespread abuses of human rights in the conflict in Chechnya, including acts of torture, and the apparent failure to check such abuses and address them speedily and effectively.

5. Recommendations

43. The Committee recommends that the State party:

(a) Make torture as defined in the Convention a distinct crime, with sufficiently severe punishment to reflect the gravity of the offence;

(b) Expedite the process of training the personnel, including the medical personnel, of all agencies involved in law enforcement and the detention of prisoners as to their powers and duties under the law;

(c) Adopt programmes to inform detainees and the public of their rights and the means available under the law to protect them;

(d) Establish effective machinery to monitor the conditions under which investigations of crimes are conducted, the conditions under which persons are held in custody and conditions in prisons;

(e) Establish an appropriate process for the prompt investigation of complaints of suspects, detainees and prisoners and the prosecution of the offenders;

(f) Radically improve conditions in prisons, including space, facilities, food and sanitation;

(g) Abolish acts, rules and regulations allowing remand in custody for longer than 48 hours without judicial authorization, and those limiting access to legal assistance. Unimpeded access to counsel should be safeguarded at all times;

(h) Establish an independent committee to investigate allegations of torture and inhuman and degrading treatment committed by the military forces of the Russian Federation and Chechen separatists, with a view to bringing to justice those against whom there is evidence tending to establish their involvement or complicity in such acts.

APPENDIX B: EUROPEAN COMMITTEE FOR THE PREVENTION OF TORTURE AND INHUMAN OR DEGRADING TREATMENT OR PUNISHMENT

Excerpts from the European Convention for the Prevention of Torture

Article 1

There shall be established a European Committee for the Prevention of Torture and Inhuman or Degrading Treatment or Punishment (hereinafter referred to as "the Committee"). The Committee shall, by means of visits, examine the treatment of persons deprived of their liberty with a view to strengthening, if necessary, the protection of such persons from torture and from inhuman or degrading treatment or punishment.

Article 2

Each Party shall permit visits, in accordance with this Convention, to any place within its jurisdiction where persons are deprived of their liberty by a public authority.

Article 7

1. The Committee shall organise visits to places referred to in Article 2. Apart from periodic visits, the Committee may organise such other visits as appear to it to be required in the circumstances.

2. As a general rule, the visits shall be carried out by at least two members of the Committee. The Committee may, if it considers it necessary, be assisted by experts and interpreters.

Article 8

1. The Committee shall notify the Government of the Party concerned of its intention to carry out a visit. After such notification, it may at any time visit any place referred to in Article 2.

2. A Party shall provide the Committee with the following facilities to carry out its task:
   (a) access to its territory and the right to travel without restriction;
   (b) full information on the places where persons deprived of their liberty are being held;

(c) unlimited access to any place where persons are deprived of their liberty, including the right to move inside such places without restriction;

(d) other information available to the Party which is necessary for the Committee to carry out its task.

In seeking such information, the Committee shall have regard to applicable rules of national law and professional ethics.

3. The Committee may interview in private persons deprived of their liberty.

4. The Committee may communicate freely with any person whom it believes can supply relevant information.

5. If necessary, the Committee may immediately communicate observations to the competent authorities of the Party concerned

Article 10

1. After each visit, the Committee shall draw up a report on the facts found during the visit, taking account of any observations which may have been submitted by the Party concerned. It shall transmit to the latter its report containing any recommendations it considers necessary. The Committee may consult with the Party with a view to suggesting, if necessary, improvements in the protection of persons deprived of their liberty.

2. If the Party fails to co-operate or refuses to improve the situation in the light of the Committee's recommendations, the Committee may decide, after the Party has had an opportunity to make known its views, by a majority of two-thirds of its members to make a public statement on the matter.

Article 11

1. The information gathered by the Committee in relation to a visit, its report and its consultations with the Party concerned shall be confidential.

2. The Committee shall publish its report, together with any comments of the Party concerned, whenever requested to do so by that Party.

3. However, no personal data shall be published without the express consent of the person concerned.

Appendix B: European Committee for the Prevention of Torture and Inhuman or Degrading Treatment or Punishment

The Committee's November 1998 Visit
Press Release

STRASBOURG, 4.12.98 - A delegation of the COUNCIL OF EUROPE's Committee for the Prevention of Torture and Inhuman or Degrading Treatment or Punishment (CPT) recently carried out a fifteen day visit to the Russian Federation (16 to 30 November 1998). It was the CPT's first visit to the Russian Federation, the Convention setting up the Committee having entered into force for Russia on 1 September 1998.

In the course of the visit, the CPT's delegation focused its attention on pre-trial detention and the treatment of persons deprived of their liberty by the Militia. In addition to visiting a number of pre-trial and Militia establishments in Moscow City and the regions of Nizhnyi Novgorod and Saratov, the delegation held extensive consultations with the Russian authorities, at both federal and regional level.

The visit was carried out by the following members of the CPT:

Constantin ECONOMIDES, Head of the Delegation (Greek)
Emilia DRUMEVA (Bulgarian)
Zdenek HAJEK (Czech)
Adam LAPTAS (Polish)
Gisela PERREN-KLINGLER (Swiss)
Jagoda POLONCOVA (Slovak).

They were assisted by three experts - Andrew COYLE (Director of the International Centre for Prison Studies, King's College, London), Enda DOOLEY (Director of Prison Medical Services, Department of Justice, Dublin) and Jean-Pierre RESTELLINI (Specialist in forensic and internal medicine, Geneva) - as well as by Trevor STEVENS (Secretary of the CPT) and Petya NESTOROVA of the CPT's Secretariat.

The delegation visited the following places:

Pre-trial establishments (SIZO)
    SIZO N° 2 ("Butyrka") in Moscow
    SIZO N° 1 in Nizhnyi Novgorod

SIZO N° 1 in Saratov

Establishments under the authority of the Ministry of Internal Affairs

Moscow

Temporary holding facility (IVS) at Moscow City Directorate of Internal Affairs (Petrovka St.)
Moscow City Regional Directorate for Combating Organised Crime
Kazanskyi Railway Station Division of Internal Affairs
Divisions of Internal Affairs at Sheremetevo-1 and 2 Airports

Central Administrative Area:
11th Division of the Militia, 2nd District Command of Internal Affairs (Barrikadnaya St.)
5th Division of the Militia, 3rd District Command of Internal Affairs (Gorky St.)
68th Division of the Militia, 7th District Command of Internal Affairs (Myasnitskaya St.)

North-East Administrative Area:
Alekseevskee District Division of Internal Affairs (Novoalekseevskaya St.)
Otradnoe District Division of Internal Affairs (Olonetskaya St.)
Temporary holding facility (IVS) (Dekabristov St.)

East Administrative Area:
Izmailovo District Division of Internal Affairs (Izmailovskaya Square)
Temporary holding facility (IVS) (Parkovaya St.)

South-West Administrative Area:
Kon'kovo District Division of Internal Affairs (Profsoyuznaya St.)

North-West Administrative Area:
Strogino District Division of Internal Affairs (Tvardovskovo St.)

Nizhnyi Novgorod

Avtozavodskoe District Division of Internal Affairs
Nizhegorodskoe District Command of Internal Affairs (N. Volzhskaya Naberezhnaya St.)

Appendix B: European Committee for the Prevention of Torture and Inhuman or Degrading Treatment or Punishment   171

Volgo-Vyatskoe Regional Directorate for Combating Organised Crime

Saratov
Engels City Command of Internal Affairs (Telegrafnaya St.)
3rd, 4th and 5th Divisions of the Militia, Engels
Saratov City Command of Internal Affairs (Moskovskaya St.)
Leninskoe District Command of Internal Affairs, Saratov (Ippodrumnaya St.)
Zavodskoe District Command of Internal Affairs, Saratov (Entuziastov Av.)
"KOBRA" unit, Saratov

Other establishments
Moscow City Hospital N° 20 (Security ward)
Transit zone at Sheremetevo-2 Airport, Moscow
Holding facility for aliens at Sheremetevo Hotel, Moscow

The Committee's September 1999 Visit
Press Release

STRASBOURG, 17.09.99 - A delegation of the COUNCIL OF EUROPE Committee for the Prevention of Torture and Inhuman or Degrading Treatment or Punishment (CPT) recently carried out a seventeen-day visit to the Russian Federation. The visit began on 30 August 1999 and was organised within the framework of the CPT's programme of periodic visits for 1999. It was the CPT's second visit to the Russian Federation. The first visit - which focused specifically on pre-trial detention and the treatment of persons deprived of their liberty by the Militia - took place in November 1998.

The visit was carried out by the following members of the CPT:

John OLDEN, Head of the delegation, 2nd Vice-President of the CPT, (Irish)
Constantin ECONOMIDES (Greek)
Andres LEHTMETS (Estonian)
Adam LAPTAS (Polish)
Jagoda POLONCOVA (Slovak)
Ole Vedel RASMUSSEN (Danish).

They were assisted by three experts - Andrew COYLE (Director of the International Centre for Prison Studies, King's College, London), Timothy

HARDING (Director of the University Institute of Forensic Medicine, Geneva) and Jean-Pierre RESTELLINI (Specialist in forensic and internal medicine, Geneva) - as well as by Petya NESTOROVA and Borys WÓDZ of the CPT's Secretariat.

The delegation visited the following places:

Establishments under the authority of the Ministry of Internal Affairs

Chelyabinsk:

Leninskoe District Command of Internal Affairs
Traktozavodskyi District Command of Internal Affairs
Directorate for Combating Organised Crime (UBOP)

St.Petersburg:

Temporary holding facility (IVS) at St.Petersburg City Command of Internal Affairs
Petrogradski District Command of Internal Affairs
Primorski District Command of Internal Affairs
35th Militia Division, Primorskyi District
52nd Militia Division, Krasnogvardeiskyi District
Joint reception and distribution centre at St.Petersburg City Command of Internal Affairs

Vologda:

City Command of Internal Affairs
City Sobering-up Centre
Reception and distribution centre for minors (Gorki Street)
Joint reception and distribution centre (Leningradskaya Street)

Establishments under the authority of the Ministry of Justice

Chelyabinsk Region:

Medical-correctional establishment (LIU) No 3, Chelyabinsk
Prison No 2, Zlatoust
Strict regime colony No 2, Chelyabinsk

Appendix B: European Committee for the Prevention of Torture and Inhuman or Degrading Treatment or Punishment

St.Petersburg City and Leningrad Region:

Educational colony for juveniles, Kolpino
Pre-trial establishment (SIZO) No 1 ("Kresty"), St.Petersburg

Vologda Region:

Colony No 5 for prisoners serving life sentences, Novozero
Inter-regional hospital (LPU) No 10, Vologda
Prison No 1, Vologda

Establishments under the authority of the Ministry of Health
Special psychiatric hospital with intensive supervision, St. Petersburg
Forensic psychiatric ward of the Territorial Psychiatric Board No 2, St. Petersburg

APPENDIX C: LETTER FROM RUSSIA'S OMBUDSMAN TO THE MINISTER OF INTERNAL AFFAIRS

Translation from Russian

December 29, 1998

STATEMENT OF THE PRESS SERVICE OF THE HUMAN RIGHTS OMBUDSMAN OF THE RUSSIAN FEDERATION

1998-12-29-002

Mr.O.O.Mironov, human rights ombudsman in the Russian Federation, sent a letter to Mr.S.V.Stepashin, Minister of Internal Affairs of the Russian Federation. The letter, inter alia, reads:

"Dear Sergei Vadimovich,

Socio-economic changes in Russia have significantly affected the human rights situation, including the rights of those who have violated the law, and whose rights cannot be addressed outside the context of human rights in Russia in general.

The Russian Ministry of Internal Affairs has undergone major changes which fall in line with the construction of a state based on democracy and the rule of law. The reform process has been completed, federal ministerial tasks and functions have been clearly defined.

The law enforcement system is overcoming shortcomings in solving and investigating grave crimes.

Efforts to strengthen law and order and public safety undertaken by federal and regional bodies of state power and by law enforcement agencies have produced certain results.

However, procuracy inquiries show that in 1997 30 thousand police officers were administratively punished, more than 1.5 thousand police officers were prosecuted for service-related crimes, 853 police officers were prosecuted for abuse of power. 50.6 thousand crimes, previously unregistered, were put on record.

Appendix C: Letter from Russia's Ombudsman to the Minister of Internal Affairs

Similar violations, directly connected with breaching civil rights and freedoms, were committed by law enforcement officials in 1998 as well.

Wide-spread violations by law enforcement officials, such as concealment of crimes, ill-treatment during investigation, various cases of abuse of power are of special concern.

Letters to the Russian ombudsman from citizens show that officials of the Ministry of Internal Affairs violate the constitutional norms and provisions of the European Convention on Human Rights, though these officials are supposed to ensure law and order and protect legitimate rights of the citizens.

Citizens refer to numerous cases of violence and cruel treatment of defendants during police inquiry, detective activities and preliminary investigation.

In most cases, such requests are sent by persons who are suspected and accused of having committed grave and extremely grave crimes; they claim that police officers resorted to physical and psychological violence in order to get confessions. /.../[336]

During personal meetings of the ombudsman with inmates in pre-trial detention facilities and prisons, every second person claimed that police officers subjected him to beatings and humiliation from the moment of detention until transfer to a pre-trial detention facility.

Press reports also mention torture, in particular, electroshock being used by police officers against detainees. /.../

On February 12, 1998, the criminal chamber of the Supreme Court of the Republic of Mordovia convicted seven police officers of the Republic of Mordovia for abuse of power, violence and personal humiliation against detained persons./.../ Six out of the seven officers were convicted to prison terms ranging from 3 to 9.5 years. The court has instructed the republic's Ministry of Internal Affairs to pay

---

[336] The names of the victims whose cases the ombudsman raised with the Ministry of Internal Affairs had been deleted from the copy of the letter that the ombudsman gave Human Rights Watch.

compensation to the victims. This six-month trial was widely covered by the media. The court ruled that torture was of a systematic nature and was committed in complicity with high-ranking officials. The Court issued a separate statement to the Russian Ministry of Internal Affairs.

Another cause for concern is the use of force by police officers against participants in economic and political protests. Thus, practically all newspapers published after October 10, 1998, mentioned about forcible dispersion of the miners' picket on the "*Gorbatyi most*" [a bridge near the building of Russia's federal government] (for example, "Cleansing at the 'hour of the jackal'", *Sovetskaia Rossia*, 13.10.98.). However, no one is responsible, everything is covered with secrecy and vagueness. It is essential that the public should know who gives orders to use force.

The public is quite concerned by the facts of certain police officers directly violating the law by openly cooperating with criminals. This has been repeatedly mentioned in the press. For example, Ie.Ukhov in his article "Werewolves in uniform" (*Trud*, 3.11.98) mentions the exposure of two police officers on the payroll of criminals.

K.Voronov in his article (*Kommersant* daily, 6.11.98) reported that a Novosibirsk regional court convicted two high-ranking police officers who took a 125 million ruble bribe to close a criminal case.

Having conveyed to you the above mentioned facts in accordance with clause 1, Article 31 of the Federal Constitutional Law on the Human Rights Ombudsman in the Russian Federation, I request you to take appropriate measures to prevent the officials of your ministry from violating constitutional rights and freedoms of the citizens.

I am awaiting your information on the measures taken.

O.O.Mironov"

APPENDIX D: RESPONSE FROM THE MINISTRY OF INTERIOR TO RUSSIA'S OMBUDSMAN

MINISTRY OF INTERNAL AFFAIRS
OF THE RUSSIAN FEDERATION
Moscow

Translation from Russian

February 2, 1999, [1] 1/2062
Ref. OM-259, December 28, 1998

        Mr.O.O.MIRONOV,
        HUMAN RIGHTS OMBUDSMAN
        IN THE RUSSIAN FEDERATION
        47, Miasnitskaia Str., Moscow-103084

On measures on strengthening respect for human rights and observance of law in the activities of the bodies and structural units of the Ministry of Internal Affairs of the Russian Federation

Dear Oleg Orestovich,

Your letter regarding violence against suspects and accused persons during police inquiry, detective activities and preliminary investigation has been closely considered by the leadership of the Russian Ministry of Internal Affairs. All the cases have been thoroughly investigated, and those guilty of ill-treatment have been appropriately punished.

The situation with the rule of law and respect for human rights in realizing the work of police departments is closely monitored by the Main departments and Departments of the Ministry, and is systematically reviewed at working sessions under the ministry leadership.

In view of the acuteness of the problem and the urgency of taking measures to strengthen observance of law and discipline in the police service and the interior troops, the Ministry has issued a number of instructions to improve personnel management, prevent violations by police officers and servicemen. Necessary steps are being taken to implement the instructions.

As a means of control and practical assistance, senior staff systematically visit subordinate structures and receive reports from the chiefs of units producing low statistics in discipline and observance of law by their personnel.

Regarding this problem, the Ministry collegium has heard reports of the Minister of the Interior of the Republic of Mordovia, heads of St. Petersburg city and Leningrad Region Chief Police Departments, Ivanovo, Kemerovo, Samara, Tambov, Novgorod, Vladimir, Tomsk, Irkutsk Police Departments, as well as of the Commanding Officer of the Interior Troops Volga Regional Command. The chiefs responsible for serious shortcomings have been administratively punished.

Thus, investigation into the Russian Procuracy General representation "On checking violations of law in investigating reports from citizens about crimes" in St. Petersburg and Leningrad Region has resulted in the decision of the Ministry Collegium (No. 3 KM of June 6, 1998) to remove and sack Lt-General of the Interior A.V.Ponidelko, Head of the Chief Police Department.

Service eligibility has been attested of the regional ministers of the interior, heads of main police departments and police departments, and their deputies for personnel management. Since February of the current year, this procedure has been initiated with respect to regional deputy ministers, heads of main police departments and police departments for criminal police.

To assist chiefs of local divisions in personnel management, more than forty instructions, information digests and theoretical recommendations, as well as reviews of the state of discipline among the personnel in the ministry and its departments, have been circulated in 1998.

Timely reaction to extraordinary incidents among the personnel has been ensured, selection criteria for candidates to join the interior service have been toughened.

Under the European Convention for the Prevention of Torture and Inhuman or Degrading Treatment or Punishment, the first ever visit of the European Committee to Russia took place from November 15 to 30, 1998; the members have inspected fourteen pre-trial detention facilities and twelve administrative detention wards of city and district police departments in Moscow, Nizhnii Novgorod and Saratov.

Appendix D: Response from the Ministry of Interior to Russia's Ombudsman

The visiting members have met governors, procurators, heads of main police departments and police departments and discussed the issues of assistance necessary to improve conditions in the police custody, as well as the issues of respect for law and human rights. The visiting members have held one hundred and twenty confidential interviews with detainees and those in custody. Sixty meetings were held with police detectives and division heads, with emphasis on the treatment of detainees, suspects and accused by police officers, on financial, logistics and medical support of these institutions.

This inspection is to produce a detailed report with specific recommendations, which, after adoption in the Council of Europe, will be forwarded to the Russian government.

To eliminate violations of discipline and law fully and completely, a whole new supervisory preventive mechanism has to be established. We believe that we will be able to provide you with the corresponding draft in the second half of 1999.

Expanded session of the Ministry collegium was already held in December, 1998 to discuss "Personnel management and personnel policy in the Russian Ministry of Internal Affairs". A concept of personnel management under current conditions has been adopted, which includes a set of measures to improve control and preventive mechanisms.

We appreciate you raising the issues and hope that a permanent working interaction will be established between the office of the human rights ombudsman in Russia and interested services of the ministry to exchange information on violations of law by the ministry personnel.

Regards,

Col-General of Justice I.N.Kozhevnikov,
Deputy Minister of Internal Affairs

APPENDIX E: DECISION OF THE PRESIDENTIAL HUMAN RIGHTS CHAMBER OF APRIL 7, 1998

Unofficial translation

Political Consultative Council under the President of the Russian Federation

The Permanent Chamber on Human Rights

DECISION
of April 7, 1998
On gross violations of human rights in the organs of the Ministry of Internal Affairs

After considering the matter of gross violations of human rights in the organs of the Ministry of Internal Affairs of the Russian Federation at a hearing, the Permanent Chamber on Human Rights notes:
Torture and cruel, degrading forms of treatment or punishment with respect to citizens in the organs of the Ministry of Internal Affairs during the pretrial stages of criminal justice administration have a massive and systematic character which makes it one of the most serious problems of abuse of power and violations of human rights.
Large number of facts about torture in Russia are mentioned in reports of Russian and international human rights organizations.
The current practice is partially related to the problems and deficiencies of legislation and ministerial normative regulations. Despite the recommendation of the United Nations Committee against Torture, such a dangerous crime as torture has not been criminalized. As a result, official statistics on the number of revealed cases do not exist. The issue of public control over the activities of the law enforcement agencies has also not been solved.
However, deficiencies in legislation cannot solely explain why citizens are not protected against lawlessness commited by Ministry of Internal Affairs agencies. Other reasons are the widespread and increasing use of of unlawful forms and methods of pressure on persons who found themselves in the criminal justice system: suspects, defendants, witnesses, as well as those detained for administrative offenses. Repressive methods (instead of methods directed towards the protection of rights) remain an element of the technology of the law enforcement agencies.

Appendix E: Decision of the Presidential Human Rights Chamber of April 7, 1998

Target indicators for the organs of the Ministry of Internal Affairs are pre-planned and reported figures (crime solving rates and crime plans).

One of the reasons for the gross violations of human rights by Ministry of Internal Affairs agencies is the swelling of and reorganization the law enforcement system, which has led to a drop in professional and moral quality of its officials.

The Chamber sees the existing situation with regard to the protection of citizens against violations of their rights by law enforcement agencies as destructive, as constituting a real threat to national security, which dictates the need to adopt urgent measures to overcome it with the joined efforts of state power, human rights organizations and the media.

Considering the above, as well as the European Convention for the Prevention of Torture and Inhuman or Degrading Treatment or Punishment, which came into force for the Russian Federation in 1998, the Chamber decided:

1. To create a working group with the aim of drafting a federal program for the struggle against torture, inhuman and degrading treatment or punishment, asking the leadership of the Ministry of Internal Affairs of the Russian Federation and the Procuracy General of the Russian Federation to assign representatives to participate in the preparation of the draft. To take into account during the preparation of the draft federal program the recommendations contained in the materials presented at the session of the Chamber.
2. To propose to the Ministry of Internal Affairs of the Russian Federation and the Procuracy General of the Russian Federation to discuss the possibility of cooperation with nongovernmental organizations in the field of monitoring respect for human rights at police precincts, departments of the Ministry of Internal Affairs, and temporary holding centers.
3. To propose to the Ministry of Internal Affairs of the Russian Federation and the Procuracy General of the Russian Federation to adopt normative acts requiring that all detainees be given a card listing their rights, as well as requiring that a duty lawyer (defender) be present at police precincts, departments of the Ministry of Internal Affairs, and temporary holding centers.
4. To propose to those who have the right of legislative initiative to develop draft laws on public control over respect for the rights of detainees and on amendments to the criminal code of the Russian Federation and the criminal procedure code of the Russian Federation, which would criminalize torture

and other forms of inhuman or degrading treatment or punishment, and to submit these to the State Duma.

The Chairman of the Permanent Chamber   V. Borshchev

Translated by Diederik Lohman

APPENDIX F: SEPARATE RULING OF SUPREME COURT JUDGE VASILII MARTYSHKIN ON TORTURE IN MORDOVIA

Unofficial translation

Case No. 2-4/98
Separate Statement

On February 12, 1998, the criminal chamber of the Supreme Court of the Republic of Mordovia, consisting of:
 Chair V.N. Martyshkin,
 lay assessors G.S. Baikovaia, V.S. Mitiaeva,
 and clerk T.M. Trushkina
 with participation of prosecutor I.A. Rusiaev,
 and lawyers L.Iu. Mel'nikova, S.V. Afanas'ev, N.V. Shmakova, I.P. Shcherbakov, V.K. Galaev, M.T. Smirnova, V.V. Gavaev,

in an open court hearing in the city of Saransk in the Republic of Mordovia, after considering the criminal case against officers of the criminal investigation department of the Ministry of Internal Affairs of Mordovia Alexander Alexandrovich Daev, Evgenii Nikolaevich Sazonov, Sergei Valentinovich Antonov on the basis of article 171(2) of the criminal code of the RSFSR, officers of the criminal investigation department of the Bol'shebereznikovskii ROVD Vladimir Il'ich Tutaev, Anatolii Nikiforovich Frolkin on the basis of article 171(2) of the criminal code of the RSFSR, officers of the criminal investigation department of the Lenin district ROVD in Saransk Alexander Evgenievich Guliaikin, Dmitrii Nikolaevich Kuflin on the basis of article 171(2) of the criminal code of the RSFSR, and Evgenii Nikolaevich Sazonov on the basis of article 175 of the criminal code of the RSFSR,

RULED:
By verdict of February 12, 1998, of the Supreme Court of the Republic of Mordovia, E.N. Sazonov was sentenced for forgery of official documents to one year of deprivation of his liberty for exceeding his authority and office, accompanied with violence, which inflicted pain on and degraded seven victims;
 Convicted on the basis of article 171(2) of the criminal code of the RSFSR:
 A.A. Daev, E.N. Sazonov to nine years and six months of deprivation of freedom each;
 A.E. Guliaikin and D.N. Kuflin to five years of deprivation of freedom each;
 S.V. Antonov to three years and six months of deprivation of freedom;

A.N Frolkin and V.I. Tutaev to three years of deprivation of freedom each. Tutaev's sentence is suspended, with a probation period of two years.

As officers of the criminal investigation department used torture and ill-treatment against the victims in office No. 343 of the building of the Mordovian MVD and office No. 306 of the Lenin district ROVD in Saransk, and in offices of the Bol'shebereznikosvkii ROVD, the Ministry of Internal Affairs of Mordovia is required to pay compensation to indemnify the moral [sic] damage in new prices:[337]

- to the mother of the deceased O.V. Igonin — Valentina Mikhailovna Igonina— 200,000 rubles;

- to police major Nikolai Andreevich Abramov — 50,000 rubles;

- to Vasilii Vasilievich Abramov — officer of the State Automobile Inspectorate, and Alexander Alexandrovich Derkaev— an Afghan veteran, who was wounded and decorated for his courage, and whose eleventh rib on the right hand side the convicted broke while torturing him with a gas mask — 30,000 rubles each;

It should be noted that all these crimes were committed before the appointment of Iu. A. Liashev to the position of Minister of Internal Affairs of the Mordovia.

The officers of the criminal investigation department of the Mordovian MVD and the officers of the investigation department of the Bol'shebereznikovskii and Lenin district ROVDs in Saransk committed the crimes between April 1994 and July 1995.

1. The court established beyond a reasonable doubt that the reasons for the conditions under which the crimes of exceeding authority and office were committed by officers of the criminal investigation department of the MVD and the Bol'shebereznikovskii and Lenin district ROVDs in Saransk were a lack of control and permissiveness by the leadership of the involved ROVD, the duty service and the leadership of the Mordovian MVD.

Thus, as the court established, in April 1994 in an MVD building,[338] in office no. 343, [police officers] Daev, Sazonov, Antonov used force during a so-called "informal questioning" before the interrogation of [criminal suspects] A.A. Derkaev, V.V. Abramov, N.A. Abramov, and others by investigator of the

---

[337] In 1998, Russia carried out a currency reform. As of January 1, 1998, it denominated its currency by scrapping three zero's of its money.
[338] MVD is the Russian acronym for Ministerstvo Vnutrennikh Del, or Ministry of Internal Affairs.

Appendix F: Separate Ruling of Supreme Court Judge Vasilii Martyshkin on Torture in Mordovia

investigative department of the MVD V.P. Ushakov. In doing so, they put a gas mask on their heads, cutting the oxygen with the aim of receiving confessions from the suspects to stealing a MTZ-80 tractor from the collective farm "Kalinin" in the Bol'shebereznikovskii district of Mordovia. [The policemen] handcuffed [the brothers] Abramov, Derkaev, and the other victims, tied their legs to the floor, pulled their head toward the legs with the belt of a kimono, and beat them. One victim in the case, police major and chief of the B. Bereznikovskii GAI, N.A. Abramov, lost consciousness. A.A. Derkaev and V.V. Abramov testified to this in court.

2. We note the cruelty and refinement of the torture used by officers Daev, Sazonov, Antonov of the investigative department of the MVD and officers Tutaev and Frolkin of the investigative department of the B. Bereznikovskii district ROVD, and officers Kuflin and Guliaikin of the Lenin district ROVD.

As V.V. Abramov testified in court, he was tied in the "konvertik" position and put on his back, [police officer] Antonov and the other MVD employees beat him with the strap of the gas mask on the scrotum. Derkaev, who sustained a broken rib during the "informal questioning," told the court that [police officer] Frolkin, after putting his foot on [Derkaev's] genitals, demanded a confession, saying that he will not need them [his genitals] anymore in life.

On July 25, 1995, [police officers] Daev, Sazonov, Guliaikin demanded a confession to armed robbery from minor A.S. Lavrent'ev in office no. 306 of the Lenin ROVD[339] and demanded that he name accomplices. They asphyxiated the minor several times with a type RP-4 gas mask. During the torture, which lasted for a long time, Lavrent'ev twice urinated on himself, and was beaten.

Unable to withstand the violence, the minor implicated his acquaintance O.V. Igonin, assuming that the latter was serving in the army. However, Lavrent'ev was mistaken, because Igonin was a student.

During the night of July 25, 1995, [police officers] Daev, Sazonov, Kuflin, Guliaikin, on the instruction of former heads of the Lenin ROVD in Saransk—Iu.I. Golov, V.A. Chekhonin—detained O.V. Igonin in the presence of his parents at his home.

Without submitting the detained O.V. Igonin to the duty officer's department [for registration], without writing a detention report, during night time—at 2:00

---

[339] ROVD is the Russian acronym for raionoe otdeleniie vnutrennykh del, or district police station.

a.m.—Daev, Sazonov, Guliaikin, Kuflin, began to force Igonin into confessing to armed robbery...after they handcuffed him and bound his legs. To that end, they all together put a gas mask [on Igonin] and cut the oxygen. When Igonin choked, they brought him to his senses and the torture session was repeated. At around 4:00 a.m. of July 26, 1995, Igonin died, unable to stand the "informal questioning," as the defendants [the policemen] called their actions with respect to the victims.[340]

3. However, despite the results of the investigation of the criminal case against Daev, Sazonov, Tutaev and Frolkin, the leadership of the Mordovian MVD did not take the necessary measures, including relieving [them] from [their] official positions. This carelessness and tolerance, the attempt to defend [the police officers] led to Daev and Sazonov committing an offence with even more grave results against minor A.S. Lavrent'ev and O.V. Igonin [341]

The procuracy of Saransk opened a criminal case under article 171(2) of the criminal code of the RSFSR against the criminal investigation officers [Daev and Sazonov] on June 7, 1994, about which the leadership of the MVD of Mordovia, the Bol'shebereznikvoskii and Lenin ROVD were informed. On July 25, 1995, investigator Savinov D.A. of the Saransk procuracy wrote the indictments against Daev, Sazonov, Antonov, Frolkin, and Tutaev.

From January 23, 1995 to May 3, 1995, defendants Daev, Sazonov, Antonov, Tutaev, and Frolkin were presented charges on the basis of articles 171(2) and 179(2) of the criminal code of the RSFSR.

Daev A.A. read all the materials of the criminal case on those charges by May 13, 1995, and Sazonov E.N. by July 20, 1995. Thus, they fulfilled the requirement of article 201 of the criminal procedure code of the RSFSR, just as the other defendants on the case (volume 2., pages 293, 296)

On July 25, 1995 investigator Savinov D.A. of the Saransk procuracy wrote the indictments against Daev, Sazonov, Antonov, Frolkin and Tutaev (volume 2, pages 314-350).

However, despite the presented charges and the completion of the investigation into the criminal case, officers of the criminal investigation department, including of the central apparatus of the UUR MVD of Mordovia,

---

[340] *Chastnoe opredelenie* by Judge Vasilii Martyshkin of the Supreme Court of the Republic of Mordovia, case 2-4/98, February 12, 1998.
[341] *Chastnoe opredelenie* by judge Vasilii Martyshkin of the Supreme Court of the Republic of Mordovia, Case 2-4/98, February 12, 1998. Emphasis added.

Daev A.A., Sazonov E.N., Antonov S.V. were not fired or relieved from their official position.

This resulted in the leadership of the UUR of the Ministry of Internal Affairs of Mordova sending Daev and Sazonov to the Leninsky ROVD in Saransk to render assistance in the investigation of a robbery committed in Saransk on the night of July 22 and 23, 1995.

Thus, on July 25, 1995, Daev and Sazonov gave instruction to Guliaikin to bring the unlawfully detained minor, A.S. Lavrentev, out from IVS-1, who, under acute torture, had named the student O.V. Igonin. They had already delivered Igonin in handcuffs to the very same office, No. 306 of the Lenin district ROVD, where a few hours later he suffocated to death in a gas mask used by Daev, Sazonov, Kuflin and Guliaikin.

4. Furthermore, on the basis of the demands presented in a petition from the lawyers and the defendants in the criminal case, the court established the following legal violations of the information center of the MVD in Mordovia.

In the period, when the investigator had presented Daev the accusation and the investigation of the case concerning A.A. Daev and other employees of investigation department of the MVD of Mordovia had been completed, A.A. Daev on July 20, 1995 collected information at the information center of Mordovia about convictions and other compromising data on the witnesses of his criminal case, who exposed the use of physical abuse during interrogations by the employees of the criminal investigation department. He did so with the permission of the deputy head of the criminal investigation department of theMVD of Mordovia (there is a signature of the official in question). The witnesses: V. U Perepletchikov, U.N. Galushkin, U.B. Manerov, I.V. Chuprin, V.U. Borisov, I.V. Mukletsov, I.A. Kulikov, V.I. Sarankin.

The court considers that there was ample foundation to dismiss Daev and Sazonov, as well as to simultaneously fire them from the Ministry of Internal Affairs, in the period of investigation into the case; besides the crimes they committed, it is also necessary to take into account that the leadership of the Mordovian MVD took disciplinary action against both of them for breaking the law in 1994 and 1995.

5. The court established beyond a reasonable doubt that the employees of the Mordovian criminal investigation department of the Ministry of Internal Affairs, the criminal investigation department of the Leninskii district ROVD

in Saransk, and the criminal investigation department of the Bol'shebereznitskii ROVD in 1994 and 1995 systematically violated articles 1-14 of the law on the police of the Russian Federation, as well as article 20 of the constitution of Mordovia and article 21 of the Russian constitution.

According to the law on the police of the Russian Federation (articles 1-5), the police of the Russian Federation are obliged to defend the life, health, rights and freedom of citizens. The Russian constitution comprises the legal foundation for this activity. The police are prohibited from using degrading treatment. The use of special devices is discussed in article 14 of the law on the police of the Russian Federation.

In accordance with article 21 of the Russian constitution and article 20 of the constitution of Mordovia: "No one shall be subjected to torture, force, or any form of cruel or degrading treatment or punishment."

These requirements of the law on the police of the Russian Federation and of the constitution of Mordovia were systematically and grossly violated by the defendants for a long period of time. And the leadership of the ROVD and the MVD of Mordovia did not interfere with these violations, in spite of the fact that the MVD has its own internal security service.

In essence the employees of the criminal investigation department, having exceeded their authority and systematically used torture and ill-treatment in their dealings with victims N.N. Shubin, I.N. Ezhikov, N.A. Abramov, A.A. Derkaev, V.V. Abramov, O.V. Igonev, and A.S. Lavrentiev in 1994 and 1995, they violated the constitutional provision stating that: "No one shall be subject to torture, force, or any form of cruel or degrading treatment or punishment."

Only thanks to the interference of the procurator and the mass media in Mordova were the human rights violations of said members of the criminal investigation department stopped.

During the detention of the victims, the police used handcuffs during the interrogation without any reason, violating article 14 of the law on the police. A gas mask was forced over his head of the suspect beforehand, and the air supply was cut off. The suspects were forced to stand with half-bent legs and stretched out arms for long periods of time, and were deprived of sleep and food for lengthy periods of time. The night time interrogations and their length testify to this. These were recorded in prison journals at IVS-2 of the Mordovian MVD and viewed by the court.

As was established during the course of the procuracy's investigation, not one of the seven victims detained by officers of the criminal investigation department were involved in committing the crimes of which they were suspected, and the case against them was dismissed for lack of evidence.

6. It has been established in court that, in violation of departmental instructions of the Ministry of Internal Affairs of the Russian Federation, police officers Majors N.A. Abramov and V.V. Abramov, following their unlawful arrest and subjection to violence, were placed in cells with criminals, which subjected the lives of the innocent police officers to danger.

As is evident from the case, Major N.A. Abramov, chief of the B. Bereznikovskii ROVD, had worked for the police for a long time and was regularly promoted, to which testified among others the former chief of the ROVD.

However, after being ill-treated with a gas mask and other violence, he and V.V. Abramov were placed in a general cell with seventeen prisoners being held for various serious crimes, as well as members of organized crime groups. N.A. Abramov was held there for twenty-six days, after which he was transferred to pretrial detention center No. 1 of the Mordovian MVD.

While being tortured at the ROVD and the MVD on April 9 and 10 of 1994, one of A.A. Derkaev's ribs was broken. However, after both he and the Abramovs were placed in IVS-2, the Mordovian MVD refused to call for a doctor, and when he requested a pen and paper, the administration of the IVS-2 gave him only a box of matches, saying, "Here's your pen and paper."

And only after A.A. Derkaev's transfer to SIZO No. 1 of the Mordovian MVD on April 26, 1994 was he given medical attention by Dr. N.I. Konakov. Derkaev was held in custody unlawfully for over forty days.

After N.A. Abramov, V.V. Abramov and A.A. Derkaev were released from custody, they were hospitalized for a long period of time. The procurator of the city of Saransk found evidence during his investigation that the Mordovian MVD had violated procedure by holding police officers V.V. Abramov and N.A. Abramov in a general cell in IVS-2 and had committed other violations. The Mordovian MVD's response indicates that the violations were in fact confirmed.

However, when questioned as witnesses during the trial hearing, the leadership of IVS-2 and several employees attempted to conceal the violations, including those committed by members of the department of criminal investigations.

A.A. Derkaev's complaints regarding the IVS-2's failure to call a doctor were not recorded in the journal of initial inspections of detainees at the IVS-2. The journal does contain a remark that during the detention of Derkaev and the Abramovs at the IVS-2, the staff doctor was on vacation.

As indicated in the journal of interrogations reviewed by the court, employees of the IVS-2 gave Derkaev and the Abramovs over to detectives Daev and Sazonov without instructions from the investigator, and the request order for the interrogation was filled out by a member of the criminal investigation department of the Mordovian MVD, while they were not part of the investigative team and did not have the right to hold interrogations.

7. Furthermore, it is widespread practice in Mordovia for suspects to be called and delivered for interrogation by members of the department of criminal investigations rather than by the convoy service, which is in violation of the law.

As happened in the criminal case currently reviewed by the Supreme Court, detective of the MVD, who delivered the victims in this case, subjected Derkaev, the Abramovs and others to physical violence with the aim of forcing them to sign confessions.

Aside from the victims (seven in the case), witnesses who had shared cells with them told the court about the widespread use of violence by police in Mordovia. They testified that after a few days of beatings by the police, N.A. Abramov and A.A. Derkaev were unable to move unassisted, and that N.A. Abramov, himself a police major, wanted to commit suicide, saying that he could no longer stand the torture to which he was subjected in room No. 343 of the MVD.

N.I. Kanakov, the doctor at SIZO No. 1, N.V. Kainov, the deputy chief of SIZO No. 1, and P.A. Suraev, head of the SIZO's investigation department, all of whom were working at the time, confirmed in court that suspects brought in from the IVS-2 of the MVD often complained about beatings by police officers, and that in particular, A.A. Derkaev arrived on April 26, 1994 with traces of violence, saying that he was beaten by members of the MVD. This was noted by the doctor at SIZO No. 1, where the traces of violence were recorded on Derkaev's dispensary chart.

The court reviewed experts' conclusions regarding the nature and severity of the victims' injuries. In court, the victims' doctors confirmed that Derkaev and the Abramovs were confined to hospital beds as a result of the violence to which they were subjected by the MVD, and the same conclusion follows from the stories of their illnesses introduced in court.

At present, the Mordovian Supreme Court is hearing another criminal case, against three members of the MVD (an investigator with the special department of the MVD, a detective of the investigative department of the MVD and a detective of the department for organized crime of the MVD) connected with an accusation of unlawful detention and attempts to coerce testimony from seventeen victims with the use of violence and harassment accused of illegally detaining and attempting to coerce testimony from 17 victims with the use of violence and harassment.

8. The court also found that leadership of the B. Bereznikovskii ROVD and the criminal investigation department of the Mordovian Ministry of Internal Affairs submitted to the investigative agencies and to the court inaccurate evaluations of several defendants involved in this case.

It was found that on April 4, 1994 in the building of the ROVD A. N. Frolkin, an officer of the OUR of the B. Bereznikovskii ROVD, and a group of other defendants beat A. A. Derkaev, forced him to wear a gas mask, and stepped on his groin. As a result, Derkaev suffered a fractured rib.

In an evaluation dated December 12, 1997 that was provided to the investigator (volume 2, page 244) and presented to the court by a lawyer and which was compiled and signed by deputy chief for personnel V. N. Kuvalev of the ROVD, and by the chief of the B. Bereznikovskii's ROVD, N. A. Vediashov, it is stated that "Frolkin strictly observes all legal norms and has reorganized his work according to the latest instructions of the government and, generally, is improving the style and methods of his conduct."

According the testimony of the victim, A. A. Derkaev, while he was being beaten by the officers of the ROVD (Frolkin and Tutaev) and by officers of the criminal investigation department of the Mordovian Ministry of Internal Affairs (Daev and Sazonov) while wearing handcuffs and lying on the floor, deputy chief of the ROVD V. A. Kusliaikin entered the room and did nothing to stop the violence being committed by the defendants, of which both Frolkin and Tutayev were his direct subordinates.

According to the testimony of Kusliaikin in court, at the time in question he was temporarily acting chief of the B. Bereznikovskii ROVD and it was precisely during this period that, with his knowledge, Shubin, Derkaev, V.V. Abramov and N.A. Abramov were arrested and illegally subjected to violence.

Kusliaikin did not initiate any disciplinary action.

S.V. Antonov, an officer of the criminal investigation department of the Mordovian Ministry of Internal Affairs, participated in the violence against the four victims, one of whom (Derkaev) suffered a fractured rib and another (V.V. Abramov) was beaten about the genitals with a belt.

In an official statement of the criminal investigation department of the Mordovian Ministry of Internal Affairs (volume 2, page 245), it is noted that "S. V. Antonov strictly observes all legal norms, is extremely scrupulous and is able to properly judge his own conduct."

The court found that A. A. Daev and E. N. Sazonov, officers of the criminal investigation department f the Mordovian Ministry of Internal Affairs, systematically in the course of "informal questions" applied torture with the use of special devices and a RSh-4 gas mask. They personally participated in six episodes of personal humiliation, including some relating to A. A. Derkaev who suffered a broken rib; to A. S. Lavrentiev, a minor who twice urinated in his pants while being tortured; to police Major N. A. Abramov, who lost consciousness while being forced to wear a gas mask; and to O.V. Igonin, who died in an investigator's office during an "informal questioning."

The court also found (on the basis of documents from the personnel department of the Mordovian Ministry of Internal Affairs; see volume 4, page 24) that Daev (July 17, 1994) and Sazonov (February 7, 1995) had been disciplined for legal violations: each officer had received a strict reprimand for violations of official procedures.

However, in evaluations provided to the court, the criminal investigation department of the Mordovian Ministry of Internal Affairs did not refer to these disciplinary measures taken against Daev and Sazonov. Moreover, despite the severity of the crimes committed by Daev and Sazonov (under article 171(2) of the criminal code of the RSFSR) and despite the fact that Sazonov also submitted a forged official document (article 175 of the criminal code of the RSFSR), the statements regarding them read (volume 2, page 247, 249): "Daev and Sazonov are responsible in the fulfillment of their official duties and strictly observe all legal norms. They have calm natures, are proper in their treatment of civilians, have received positive evaluations and both possess proper restraint and erudition. Daev and Sazonov are respected and admired within the criminal investigations unit of the Ministry of Internal Affairs."

However, the laudatory tone of these evaluations of Daev, Sazonov, Antonov and others does not correspond with the extreme severity of the actions they committed.

It is the opinion of the court that officers who have been disciplined for systematic violations of legal norms, who have committed serious crimes against the lives and health of the citizens that they are obliged to protect, and who have systematically violated article 20 of the Mordovian Constitution and article 21 of the Constitution of the Russian Federation which prohibit the use of torture cannot be regarded with respect and admiration by any responsible member of the criminal investigations unit of the Ministry of Internal Affairs of Mordovia.

Therefore, the Supreme Court of Mordovia cannot accept the conclusions of the above-mentioned statements.

9. The following relates to the serious inadequacies in selecting and managing the officers of the detective units of the Mordovian Ministry of Internal Affairs and to the poor evaluation of the personal qualities of individuals applying for positions within the criminal investigations unit.

Criminal investigation unit officers V.I. Tutaev, D.N. Kuflin and A.E. Guliaikin committed crimes within one year of beginning work with the unit. A.E. Guliaikin committed crimes just one month after beginning work with the ROVD.

D.N. Kuflin was reprimanded by the Mordovian Ministry of Internal Affairs for legal violations on May 25, 1995. He received an official conduct warning (volume 6, page 110). Two months later, on July 25, 1995, Kuflin committed a crime with a group of other individuals and subsequently (August 25, 1995) was dismissed from the ROVD.

A.A. Daev and E.N. Sazonov, both officers of the ciminal investigations unit of the Ministry of Internal Affairs in 1994 and 1995, each received two reprimands for violations of legal norms. Each was given a strict reprimand and an official conduct warning (volume 4, page 24).

V.I. Tutaev and A.E. Guliaikin had no special training for police work.

The following information attests to the formalistic attitude of the ROVD of the city of Saransk regarding the trial period of employment of A.E. Guliaikin in the criminal investigations unit and the poor evaluation of his personal qualities.

According to order No. 207 of the Mordovian Ministry of Internal Affairs issued on June 6, 1995, A.E. Guliaikin was appointed a regular officer of the criminal investigations unit of the Saransk ROVD (volume 6, page 97-101), as he was considered to have completed an abbreviated trial employment period that ended on June 10, 1995.

On the night of June 25-26, 1995, A.E. Guliaikin, together with Kuflin, Daev and Sazonov, committed a crime against O.V. Igonin. Earlier the same day, Guliaikin, together with Daev and Sazonov, tortured a minor, A.S. Lavrentiev, by forcing him to wear a gas mask.

Despite the fact that A.E. Guliaikin and D.N. Kuflin were caught red-handed in ROVD office number 306 with the body of O.V. Igonin, a request that had been submitted to the Ministry of Internal Affairs of Russia asking that Guliaikin be promoted to the rank of lieutenant was not revoked. After the crime that Guliaikin committed, order number 658 of the Ministry of Internal Affairs of the Russia (dated August 1, 1995) promoted him to the rank of lieutenant (volume 6, page 99).

Shortly thereafter, Guliaikin was dismissed and arrested.

Despite the fact that Frolkin, Antonov and Tutaev faced criminal charges and that investigators of the prosecutor's office had requested their dismissal, continued to work in the organs of the Ministry of Internal Affairs and attempted to obstruct justice in this case and to influence the victims, for which they were (together with Kuflin) arrested on November 18, 1997.

As is evident from the files and documents obtained by the court from the Mordovan prosecutor's office, and from a presentation of the procurator of Mordovia, other officers had previously committed serious crimes for which they had been convicted. These facts were confirmed in court by chiefs of the Lenin district ROVD and the IVS-2, by deputy Minister of Internal Affairs V.S. Razin and by the chief of the criminal investigations unit of the Ministry of Interior V. M. Glinskii.

From the testimony of these witnesses and from documents and copies of official sentences, it was established that the following employees of the Mordovian Ministry of Internal Affairs had been convicted by the Mordovian Supreme Court:

- On July 10, 1996, V.N. Khaidukov, chief of IVS-1, was convicted under article 108 of the criminal code of the RSFSR. IVS-1 employees M.P. Igoshkin and Iu.A. Molov were also convicted of crimes committed on the territory of the IVS in connection with the same case;
- On July 22, 1996, A.N. Iurkin, an officer of the Saransk city department of internal affairs, was convicted under articles 102(a, e, i and n); article 108(1); article 117(4); article 145(2); article 146(2a and g); and article 210 of the criminal code of the RSFSR. Having been convicted of several murders and robberies, Iurkin was sentenced to death.
- On February 2, 1997, A. Mitreikin, an officer of the convoy service of the ROVD in Zubovo-Poliansk, was convicted under article 102 (a, e, and d); article 146(3); article 145(2); and article 210 of the criminal code of the RSFSR. He was sentenced to death for the murders of two individuals committed during a robbery attempt.

All these examples attest to the inadequately effective training work conducted with the staff of the departments of the Mordovian Ministry of Internal Affairs.

Appendix F: Separate Ruling of Supreme Court Judge Vasilii Martyshkin on Torture in Mordovia

10. The Mordovian Supreme Court considers it necessary to draw the attention of the Russian Ministry of Internal Affairs to the courage and fortitude of the victim in the case of Major Nikolai Andreevich Abramov of the B. Bereznikovskii ROVD, which facilitated the exposure of the criminals and solving of the crime.

From the profile drawn during the case from his place of work, place of residence, and testimony given in court by the heads of the Bol'shebereznikovskii ROVD and colleagues, the characterization of Major N.A. Abramov can be only positive. N.A. Abramov, head of the regional State Automobile Inspection, prosecuted unlawfully on suspicion of stealing an MTZ-80 tractor from the Kalinin collective farm of the B. Bereznikovskii region of Mordova, courageously tolerated the degradation and humiliation by the criminal investigation department employees A.A. Daev, E.N. Sazonov, and S.V. Antonov, who subjected him to violence with a gas mask Rsh-4 and special devices, and to detention with criminals in a general cell at IVS-2 of the MVD. After recuperating, N.A. Abramov, as indicated in the case materials, has continued to work scrupulously at the Bol'sheberznikovskii ROVD as a precinct officer.

As established by the court in the given case, N.A. Abramov, while unlawfully held in custody for 26 days, was the only one of seven victims in the criminal case able to withstand all types of physical violence to which he was subjected by his former colleagues, and never slandered anyone or showed weakness. He displayed a high level of awareness and fortitude in assisting in uncovering this crime and exposing figures in internal affairs agencies who disgraced their profession.

Therefore, the Supreme Court of Mordovia requests that the Ministry of Internal Affairs of Russia recognize the courage and fortitude of the victim, N.A. Abramov, who demonstrated the finest qualities of a police officer, and regardless of the degradation and violence to which he was subjected, continues to conscientiously fulfill his duties.

The Supreme Court of Mordovia has deemed it necessary to draw the attention of the Ministry of Internal Affairs of Russia and the Procurator General of Russia the causes and conditions revealed to have facilitated commission of crimes in the organs of the Ministry of Internal Affairs of Mordovia, the violation of civil rights during so called "informal questioning," and detention in Mordovia, with the aim of averting them in the future, not only on the territory of Mordovia but in all regions and republics of the Russian Federation.

Guided by articles 21(1) and 321 of the criminal procedure code of the RSFSR, the Supreme Court of Mordovia

HAS DETERMINED:

1. In the aim of preventing such violations in the future, to draw the attention of the Ministry of Internal Affairs of Russia to the causes and conditions which facilitated commission of crimes in the organs of the Ministry of Internal Affairs of Mordovia and violation of civil rights during so called "informal questioning," during which torture and coercion were used by members of the department of criminal investigations.

2. To bring to the attention of the Ministry of Internal Affairs of Russia the courage and fortitude displayed by Major Nikolai Andreevich Abramov of the Bol'shebereznikovskii ROVD of Mordovia in fulfilling his duties, which allowed for the uncovering of the crime in question.

To bring this particular ruling to the attention of the General Procurator of Russia.

In accordance with article 21(6) of the criminal procedure code of the Russian Federation, the Ministry of Internal Affairs must take the necessary measures regarding this ruling and report the results to the Supreme Court of Mordova.

The ruling can not be appealed, but the procurator can launch a protest through the Supreme Court of Mordovia to the Supreme Court of Russia.

Signed

Chairman:

Lay assessors:

V.N. Martyshkin

Translated by Diederik Lohman, Genine Babakian, Robert Coalson, and Will Irving.